MCSE Exam Notes™: TCP/IP for NT® Server 4

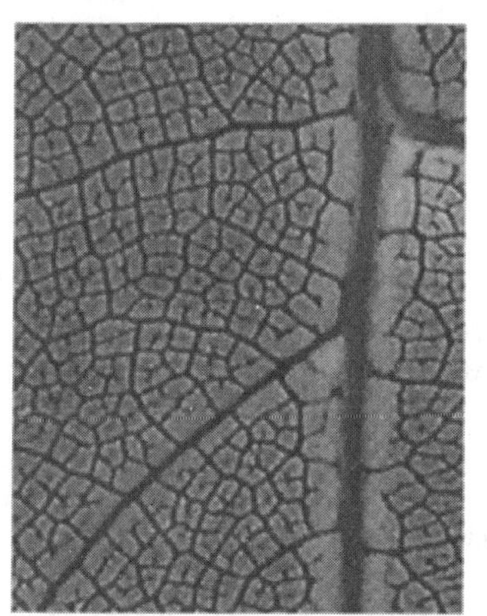

Gary Govanus

San Francisco • Paris • Düsseldorf • Soest

Associate Publisher: Guy Hart-Davis
Contracts and Licensing Manager: Kristine Plachy
Acquisitions & Developmental Editor: Neil Edde
Editor: Valerie Haynes Perry
Project Editor: Davina Baum
Technical Editor: Darin McGee
Book Designer: Bill Gibson
Graphic Illustrator: Tony Jonick
Electronic Publishing Specialist: Adrian Woolhouse
Production Coordinator: Susan Berge
Indexer: Rebecca Plunkett
Cover Designer: Archer Design
Cover Illustrator/Photographer: FPG International

Screen reproductions produced with Collage Complete.

Library of Congress Card Number: 98-86627

ISBN: 0-7821-2307-4

Manufactured in the United States of America

10 9 8 7 6 5 4 3 2 1

November 1, 1997

Dear SYBEX Customer:

Microsoft is pleased to inform you that SYBEX is a participant in the Microsoft® Independent Courseware Vendor (ICV) program. Microsoft ICVs design, develop, and market self-paced courseware, books, and other products that support Microsoft software and the Microsoft Certified Professional (MCP) program.

To be accepted into the Microsoft ICV program, an ICV must meet set criteria. In addition, Microsoft reviews and approves each ICV training product before permission is granted to use the Microsoft Certified Professional Approved Study Guide logo on that product. This logo assures the consumer that the product has passed the following Microsoft standards:

- The course contains accurate product information.
- The course includes labs and activities during which the student can apply knowledge and skills learned from the course.
- The course teaches skills that help prepare the student to take corresponding MCP exams.

Microsoft ICVs continually develop and release new MCP Approved Study Guides. To prepare for a particular Microsoft certification exam, a student may choose one or more single, self-paced training courses or a series of training courses.

You will be pleased with the quality and effectiveness of the MCP Approved Study Guides available from SYBEX.

Sincerely,

Holly Heath
ICV Account Manager
Microsoft Training & Certification

MICROSOFT INDEPENDENT COURSEWARE VENDOR PROGRAM

This book is dedicated to three of my favorite people in the whole world. First, to my wife, Bobbi. Thank you for being a part of my life.

Then there are the little people, my two grandchildren, Branny and CJ. May you grow up to take advantage of all of the new vistas offered by the growth of technology.

Acknowledgments

If I had my way, this book would be printed on 11X17 stock and anyone who had anything to do with it would get their name on the cover! Why should I be the only one with credit where people can see it? Because I am pretty sure that won't happen, let me try and go over all those people I have to thank.

First things first. Writing a book is a lot of work and it requires sacrifices on the part of those closest to the author. I am blessed with a wonderful, understanding family who doesn't get upset when I lock myself away in a little room for hours on end typing. I am sure they would like me to spend more time with them, but never once have they complained. So, to my wife Bobbi, my daughter Denise, my daughter Dawn, my parents, and my beautiful grandchildren, thank you.

It really is unfair that I get all the credit because I do so little of the work. There are so many other people who have worked on this book it is amazing. I have never met any of them, but they are all great to work with. First of all, the person who had enough faith in me to give me the project, Neil Edde, the developmental editor for this book. Neil is truly a masochist; he just keeps giving me more and more stuff to work on and for that, I thank him.

Davina Baum, the project editor for this project, has kept me on the straight and narrow for the second time. She knows just how to work with me to make sure things get in on time and just the way she wants them, all the while making me think it's my idea. She is great to work with and I hope I am assigned to her permanently!

Valerie Haynes Perry was the editor on this project. It was her responsibility to make sure that what I wrote came out making sense. My problem is my brain sometimes works faster than my fingers and all the information does not get down on paper. Valerie has found all the holes and plugged them. Believe me, there were a lot of holes. She has worked tirelessly on this project. I really think she should look to a career change; it seems that no matter when I sent her an e-mail, she responded immediately. She spends so much time on AOL, she qualifies for the title, “geek-wannabe.” For all the work she put in, Valerie deserves a ton of credit.

Darin McGee was the technical editor. He had the unenviable task of checking to make sure all my technical facts were right. Whenever there is some procedure in the book or a statement that says “this works this way,” it was up to Darin to make sure it actually operated as advertised. When he found discrepancies, he was very kind in the way he straightened me out. Never did he say, “Yo, dummy, were you sleeping when you did this?” though he probably thought it many times.

Finally, there are all those people who work for Sybex who I had no contact with, people like Susan Berge, the production coordinator, Adrian Woolhouse, electronic publishing specialist, and Bill Gibson, book designer.

To everyone who worked on the project, thanks!

Table of Contents

Introduction

If you've purchased this book, you are probably chasing one of the Microsoft professional certifications: MCP, MCSE, or MCT. All of these are great goals and they are also great career builders. Glance through any newspaper and you'll find employment opportunities for people with these certifications—these ads are there because finding qualified employees is a challenge in today's market. The certification means you know something about the product, but more importantly, it means you have the ability, determination, and focus to learn—the greatest skill any employee can have!

You've probably also heard all the rumors about how hard the Microsoft tests are—believe us, the rumors are true! Microsoft has designed a series of exams that truly test your knowledge of their products. Each test covers not only the materials presented in a particular class, but also the prerequisite knowledge for that course. This means two things for you—that first test can be a real hurdle and each test *should* get easier because you've studied the basics over and over.

This book has been developed in alliance with the Microsoft Corporation to give you the knowledge and skills you need to prepare for one of the key exams of the MCSE certification program: TCP/IP for NT Server 4.0. Reviewed and approved by Microsoft, this book provides a solid introduction to Microsoft networking technologies and will help you on your way to MCSE certification.

Is This Book for You?

The *MCSE Exam Notes* books were designed to be succinct, portable exam review guides that can be used either in conjunction with a more complete study program (such as a book, CBT courseware, or classroom/lab environment) or as an exam review for those who don't feel the need for more extensive test preparation. It isn't our goal to "give the answers away," but rather to identify those topics on which you can expect to be tested and to provide sufficient coverage of these topics.

Perhaps you've been working with Microsoft networking technologies for years now. The thought of paying lots of money for a specialized MCSE exam preparation course probably doesn't sound too appealing. What can they teach you that you don't already know, right? Be careful, though. Many experienced network administrators have walked confidently into test centers only to walk sheepishly out of them after failing an MCSE exam. As they discovered, there's the Microsoft of the real world and the Microsoft of the MCSE exams. It's our goal with these *MCSE Exam Notes* books to show you where the two converge and where they diverge. After you've finished reading through this book, you should have a clear idea of how your understanding of the technologies involved matches up with the expectations of the MCSE test makers in Redmond.

Or perhaps you're relatively new to the world of Microsoft networking, drawn to it by the promise of challenging work and higher salaries. You've just waded through an 800-page MCSE study guide or taken a class at a local training center. Lots of information to keep track of, isn't it? Well, by organizing the *MCSE Exam Notes* books according to the Microsoft exam objectives, and by breaking up the information into concise manageable pieces, we've created what we think is the handiest exam review guide available. Throw it in your briefcase and carry it to work with you. As you read through the book, you'll be able to identify quickly those areas you know best and those that require more in-depth review.

NOTE The goal of the *MCSE Exam Notes* series is to help MCSE candidates familiarize themselves with the subjects on which they can expect to be tested in the MCSE exams. For complete, in-depth coverage of the technologies and topics involved, we recommend the *MCSE Study Guide* series from Sybex.

How Is This Book Organized?

As mentioned above, this book is organized according to the official exam objectives list prepared by Microsoft for the TCP/IP for NT Server 4.0 exam. The chapters coincide with the broad objectives groupings, such as planning, installation and configuration, connectivity, monitoring and optimization, and troubleshooting. These groupings are also reflected in the organization of the MCSE exams themselves.

Within each chapter, the individual exam objectives are addressed in turn. Also in turn, the objectives sections are further divided according to the type of information presented.

Once the planning has been completed in Chapter 1, we will look at how to install and configure TCP/IP in Chapter 2. This is where we get into the meat of TCP/IP—things such as subnet masks, scopes for DHCP, the differences between an LMHOSTS file and the HOSTS file, and how to route IP.

Chapter 3 will show you how to connect your NT-based network to other systems, such as a UNIX host. It also discusses how to configure a Remote Access Service (RAS) server for use on an IP network and how to browse a multiple-domain network.

A network of any size will have some bottlenecks. Many of these can be avoided by monitoring your network. Monitoring shows if your planning provides the appropriate results. Chapter 4 deals with the monitoring and optimization of networks running TCP/IP.

Finally, Chapter 5 will discuss how to troubleshoot problems. This chapter brings out the Microsoft utilities that are available to help you diagnose where the issues lie and how to fix them. Problems on a TCP/IP network seem to fall into either addressing or name resolution, so we will look at both aspects.

Critical Information

This section presents the greatest level of detail on information that is relevant to the objective. This is the place to start if you're unfamiliar with or uncertain about the technical issues related to the objective.

Necessary Procedures

Here you'll find instructions for procedures that require access to a lab computer for their completion. From installing operating systems to modifying configuration defaults, the information in these sections addresses the hands-on requirements for the MCSE exams.

NOTE Not every objective has procedures associated with it. For such objectives, the Necessary Procedures section has been left out.

Exam Essentials

In this section, we've put together a concise list of the most crucial topics of subject areas that you'll need to comprehend fully prior to taking the MCSE exam. This section can help you identify those topics that might require more study on your part.

Key Terms and Concepts

Here we've compiled a mini-glossary of the most important terms and concepts related to the specific objective. You'll understand what all those technical words mean within the context of the related subject matter.

Sample Questions

For each objective, we've included a selection of questions similar to those you'll encounter on the actual MCSE exam. Answers and explanations are provided so you can gain some insight into the test-taking process.

NOTE For a more comprehensive collection of exam review questions, check out the *MCSE Test Success* series, also published by Sybex.

How Do You Become an MCSE?

Attaining Microsoft Certified Systems Engineer (MCSE) status is a challenge. The exams cover a wide range of topics and require dedicated study and expertise. However, this is why the MCSE certificate is so valuable. If achieving the MCSE were too easy, the market would be quickly flooded by MCSEs and the certification would become meaningless. Microsoft is keenly aware of this fact and has taken steps to ensure that the certification means its holder is truly knowledgeable and skilled.

To become an MCSE, you must pass four core requirements and two electives. Most people select the following exam combination for the MCSE core requirements for the most current track:

Client Requirement

70-073: Implementing and Supporting Windows NT Workstation 4.0
or

70-064: Implementing and Supporting Microsoft Windows 95

Networking Requirement

70-058: Networking Essentials

Windows NT Server 4.0 Requirement

70-067: Implementing and Supporting Windows NT Server 4.0

Windows NT Server 4.0 in the Enterprise Requirement

70-068: Implementing and Supporting Windows NT Server 4.0 in the Enterprise

Electives

Some of the more popular electives include the following:

70-059: Internetworking Microsoft TCP/IP on Microsoft Windows NT 4.0

70-087: Implementing and Supporting Microsoft Internet Information Server 4.0

70-081: Implementing and Supporting Microsoft Exchange Server 5.5

70-026: System Administration for Microsoft SQL Server 6.5

70-027: Implementing a Database Design on Microsoft SQL Server 6.5

70-088: Implementing and Supporting Microsoft Proxy Server 2.0

70-079: Implementing and Supporting Microsoft Internet Explorer 4.0 by Using the Internet Explorer Administration Kit

---

TIP This book is a part of the *MCSE Exam Notes* series that is published by Network Press (Sybex). It covers four core requirements and your choice of several electives—the entire MCSE track!

Where Do You Take the Exams?

You may take the exams at any one of more than 800 Sylvan Prometric Authorized Testing Centers around the world. For the location of a testing center near you, call (800) 755-EXAM (755-3926). Outside the United States and Canada, contact your local Sylvan Prometric Registration Center. You may also register for an exam with Sylvan Prometric via the Internet. The Sylvan site can be reached through the Microsoft Training and Certification site, `www.microsoft.com\train_cert\`, or at `http://www.slspro.com/msreg/microsoft.asp`.

Follow these steps to register for a Microsoft Certified Professional exam:

1. Determine the number of the exam you want to take.
2. Register with Sylvan Prometric. At this point you will be asked for advance payment for the exam. At this writing, the exams are $100 each. Exams must be taken within one year of payment. You can schedule exams up to six weeks in advance or as late as one working day prior to the date of the exam. You can cancel or

reschedule your exam if you contact Sylvan Prometric at least two working days prior to the exam. Same-day registration is available in some locations, although this is subject to space availability. Where same-day registration is available, you must register a minimum of two hours before test time.

3. After you receive a registration and payment confirmation letter from Sylvan Prometric, call a nearby Sylvan Prometric Testing Center to schedule your exam.

When you schedule the exam, you'll be provided with instructions regarding appointment and cancellation procedures, ID requirements, and information about the testing center location.

What the TCP/IP Exam Measures

The people who write the exams for Microsoft want to make sure that you are a very well-rounded network administrator. The MCSE designation is kind of a Liberal Arts degree in Networking; you need to know something about multiple topics.

That philosophy shows in the TCP/IP exam and in the way the questions are worded. As you study, try to think like an exam writer. What would you write questions about?

- Is there some special terminology that Microsoft uses?
- Are there tips presented on topics such as troubleshooting?
- Is a specific way of doing something stressed over and over?
- Is there something about the subject that is very specific, such as IP addressing, subnetting, host addresses, and network designations?

All of these are tips that the information may show up on the test.

A TCP/IP exam measures your understanding of the concept and how well you know the procedures. You should know the reasoning behind procedures as well as the procedures themselves. If you know the subject matter and can understand and work with the protocol by installing and using TCP/IP, you should do great on the exam.

How Microsoft Develops the Exam Questions

Microsoft's exam development process consists of eight mandatory phases. The process takes an average of seven months and contains more than 150 specific steps. The phases of Microsoft Certified Professional exam development are listed here.

Phase 1: Job Analysis

Phase 1 is an analysis of all the tasks that make up the specific job function based on tasks performed by people who are currently working in that job function. This phase also identifies the knowledge, skills, and abilities that relate specifically to the certification for that performance area.

Phase 2: Objective Domain Definition

The results of the job analysis provide the framework used to develop exam objectives. The development of objectives involves translating the job function tasks into a comprehensive set of more specific and measurable knowledge, skills, and abilities. The resulting list of objectives, or the *objective domain*, is the basis for the development of both the certification exams and the training materials.

NOTE The outline of all *MCSE Exam Notes* books is based upon the official exam objectives lists published by Microsoft. Objectives are subject to change without notification. We advise you to check the Microsoft Training and Certification Web site (`www.microsoft.com\train_cert\`) for the most current objectives list.

Phase 3: Blueprint Survey

The final objective domain is transformed into a blueprint survey in which contributors (technology professionals who are performing the applicable job function) are asked to rate each objective. Based on the contributors' input, the objectives are prioritized and weighted. The actual exam items are written according to the prioritized objectives. The blueprint survey phase helps determine which objectives to measure, as well as the appropriate number and types of items to include on the exam.

Phase 4: Item Development

A pool of items is developed to measure the blueprinted objective domain. The number and types of items to be written are based on the results of the blueprint survey. During this phase, items are reviewed and revised to ensure that they are

- Technically accurate
- Clear, unambiguous, and plausible
- Not biased toward any population, subgroup, or culture
- Not misleading or tricky
- Testing at the correct level of Bloom's Taxonomy
- Testing for useful knowledge, not obscure or trivial facts

Items that meet these criteria are included in the initial item pool.

Phase 5: Alpha Review and Item Revision

During this phase, a panel of technical and job function experts reviews each item for technical accuracy, answers each item, and reaches a consensus on all technical issues. Once the items have been verified as technically accurate, they are edited to ensure that they are expressed in the clearest language possible.

Phase 6: Beta Exam

The reviewed and edited items are collected into a beta exam pool. During the beta exam, each participant has the opportunity to respond to all the items in this beta exam pool. Based on the responses of all beta participants, Microsoft performs a statistical analysis to verify the validity of the exam items and to determine which items will be used in the certification exam. Once the analysis has been completed, the items are distributed into multiple parallel forms, or versions, of the final certification exam.

Phase 7: Item Selection and Cut-Score Setting

The results of the beta exam are analyzed to determine which items should be included in the certification exam based on many factors, including item difficulty and relevance. Generally, the desired items are answered correctly by 25 percent to 90 percent of the beta exam candidates. This helps ensure that the exam consists of a variety of difficulty levels, from somewhat easy to extremely difficult.

Also during this phase, a panel of job function experts determines the cut score (minimum passing score) for the exam. The cut score differs from exam to exam because it is based on an item-by-item determination of the percentage of candidates who would be expected to answer the item correctly. The experts determine the cut score in a group session to increase the reliability.

Phase 8: Live Exam

Once all the other phases are complete, the exam is ready. Microsoft Certified Professional exams are administered by Sylvan Prometric.

Tips for Taking Your TCP/IP Exam

Here are some general tips for taking your exam successfully:

- Arrive early at the exam center so you can relax and review your study materials, particularly tables and lists of exam-related information.
- Read the questions carefully. Don't be tempted to jump to an early conclusion. Make sure you know *exactly* what the question is asking.
- Don't leave any unanswered questions. They count against you.
- When answering multiple-choice questions you're not sure about, use a process of elimination to get rid of the obviously incorrect questions first. This will improve your odds if you need to make an educated guess.
- Because the hard questions will eat up the most time, save them for last. You can move forward and backward through the exam.

- This test has many exhibits (pictures). It can be difficult, if not impossible, to view both the questions and the exhibit simulation on the 14- and 15-inch screens that are usually found at the testing centers. Call around to each center and see if 17-inch monitors are available. If they aren't, perhaps you can arrange to bring in your own. Failing this, some have found it useful to quickly draw the diagram on the scratch paper provided by the testing center and use the monitor to view the question.
- Many participants run out of time before they are able to complete the test. If you are unsure of the answer to a question, you may want to choose one of the answers, mark the question, and go on—an unanswered question does not help you. Once your time allocated for the exam is up, you cannot go on to another question. However, you can remain on the current question indefinitely when the time runs out. Therefore, when you are almost out of time, go to a question you feel you can figure out—given enough time—and work until you feel you have got it (or the night security guard boots you out).
- You are allowed to use the Windows calculator during your test. However, it may be better to memorize a table of the subnet addresses and to write it down on the scratch paper supplied by the testing center before you start the test. Be familiar with the calculator and know how to switch between binary and decimal. The calculator can be a great help on those tricky subnet questions.

Once you have completed an exam, you will be given immediate, online notification of your pass or fail status. You will also receive a printed Examination Score Report indicating your pass or fail status and your exam results by section. (The test administrator will give you the printed score report.) Test scores are automatically forwarded to Microsoft within five working days after you take the test. You do not need to send your score to Microsoft. If you pass the exam, you will receive confirmation from Microsoft, typically within two to four weeks.

Contact Information

To find out more about Microsoft Education and Certification materials and programs, to register with Sylvan Prometric, or to get other useful information, check the following resources. Outside the United States or Canada, contact your local Microsoft office or Sylvan Prometric testing center.

Microsoft Certified Professional Program—(800) 636-7544
Call the MCPP number for information about the Microsoft Certified Professional program and exams and to order the latest Microsoft Roadmap to Education and Certification.

Sylvan Prometric Testing Centers—(800) 755-EXAM (755-3926)
Call Sylvan Prometric to register to take a Microsoft Certified Professional exam at any of their over 800 testing centers around the world.

Microsoft Certification Development Team—Web: `http://www.microsoft.com/Train_Cert/mcp/examinfo/certsd.htm`
Contact the Microsoft Certification Development Team through their Web site to volunteer for participation in one or more exam development phases or to report a problem with an exam. Address written correspondence to:

Certification Development Team

Microsoft Education and Certification

One Microsoft Way

Redmond, WA 98052

Microsoft TechNet Technical Information Network—(800) 344-2121
This is an excellent resource for support professionals and system administrators. Outside the United States and Canada, call your local Microsoft subsidiary for information.

How to Contact the Author

Gary Govanus can be reached at ggovanus@psconsulting.com.

CHAPTER 1

Planning

Microsoft Exam Objectives Covered in This Chapter:

- **Given a scenario, identify valid network configurations.** *(pages 3 – 23)*

What is a valid network configuration? A *valid network configuration* involves the proper use of the tools that you have in hand to facilitate communications. In this case, the tool that you will be using is the TCP/IP protocol suite.

Planning involves the ability to devote hours to the study of how to avoid a problem, rather than spending days trying to fix it. With a large TCP/IP installation, planning can make the difference between being really efficient and being overwhelmed by trouble calls. Planning is the difference between workstations being able to access the right resources and having a frustrated end user who cannot access the Internet. Planning involves simple things, such as the proper placement of Dynamic Host Configuration Protocol (DHCP) servers, Domain Name Service (DNS) systems, and Windows Internet Name Service (WINS) systems. It addresses the more mundane things, such as making sure the company has enough IP addresses and that the addresses that have been assigned actually reside in the appropriate subnets. If all this looks like alphabet soup, don't panic, it should make some sense by the end of this chapter.

If you are *really* fortunate, you get to plan your own implementation of TCP/IP. If you are like most people, you get to work on a network that other people laid out, and you get to implement the corporate strategy. Some people are "lucky" enough to come in and clean up a network that someone implemented without planning. That is always a joyous occasion.

For the purpose of this chapter, it is assumed that your corporate network has no TCP/IP implementation strategy and you are the one responsible for a WAN (wide area network) rollout of the new protocol. This chapter lays out some of the things to think about in your rollout.

Given a scenario, identify valid network configurations.

It all starts with planning. There are a lot of issues to be raised in the planning process. The exam writers seemed to recognize this and they spent much of their time writing questions about planning.

Critical Information

TCP/IP is an acronym for Transmission Control Protocol/Internet Protocol. It is most commonly thought of as the protocol of UNIX and the Internet. Calling TCP/IP a protocol is like calling an encyclopedia a book. TCP/IP is really made up of a multitude of different protocols that combine to provide communications between two computers. The types of communications that each of these protocols provides depends on the purpose of the communication.

UNIX is the greatest operating system ever designed by a committee that never met. When the operating system was originally written, it was published and other people tried it and liked it. Like most blossoming technologies, users wanted more. In this case, the developers of UNIX simply provided the code and the wherewithal for the users to write the utilities they wanted. When the utilities were written, the new version of UNIX was re-posted, people used it, they wanted more, and the evolution continued.

The Internet is unique because it is a multinational entity without an owner, or even an official governing body. There is no Internet CEO who decides what goes where and who can do what. Instead, there are a variety of committees, task forces, and advisory groups that make up the standards that govern the Internet and computer communication. The process is much more democratic than you might believe.

The Internet and TCP/IP are both constantly changing. The change to TCP/IP will start with something called a Request For Comment or RFC. When an RFC is published, it is given a unique number and made available to anyone who would like to subscribe. When an RFC is distributed, anyone can comment, from someone who deeply understands the inner workings of the protocol to a novice who may just have an idea; it doesn't matter. After the subject has been kicked around for awhile, the RFC begins to take a more solid format and at this time the task force or authority responsible for the RFC will assign it a designation that lets the world know where this RFC is in the standards process.

So how do you create an RFC? The process starts when someone wants to formalize a topic, writes a document describing the issue, and mails it to Jon Postel (Postel@ISI.EDU). Postel acts as a referee for the proposal. Anyone wishing to take part in the discussion then comments on the topic. The proposal itself may go through multiple revisions. Should it be generally accepted as a good idea, it will be assigned a number and filed with the RFCs.

An RFC goes through five stages, which don't appear to be formal, but they generally include the following:

Draft standard stage: This is the first stage. It can be likened to an early discussion stage. This is where things are really loose and the community is just trying to get an idea of what should be placed in the RFC.

Proposed standard stage: Once the RFC has been roughed out, it then moves to the more formalized proposed standard stage. At this stage the Internet community works out the details of the standard.

Experimental stage: Once the details are worked out, then it must be determined if the procedure will actually work; this is where the experimental stage comes into play.

Standard stage: Once all the preparation and testing have been completed, the document has earned the right to be called a *standard*.

Obsolete or historic stage: Like most things in computing, even standards have a shelf life. After a standard has done its job and technology has moved on, the standard can be moved to the obsolete or historic category.

In addition to these five stages of a standard, the following five classifications can be associated with each RFC:

Classification	Comments
Required	This RFC must be implemented.
Recommended	The Internet community recommends that this standard be implemented.
Elective	You can implement this standard if you want to, but you don't have to.
Limited	This standard is only to be implemented in very specific circumstances.
Not Recommended	Isn't it nice to know that even the esteemed members of the Internet community sometimes come up with ideas that go over like the proverbial lead balloon?

So, when someone talks about an RFC for the Ethernet standard, you know that the RFC has reached the stage where it is pretty much written in stone. This particular standard is the way things are going to be for a while. If the standard is for something such as the Ethernet 802.2 frame type, the standard is required. That means anyone making use of the Ethernet 802.2 frame type must follow the information in the RFC, or the new product simply will not work.

If you are interested in looking at an RFC, go to the InterNIC FTP site at ds.internic.net. Look for the index of RFCs in the RFC directory. RFCs are numbered, so if you miss the index file, you may end up with an RFC that is of little or no interest to you.

If you do not have access to the FTP server, you can also request RFCs through e-mail. The process is automated and you can access it by sending e-mail to mailserv@ds.internic.net and including the following line in the text of your e-mail:

document-by-name RFCxxxx (replace the "xxxx" with the actual number)

If you are looking for the RFC index, use this text:

Document-by-name rfc-index

RFCs are fascinating things. Besides being tremendous technical resources available on just about any topic that relates to the Internet, an RFC is like a cyber sleeping pill. If you think studying for your TCP/IP will put you to sleep, just try an RFC on for size!

All this information is really fascinating, but don't sweat it for the test. You need to know about RFCs for your working life, but testing will not be impacted. I have found RFCs to be particularly useful in social situations where you are confronted by someone you may not want to spend time with. You may get a reputation as being somewhat boring, but your real friends will know what a witty and charming person you are. As for the others, heck, you didn't want to talk to them anyway!

The DOD Model and the TCP/IP Suite

To understand the TCP/IP suite, you must first understand how communication occurs between two computers. One reference point that is used to describe communications is the Open System Interconnect (OSI) seven-layer model. Because TCP/IP was originally written to specifications laid out by the Department of Defense (DOD), there is a special four-layer DOD model used as a reference. Figure 1.1 shows how the seven layers of the OSI model equate to the four layers of the DOD model.

By the time you have reached this stage in your MCSE testing, you have passed the Networking Essentials test. The seven layers of the OSI model are described in that courseware, so you should be

FIGURE 1.1: The OSI model and the DOD model compared

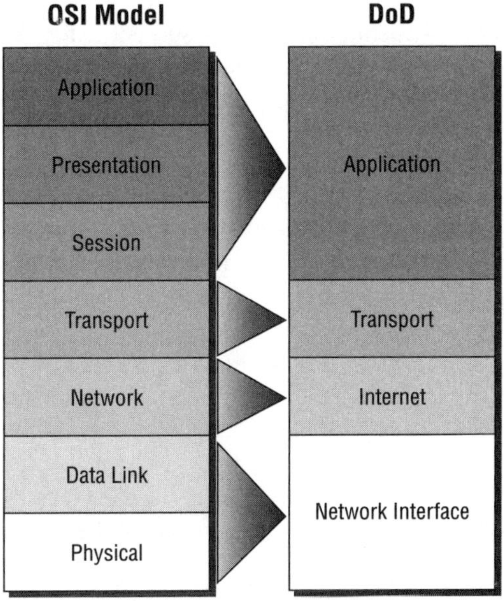

familiar with it. Knowing how the four layers of the DOD model map to the seven layers of the OSI model is important for testing purposes. Knowing what each of the different protocols are responsible for will help you understand material later in the book.

The Network Interface Layer

The bottom layer of the DOD model is the *Network Interface layer.* This layer specifies how the computers will put signals on the physical network. The standards set at the Network Interface layer are specifications for technologies, such as Ethernet and Token Ring.

The Internet Layer

One step up the ladder is the *Internet layer.* The protocols at the Internet layer are responsible for the addressing and delivery of packets from one computer to another. The protocols at the Internet layer allow you to access the Microsoft home page from anywhere in the world.

These are the common Internet layer protocols of the TCP/IP suite and the tasks they perform:

Internet Protocol (IP): IP is responsible for the addressing and routing of datagrams from one computer to another. IP also handles the delivery of datagrams from one host to another.

NOTE Communications between computers is done by the transmission of binary digits (1's and 0's). In order for the sending and receiving computers to know what these digits represent, the digits must be grouped together in some logical format. The naming of this grouping changes at various levels of the DOD model. At the Internet layer, the grouping is referred to as a datagram. Upper layers of the DOD model may refer to this grouping as a packet or frame.

Internet Control Message Protocol (ICMP): This is the tattletale protocol. ICMP carries the messages that report the errors that have occurred in packet delivery.

Address Resolution Protocol (ARP): Each host is identified by several addresses. The first address is the Media Access Control layer or MAC address. This is the Network Interface layer address that is specific to the network interface card (NIC) in the computer. An MAC address will take the format of 00-60-08-02-4D-D1. The Internet layer address, or IP address, takes the form of 207.98.156.52. It is up to the Address Resolution Protocol to resolve or equate the IP address (207.98.156.52) to the MAC address of 00-60-08-02-4D-D1.

The Transport Layer

The *Transport layer* of the DOD model is responsible for transporting the data from one computer to another. If you think of this transmission like a phone call, it would be up to the Transport layer to dial the phone and make sure the connection stayed open from the time you said "Hello" until the time you said "Good-bye."

These are the TCP/IP protocols at the Transport layer:

Transmission Control Protocol (TCP): TCP is a reliable method of delivering data from one host to another. It uses a connection-oriented communication method to perform packet delivery and error detection. TCP will perform data recovery if a packet is damaged in transit. It provides a guaranteed delivery of the information.

User Datagram Protocol (UDP): UDP is a connection-less method of delivery. A UDP packet makes a best effort to deliver a packet. If the packet is damaged in transit, it is up to the application to discover the problem and ask for a retransmission.

The Application Layer

Finally, we reach the Application layer of the DOD model. Don't get carried away by the term "application"; this term does not describe programs, such as Excel or Word. The protocols at the Application layer describe processes that are used in the background to print, copy files, resolve names and addresses, and so on. Only the most sophisticated of end users will recognize their existence and function.

Some of the Application layer protocols and applications include the following:

File Transfer Protocol (FTP): FTP works to transfer files to and from hosts.

Telnet: This utility allows a takeover of the host. You can create a Telnet session to issue commands to a remote computer.

Domain Name Service (DNS): DNS is a name resolution system that will equate a name, such as www.microsoft.com to an IP address, such as 207.68.156.52.

Windows Internet Name Service (WINS): WINS is a name resolution system that resolves the Windows NetBIOS names to a physical address.

Simple Network Management Protocol (SNMP): SNMP provides the resources for proactive network management. It provides information on the stability of the resources and workstations on your network.

Dynamic Host Configuration Protocol (DHCP): DHCP provides the dynamic addressing and configuration of workstations on a TCP/IP network.

Planning Considerations

For the sake of planning an efficient network utilizing TCP/IP there are several areas that need to be addressed, primarily the following ones:

- Proper use of an addressing scheme for a TCP/IP network. This includes knowing how many addresses your network will require.
- Proper use of DHCP servers throughout the network.
- Proper use of Hosts and LMHOSTS files in a TCP/IP environment.
- Proper use of DNS in the network environment.
- Proper use of WINS servers throughout the network.
- Proper use of SNMP in the network environment.

Configuration of an Addressing Scheme for a TCP/IP Network

Before you can start planning how to deploy IP addresses across your network infrastructure, you have to know how many addresses your system will actually need. Each host or network component is identified by a unique IP address. Here's a good rule of thumb to follow: if a network interface card is installed, it needs at least one IP address. Some network cards can have multiple IP addresses.

An IP address is made up of two parts, a network address and the host address. In addition to knowing how many hosts or network components you have on your network, you also have to know how many physical network segments your network contains.

TIP A host is defined as any component on your network that communicates using IP. Hosts can be workstations, servers, printers, routers, bridges, and so on. If a host has more than one network interface card (NIC), each card must have its own unique IP address. If a host has multiple NICs, Microsoft refers to that host as being multihomed. This term will come up often in this book.

An IP address is a 32-bit long number that is divided up into four 8-bit fields. These fields are called *octets*. Each octet is separated by a period and each octet represents a decimal number in the range of 0 to 255. An example of an IP address is 207.68.156.52. The IP address, 207.68.156.52, is assigned to Microsoft on the World Wide Web.

SEE ALSO The assignment of actual IP addresses to each network component will be discussed in Chapter 2, "Installation and Configuration." At this point, we are simply interested in the number of physical network segments your network has, and the number of hosts.

So, how do you find this addressing information? Usually, by locating the wiring diagrams of your network. For some of you, this may be unfamiliar territory. Many administrators have heard of the term documentation, but they are so busy running the network that documenting their work is a dream not a reality. You know who you are! You also knew all along that someday this was going to come back and bite you. It just happened!

If you are one of those administrators smugly sitting back with a grin on your face, knowing exactly where to get an up-to-date map of your network that shows every workstation on the network, with every network segment and router labeled, congratulations. The rest of us are very envious. That up-to-date map is exactly what you are going to need.

When you have the documentation it is simply a matter of counting the number of physical network segments and the number of hosts on each segment. As you are counting, use the following tips:

- Unpopulated segments between routers count as a network segment.
- Each network card in a host needs its own IP address. If you have a multihomed server or a multihomed router with five network cards in it, that multihomed router or multihomed server will require at least five IP addresses.
- As you are busy counting, plan for growth. The numbers you come up with at this stage of the process will be important later, so make sure you take into account the new expansion project that will add 50 more users to a segment.

To illustrate, look at Figure 1.2 below. This is a map of small network that is spread out over three buildings. Each building has its own server and each of the buildings is connected by a router.

FIGURE 1.2: Map of a small network

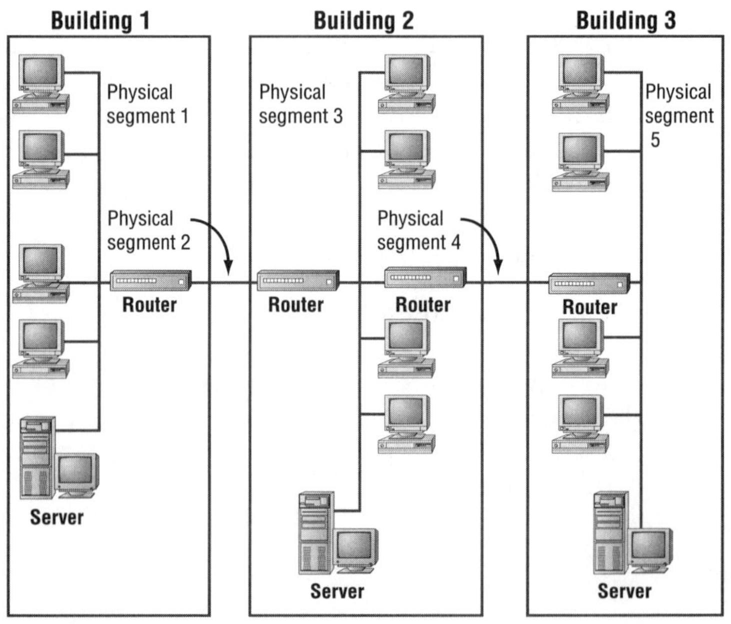

As you see, there are five physical network segments. Each network segment needs a current maximum of seven host addresses (one for the server, one for each workstation, and one for each side of the router). Because this is a high-level network overview, we don't care which network exists in which building. We are only interested in the five physical network segments.

After you conclude this stage of the planning, you should have a diagram that shows the number of physical network segments and the number of hosts on each segment. To move on to the next step, you should be able to say with confidence that your network will have x number of segments with a maximum of y number of hosts on each segment. Remember to take into account growth.

DHCP Servers in the Network

How big is your network? If you look at the figure above, my example shows six network segments with a maximum of six hosts on a segment. Two of the segments are unpopulated, so I would have to assign no more than 36 (6x6) unique IP addresses. That does not sound like too much work, does it? Your numbers may differ considerably. You may be looking at the assignment of several hundred (or thousand) unique IP addresses. That does sound like a lot of work, doesn't it?

Dynamic Host Configuration Protocol (DHCP) can come to the rescue. You can configure one or more DHCP servers to provide automatic addressing and gateway information for every host. When a DHCP server provides an address to a host, it is said the host is *leasing* the DHCP address.

Some systems on a segment may not be able to take advantage of DHCP. Because the system (usually a server or a router) needs to maintain the same IP address all the time, it must have a permanent or static address, not a leased address. In that case, the address must be manually configured.

When you configure a server to provide DCHP addresses, you give the server a block of addresses to assign. This block is referred to as a *scope of addresses*. DHCP can also provide the appropriate subnet mask and information about the gateway that serves that segment.

Host computers are then configured to go out and look for a DHCP server when the host boots. Using a process called BOOTP, the host asks the DHCP server for information. The DHCP server then gives the host an IP address with the appropriate subnet mask and the IP address of the gateway. From the administrator's point of view, configuring DHCP servers saves you the trouble of going to each of the hosts and manually entering an IP address.

Clients accessing a DHCP server do not need to be on the same side of a router or even on the same subnet as the DHCP server. While BOOTP does not travel well across routers or subnets, you can configure a DHCP relay agent. A *relay agent* simply listens for a BOOTP request, then forwards the request directly to the DHCP server. The computer acting as the DHCP relay agent needs to be running either Windows NT Workstation or Windows NT Server, and the relay agent does needs to be on the same subnet as the host computers.

SEE ALSO Configuring a computer to be a BOOTP relay agent will be covered in Chapter 2.

HOSTS and LMHOSTS Files in a TCP/IP Environment

Have you ever wondered how TCP/IP manages to turn the IP address of 207.68.156.52 into a somewhat user-friendly name, such as www.microsoft.com? Actually, there are several ways of handling the transformation.

In the early days of the Internet, when there were just a few computers on the network, system administrators manually kept track of where things were by updating a text file called the Hosts file. The format of the Hosts file wasn't anything special. As a matter of fact, if your workstation is running Windows *9x*, you have the following HOSTS.SAM file located in your C:\Windows directory:

```
# Copyright (c) 1998 Microsoft Corp.
#
# This is a sample HOSTS file used by Microsoft TCP/IP
stack for Windows98
```

```
# This file contains the mappings of IP addresses to
host names. Each
# entry should be kept on an individual line. The IP
address should
# be placed in the first column followed by the
corresponding host name.
# The IP address and the host name should be separated
by at least one
# space.
#
# Additionally, comments (such as these) may be
inserted on individual
# lines or following the machine name denoted by a '#'
symbol.
#
# For example:
#
102.54.94.97    rhino.acme.com     # source server
38.25.63.10    x.acme.com       # x client host
127.0.0.1localhost
```

The HOSTS file can be edited with any text editor. It is saved without an extension, in a location where the operating system will find it. In the case of Windows, that would be the C:\Windows directory. On some systems, especially UNIX-based servers, the HOSTS file is stored in the ETC directory. Notice the use of the # (pound) sign. In a HOSTS file, the pound sign serves only one purpose—to designate what follows as a comment that should be ignored.

The HOSTS file resolves IP addresses to host computer names. If someone were to type in the name, rhino.acme.com, the system would know to find host address 102.54.94.97. When a new system would come online, or the system administrator would find a new IP address that needed to be accessed quickly, the administrator would make a new entry in the local HOSTS file.

TIP An explanation of the HOSTS file was included to make the discussion of the LMHOSTS file easier to understand. The HOSTS file is common in the IP world, but for testing purposes, the LMHOSTS file is the one you want to focus on. There will be a few questions on the HOSTS file, but the LMHOSTS file is an exam writer's favorite.

In the world of Windows NT, the HOSTS file is still being used, but another file, the LMHOSTS file, helps with NetBIOS name resolution. NT uses LMHOSTS to map IP addresses to NetBIOS computer names. The LMHOSTS file is located in the <drive letter>\<system root>\System32\Drivers\etc directory and looks like this:

```
#LMHOSTS file for PSCONSULTING. Created 4/16/98
210.47.26.50        Bobbi
210.47.26.51        Cris
210.47.26.52        Denise
210.47.26.53        Brandice
210.47.26.54        CJ
210.47.26.55        PSCONSULT#PRE#DOM:PSDOM
210.47.26.56        PSService#PRE
#BEGIN_ALTERNATE
#INCLUDE \\PSCONSULT\SYSTEM32\DRIVERS\ETC\LMHOSTS
#INCLUDE \\PSSERVICE\SYSTEM32\DRIVERS\ETC\LMHOSTS
#END_ALTERNATE
```

So, you have noticed that this file looks a little different from the traditional HOSTS file. Notice the use of the # (pound) sign. In an LMHOSTS file, the pound sign serves two purposes. On the first line, it designates a comment line. In the rest of the file, it serves to set off key words.

SEE ALSO For testing purposes, you should know that the LMHOSTS file resolves NetBIOS computer names to TCP/IP addresses. There will be a more complete discussion of the LMHOSTS file and keywords in Chapter 2, "Installation and Configuration."

DNS in the Network Environment

Another way of statically maintaining a name to address resolution service is to use DNS, or Domain Name Service. If your network is not connected to the Internet, configuring one of the servers on your network to be a DNS server will provide a single point of administration for host name resolution. If your network is hooked to the Internet, DNS management is usually handled by your Internet service provider (ISP). You just point your workstations to the ISP's DNS server or any DNS server on the Net.

Microsoft DNS provides resolution of computer host names to IP addresses for systems that cannot take advantage of dynamic name resolution provided by WINS. In other words, it is DNS that makes the name microsoft.com equate to an IP address of 207.68.156.52.

SEE ALSO For the Planning section on the exam, you will need to know that DNS provides name resolution for computers that are not capable of using WINS name resolution. These include Macs or UNIX workstations on your network. We will discuss how to implement DNS in Chapter 2, "Installation and Configuration."

WINS Servers in the Network

Windows Internet Name Service (WINS) provides name and address resolution for computers with NetBIOS or Windows names. Unlike DNS or the HOSTS and LMHOSTS files, WINS is dynamic. When a Windows-based computer named \\ntserver comes online it can register that name with a WINS server. Then, whenever a client needs to find the \\ntserver computer, the client can query the WINS server for the location. Notice that the NetBIOS name can be different from the DNS name.

Because your network may have multiple subnets, it is possible to have multiple WINS servers on your network. In this case, the multiple servers can be configured to exchange their databases so the information on all WINS servers is consistent.

A computer that is configured to provide the DNS service can also be configured to provide WINS name resolution.

SEE ALSO WINS implementation is a very common exam question. If the scenario-based questions mention nothing but Windows, Windows 9*x*, and NT-based computers, you can almost be certain the answer will revolve around WINS. The implementation of WINS will be covered in Chapter 2, "Installation and Configuration."

SNMP in the Network Environment

Simple Network Management Protocol (SNMP) provides the means for proactive network management. Implementing SNMP on routers, servers, and just plain computers can provide SNMP managers the opportunity to query the network to find out what it happening.

NOTE SNMP consists of several parts, including the SNMP agent and the SNMP manager. An SNMP agent can be configured to send a message when it comes up or goes down, for example. In order for the agent to be effective, there must be an SNMP manager to receive the message and process it.

Microsoft does not have applications that serve as an SNMP manager; however, there are several third-party vendors that provide this capability.

TIP For exam purposes, it is important to know that SNMP exists and that NT systems can be SNMP agents.

Necessary Procedures

NOTE This "Necessary Procedures" section was designed to outline installation and configuration procedures and there are none. This note is for informational purposes only.

Exam Essentials

Planning is a difficult section to get a handle on because so much of it will be covered in future chapters. However, there are certain things that the exam writers did feature. These points are discussed below.

Know how to determine how many IP addresses you will need. Subnetting will be covered in the next chapter, but for this objective, you need to know how many IP addresses you will need. The number of IP addresses will equal the number of network interface cards (NICs) in host computers, plus an IP address for each router interface.

Know how to implement DHCP and the DHCP relay agent. Dynamic Host Configuration Protocol (DHCP) is used to dynamically assign IP addresses, subnets, and gateway information to workstations. DHCP can be used across routers if a DHCP relay agent is employed.

Know how an LMHOSTS file is used. An LMHOSTS file is used to resolve IP addresses to a NetBIOS computer name. LMHOSTS is a static file that must be edited using a text editor.

Know how a HOSTS file is used. A HOSTS file is used to resolve IP addresses to a DNS computer name. HOSTS is a static file that must be edited using a text editor.

Know how DNS and WINS interact. Domain Name Service (DNS) and Windows Internet Name Service (WINS) resolve a name to an IP address. DNS uses the DNS name while WINS resolves

NetBIOS names to IP addresses. An NT Server can be configured to provide both DNS and WINS resolution.

Key Terms and Concepts

Whenever you start talking about protocols, you start using lots of acronyms.

Address Resolution Protocol (ARP): Each host is identified by several addresses. The first address is the Media Access Control layer or MAC address. This is the Network Interface layer address that is specific to the network interface card (NIC) in the computer. A MAC address will take the format of 00-60-08-02-4D-D1. The Internet layer address, or IP address, takes the form of 207.98.156.52. It is up to the Address Resolution Protocol to resolve or equate the IP address (207.98.156.52) to the MAC address of 00-60-08-02-4D-D1.

Department of Defense (DOD) model: A four-level model that standardizes how communications occur between computers.

Domain Name Service (DNS): A name resolution system that will equate a name, such as www.microsoft.com, to an IP address, such as 207.68.156.52.

Dynamic Host Configuration Protocol (DHCP): DHCP provides dynamic addressing and configuration and workstations on a TCP/IP network.

File Transfer Protocol (FTP): FTP works to transfer files to and from hosts.

Internet Control Message Protocol (ICMP): This is the tattletale protocol. ICMP carries the messages that report the errors that have occurred in packet delivery.

Internet Protocol (IP): IP is responsible for the addressing and routing of datagrams from one computer to another. IP is also responsible for the delivery of datagrams from one host to another.

Open System Interconnect (OSI) model: This model is used to provide a reference point when discussing protocols.

Protocol: A set of rules or standards that specifies how systems will communicate.

Proxy server: A server that caches requests for the World Wide Web to help provide faster response from the Internet.

Simple Network Management Protocol (SNMP): SNMP provides the resources for proactive network management. It provides information on the stability of the resources and workstations on your network.

Subnet: A portion of the network, usually a physical network segment

Subnet mask: A 32-bit value that determines which part of a TCP/IP address specifies the network and which part specifies the unique host address.

Telnet: A utility that allows a takeover of the host. You can create a Telnet session to issue commands to a remote computer.

Transmission Control Protocol (TCP): A reliable method of delivering data from one host to another. TCP uses a connection-oriented communication method to perform packet delivery and error detection. TCP will perform data recovery if a packet is damaged in transit. It provides a guaranteed delivery of the information.

User Datagram Protocol (UDP): A connection-less method of delivery. A UDP packet makes a best effort to deliver a packet. If the packet is damaged in transit, it is up to the application to discover the problem and ask for a retransmission.

Windows Internet Name Service (WINS): A name resolution system that resolves the Windows NetBIOS names to a physical address.

Sample Questions

1. Your computer network consists of 35 Windows NT Workstations, each with one network interface card (NIC). In addition, it has four NT Servers with three interface cards each and four routers, each with three interface cards. How many IP addresses will you need?

   A. 43

   B. 47

   C. 59

   D. 94

   Answer: C. You will need 59 IP addresses, 35 for each of the workstations, 12 for the servers, and 12 for the routers.

2. You have configured an NT Server to pass out IP addresses using DHCP. All the computers that are attached to the same subnet as the DHCP server receive the addresses without a problem. Computers that are on a different subnet do not receive an address. What has to be done so the computers on the other subnet can receive addresses from this server?

   A. You cannot pass out IP addresses to systems on a different subnet.

   B. DHCP must not be configured correctly. Just assign the addresses manually.

   C. Install and configure DNS and WINS to solve the problem.

   D. You must configure a DHCP relay agent.

   Answer: D. To provide IP addresses across a router, you must configure a system to act as a DHCP relay agent.

3. Two address resolution protocols are:

   A. DNS

   B. WINS

   C. DHCP

   D. IP

   Answer: A and B. DNS will resolve DNS names to IP addresses and WINS will resolve NetBIOS computer names to IP addresses.

4. The DOD model has how many layers?

   A. Three

   B. Four

   C. Five

   D. Six

   E. Seven

   Answer: B. The DOD model has four layers. The OSI model has seven layers.

2

Installation and Configuration

Microsoft Exam Objectives Covered in This Chapter:

Given a scenario, select the appropriate services to install when using Microsoft TCP/IP on a Microsoft Windows NT Server computer. *(pages 29 – 36)*

On a Windows NT Server computer, configure Microsoft TCP/IP to support multiple network adapters. *(pages 37 – 42)*

Configure scopes by using DHCP Manager. *(pages 43 – 52)*

Install and configure a WINS Server. *(pages 52 – 83)*

- Import LMHOSTS files to WINS.
- Run WINS on a multihomed computer.
- Configure WINS replication.
- Configure static mappings in the WINS database.

Configure subnet masks. *(pages 83 – 109)*

Configure a Windows NT Server computer to function as an IP router. *(pages 109 – 127)*

- Install and configure a DHCP relay agent.

Install and configure the Microsoft DNS Server service on a Windows NT Server computer. *(pages 127 – 146)*

- Integrate DNS with other name servers.
- Connect a DNS server to a DNS root server.
- Configure DNS server roles.

Configure HOSTS and LMHOSTS files. *(pages 147 – 155)*

Configure a Windows NT Server computer to support TCP/IP printing. *(pages 155 – 162)*

Configure SNMP. *(pages 163 – 171)*

This is really quite the chapter, isn't it? It covers a lot of ground from the installation of the protocol to making sure that every workstation can find every other workstation on the network.

When you look at the objectives that Microsoft presents, the information seems to skip around and not be presented in any logical order. To make the flow of the chapter a little easier to understand, let's see how each of the sections works together.

Before we can configure our network, we must know what services will be needed. Some of these services were discussed in Chapter 1, “Planning.” Here, we'll look at how to apply that information to a real network.

In order to make use of some of these services, you will usually have a pretty large network. Services such as DHCP or DNS may not be necessary in a network of 20 computers. Just as beauty is in the eye of the beholder, so are some definitions. For our purposes, the term “large networks” will mean a network with multiple servers each with multiple adapters, all using and routing TCP/IP to keep in touch with workstations throughout the system.

With the server successfully talking TCP/IP on all fronts, the workstations need to get into the act. To facilitate workstation configuration, it is necessary to provide IP addresses to the masses. The service that will do that is DHCP (Dynamic Host Configuration Protocol), so we will configure different DHCP scopes for each subnet.

A network does not live on IP alone; there must be some name resolution. Once both ends of the communication chain can participate in the “discussion,” there must be a way for those two ends to find each other. In Chapter 1, “Planning,” name-to-address resolution methods were briefly touched on. Now is the time to handle the installation and deployment of WINS (Windows Internet Name Service). WINS has many facets and it takes advantage of Microsoft's favorite protocols, so there is a lot to be covered here.

Next comes the objective of subnet masking. Until you can determine how many subnets your network is going to need and what address ranges you have to work with, everything else will be difficult, if not impossible. Subnetting is an exact science that blends your best logic and math skills.

When you add multiple adapters into a server, you are creating multiple subnets, so you will have to route IP from one subnet to another. The objective on routing will discuss how to do that.

DNS (Domain Name Service) is one of those "gee whiz" topics. The service is simple in its design, yet elegant in its deployment. The fact that it works at all is a constant amazement.

NOTE The exam writers seem to have tied together DNS with WINS. Know how the two complement each other.

Once the DNS section is completed, all the hosts on your network should be able to find each other using either WINS or DNS. If they can't find each other, there are the stand-by HOSTS files and the LMHOSTS files.

There must be something for the hosts to do on the network, so we will cover the topic on configuring TCP/IP printing.

Finally, we have to keep track of all those services on the network, so SNMP will be installed and configured.

Does this look like it's going to be a lot of material? It is! Some of the topics covered are conceptually very easy to understand. Others may take a little work, especially the section on subnetting and addressing. Take it slow and review when necessary. There are places you can go to get another slant on the discussion, if you choose.

SEE ALSO For some hints on other areas, you can start by looking at *MCSE: TCP/IP for NT Server 4 Study Guide,* 3rd Edition by Todd Lammle with Monica Lammle and James Chellis (Sybex, 1998).

If that doesn't do it for you, go out to the Internet and use your favorite search engine to find information on subnetting. There are some interesting discussions on the topic and several different ways of approaching the subject. I will approach the subnet section in the way that seemed to make the most sense to me, and hopefully, you will find it as clear as I did.

If you are not a TCP/IP expert, make sure you dedicate some time to this chapter. Because this chapter contains the most material, the exam writers spent the most time with it. You are going to find lots of questions on the exam about subnets and host id's as well as all the services. Good studying!

Given a scenario, select the appropriate services to install when using Microsoft TCP/IP on a Microsoft Windows NT Server computer.

What kinds of services are we talking about here? There are all kinds of services that can be installed on an NT Server to make life using TCP/IP just a little bit easier. Some of these services have been discussed in Chapter 1, “Planning,” and others will be elaborated on in later chapters. This objective will stress how to utilize these services in a TCP/IP environment and how the services can all work together.

Critical Information

When you select Control Panel ➢ Network and click on the Services tab, there are all sorts of services that can be configured for TCP/IP. These are some of the most notable ones:

- An NT Server can be configured for either a Dynamic Host Configuration Protocol (DHCP) client or a DHCP server.
- You can configure the server to aid intranet or Internet browsing by becoming a Domain Name System (DNS) server.
- If you want to allow your system to be used to host Web pages or allow access to files via the File Transfer Protocol (FTP), you can install and configure the Internet Information Server (IIS).
- If you have a large contingent of TCP/IP users, many times it will include UNIX hosts. These hosts need to print and the NT Server can be configured to provide Microsoft TCP/IP printing.
- The Network Monitor Tools and Agent service will allow the system administrator to capture and view packets on the network. The Network Monitor will also allow you to do some rudimentary network management and performance monitoring, including judging the impact of some of the TCP/IP services.
- One of the reasons system administrators decide to use TCP/IP is because it is a routable protocol. One of the network services available to NT Server is the Routing Information Protocol or RIP. RIP is a distance vector protocol that can dynamically update its route tables.
- For the network that needs more proactive management, Simple Network Management Protocol (SNMP) can be installed. Using SNMP, an NT Server can become an agent, providing a third-party Network Management package with information on the health of the server and the health of the network.
- Some networks need more than DNS to resolve names. In the case of the Windows network, you can add Windows Internet Name

Service (WINS) to the NT Server. WINS will provide NetBIOS computer name resolution to IP addresses.

Dynamic Host Configuration Protocol (DHCP)

One of the biggest challenges of using TCP/IP is the management of IP addresses, subnets, and gateways. Each TCP/IP host must have a unique IP address and this can involve some serious management time. Each host will reside on a subnet and if more than one subnet exists on the network, each host will need to know how to get to the next segment. To cross to a different subnet, each host must know the address of the gateway. For the network that uses manual configuration of IP addressing, there are many areas where a sudden case of "fat fingered typing" can screw up communication.

Installing DCHP will allow you to automatically assign IP addresses, subnet masks, WINS Server(s), and default gateways, making the process all but foolproof. There are still some "gotchas" to the process, but we will look at those later in this objective.

Domain Name System (DNS)

DNS is one of the foundations of the Internet. When a browser requests http:\\www.microsoft.com something has to resolve that name to an IP address and finally to a hardware address. The DNS will resolve the name to an IP address and provide the information to get the packets to the right destination.

Internet Information Server (IIS)

IIS is the subject of a completely different test, so not much space will be devoted to it in this book. You will need to install IIS if you want to make file transfer available to users via the File Transfer Protocol (FTP).

FTP is one of the more visible protocols in the TCP/IP suite. If you want to transfer files reliably between foreign hosts (computers running NT Workstation and UNIX, for example) one common method would be FTP. Because FTP makes use of TCP, it provides for a reliable connection. FTP also offers several layers of security. You can require the systems trying to access the file to log on to the FTP site or you can allow anonymous access to the site so anyone can access the files. This security can be divided so one folder allows anonymous access and a subfolder requires a more stringent authentication.

TCP/IP Printing

More and more networks are diversifying. The days of a network that serves one operating system are a thing of the past. Now, the network may host Windows 3.11 clients, Windows 9*x* clients, Windows NT Workstations, UNIX systems, OS/2 systems, and Macintosh systems.

Installing TCP/IP printer support accomplishes several goals. TCP/IP printing allows workstation clients to print to a printer that has its own IP address, UNIX systems can access printers configured as part of the NT network, and non-UNIX systems can print to printers on the UNIX network.

Network Monitor Tools and Agents

Network Monitor Tools and Agents will allow you to capture and analyze network packets that have been sent to and from the host computer. This utility is really kind of a subset of the Network Monitor service included with Microsoft's System Management Server or SMS. Network Monitor Tools and Agents can be installed without installing all of SMS.

Once the data has been captured, you can create a graphical representation of the current network activity or just get the numerical overview of the total network activity during the capture period. If you need a more granular breakdown of statistics, you can use the Session Stats screen, which displays communication information between two particular computers during a specific session. The Station Stats window shows all network activity for that particular workstation.

SEE ALSO Network Monitor Tools and Agents will be covered in Chapter 4, "Monitoring and Optimization."

Routing Information Protocol (RIP)

TCP/IP supports two different types of routing packets from one network to another network—static routing and dynamic routing. *Static routing* is the manual configuration of route tables. *Dynamic routing* means the routing protocol determines where the links are between networks and maintains its own route table. If you decide not to use static routing, NT Server supports RIP.

NOTE NT also supports another TCP/IP routing protocol—Open Shortest Path First (OSPF). At the time this book was being written, only RIP was supplied with NT Server; OSPF was available by download.

Simple Network Management Protocol (SNMP)

For a large network, having SNMP running is not an option, it is a necessity. SNMP allows network administrators to be proactive in troubleshooting problems on the network. In addition, SNMP allows for the gathering of statistics so you can manage the growth of the network.

By default, Windows NT will allow you to configure your servers and workstations as SNMP agents. An additional product, such as SMS or Hp OpenView, is necessary to take full advantage of SNMP.

Windows Internet Name Service (WINS)

When you install a Windows 32-bit product, you have to provide a name for the computer. That name is referred to as the *computer name* or *NetBIOS name*. Somehow, this NetBIOS name needs to be resolved to an IP address or to a network hardware address. WINS is the service that makes this possible. If your network is going to have many computers on it, WINS is a service you will need to provide fast name resolution.

Installing WINS is very important when your network consists of a majority of Windows computers.

Necessary Procedures

NOTE Installation and configuration of most of these services will be done as part of later objectives in this chapter.

Exam Essentials

The TCP/IP exam has many "situational" questions. Any objective that starts out with the words "Given a scenario" will see more than its share of those kinds of questions.

Know what DHCP does. DHCP will automatically assign clients an IP address, provide the subnet mask, point the client toward the right gateway, provide the IP address of the nearest WINS Server and configure the client for the appropriate WINS Node type.

Know what DNS does. DNS resolves host names to IP addresses. DNS can be configured to work with WINS so both NetBIOS names and hosts names are resolved quickly.

Know what WINS does. WINS resolves NetBIOS names to IP addresses. It can be used with DNS to provide resolution for both Net-BIOS computer names and DNS host names quickly and efficiently.

Know what SNMP does. SNMP provides a means for network management. SNMP consists of an SNMP agent and an SNMP manager. The SNMP agent is available as part of NT. The SNMP manager can be the System Management Service (SMS) or a third-party implementation.

Know what RIP does. RIP is a routing protocol that allows dynamic configuration of route tables.

Know what product you have to install to get FTP services. You must install IIS to have the capability of creating an FTP server.

Key Terms and Concepts

DHCP (Dynamic Host Configuration Protocol): Allows automatic assignment of IP addresses and other information.

DNS (Domain Name System): A way of resolving computer host names to IP addresses.

FTP (File Transfer Protocol): A connection-oriented Application layer program for the transfer of files from one host to another.

IIS (Internet Information Server): Provides FTP server functionality.

RIP (Routing Information Protocol): Part of the TCP/IP protocol suite that provides IP routing across different subnets.

SNMP (Simple Network Management Protocol): An industry standard protocol that allows applications to view the health of the network and monitor hosts.

WINS (Windows Internet Name Service): A Microsoft implementation of resolving NetBIOS computer names to IP addresses.

Sample Questions

1. Your network consists of three Windows NT Servers, 100 Windows NT Workstations, and 350 Windows 9*x* workstations. You are concerned about address resolution of NetBIOS computer names. Given this scenario, which TCP/IP service should you use?

   A. DHCP

   B. DNS

   C. WINS

   D. RIP

   Answer: C. DHCP is responsible for IP address assignments, not resolution. RIP is a routing protocol. That leaves DNS and WINS. By default, DNS host names are the NetBIOS computer name, but the Microsoft approved answer would be WINS. Look for a scenario with all Microsoft products and think WINS.

2. Your network consists of three Windows NT Servers, 100 Windows NT Workstations, 350 Windows 9*x* workstations, and 100 UNIX hosts. You are concerned about address resolution by either host name or computer name. Given this scenario, which TCP/IP services should you use?

   A. DHCP

   B. DNS

   C. WINS

   D. RIP

   Answer: B and C. DNS can handle resolving the host names and WINS can resolve the NetBIOS names.

3. The two methods of route discovery are:

   A. Dynamic and static

   B. Automatic and manual

   C. Static and automatic

   D. Manual and static

   Answer: A. The two methods of route discovery listed are static and dynamic route discovery. RIP uses a dynamic approach.

4. Your boss says that she wants the company's customers to be able to download the latest price list from the company FTP site. At this stage, the company has TCP/IP installed, but there is no company FTP site. What needs to be installed so you can configure an FTP server?

   A. System Management Services (SMS)

   B. Backup Exec

   C. RIP

   D. Internet Information Server (IIS)

   Answer: D. Internet Information Server must be installed to give you the ability to create an FTP server.

On a Windows NT Server computer, configure Microsoft TCP/IP to support multiple network adapters.

This objective is rather deceiving. While it is important to know how to configure an NT Server with multiple network cards to support TCP/IP, the real reason for the objective is to lay some groundwork for information yet to come. In this objective, we are going to define some terms and develop some concepts that will be used throughout the book and on the test.

Critical Information

The simple act of installing another network card takes on some larger proportions when you are using TCP/IP. In effect, you are creating another network segment and each time you create another network segment, you are creating another TCP/IP subnet. When you create a new subnet, you need to assign the subnet a new network number. How are the systems on this new network segment going to receive IP addresses? If you use DHCP, you will have to configure a DHCP scope and server for this segment or configure one of the computers on the segment to be a DHCP relay agent. What about name resolution, will there have to be a WINS Server involved for the subnet? If so, make sure the server can handle the increased workload. See what I mean, just adding a new network card to a server has all sorts of ramifications that will be covered later in this chapter.

When you add a second network card to a server, you are creating a router. Obviously, this is not a dedicated router because this computer has server stuff to do besides its job as a router. Adding a second network card to a server also gives the computer some new names. It suddenly becomes a multihomed computer or perhaps a multihomed system.

A *multihomed computer* is any computer that has two or more IP addresses. A *multihomed system* is any multihomed computer that has two or more network cards bound to separate physical networks.

TIP The terms multihomed computer and multihomed system will show up on the test, so it is important that you know how to differentiate between the two.

NOTE A network card can have multiple IP addresses assigned to it.

To turn a computer running NT Server into a router, you must perform the following tasks:

- Install a second network card.
- Connect the card to another physical segment.
- Assign the card a network address, a host address, and a subnet mask.
- Enable IP routing.

Once you have enabled IP routing, the server/router will be aware of only the subnets to which it is physically attached. If you want the system to know about all the subnets on your network, you will either have to manually configure the route table or enable the Routing Information Protocol (RIP).

Necessary Procedures

Once the network card has been installed and plugged into your network, it is time to configure the card to communicate using TCP/IP. Because we haven't gotten around to talking seriously about things such as DHCP, IP addressing, and subnets yet, some assumptions must be made. The first assumption will be that you have two network cards in your server, you must add support for the TCP/IP protocol, and configure the first network card to have an IP address of 210.47.26.33 with a subnet mask of 255.255.255.224. In addition, the system will point to a gateway at 210.47.26.1. The second card will be on a different subnet, so its card address will be 210.47.26.65 using a subnet mask of 255.255.255.224. It will also point to the gateway at 210.47.26.1. IP routing will be turned on.

The first thing to do is check that TCP/IP support is loaded on the computer. TCP/IP is the default protocol of NT, but if you didn't install the operating system yourself, it is always best to check.

1. Select Start ➤ Settings Control Panel ➤ Network ➤ Protocols and if TCP/IP support is already loaded, your screen should look like the one shown here:

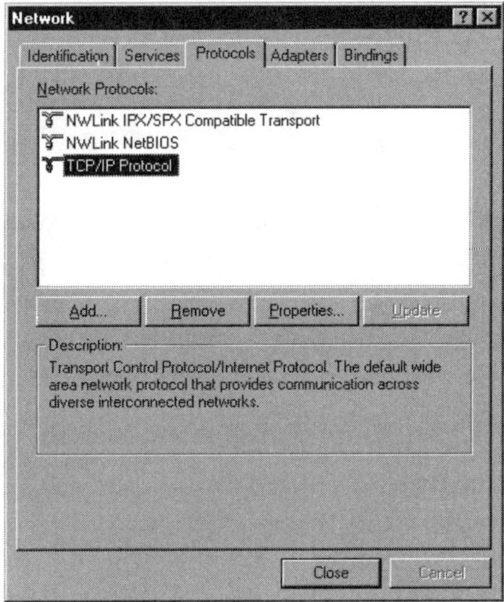

2. Highlighting TCP/IP Protocol and clicking on the Properties button will give you access to the screen to configure the cards with the assigned TCP/IP addresses. The following screen shows a

system with two network cards installed and the IP information for the first card.

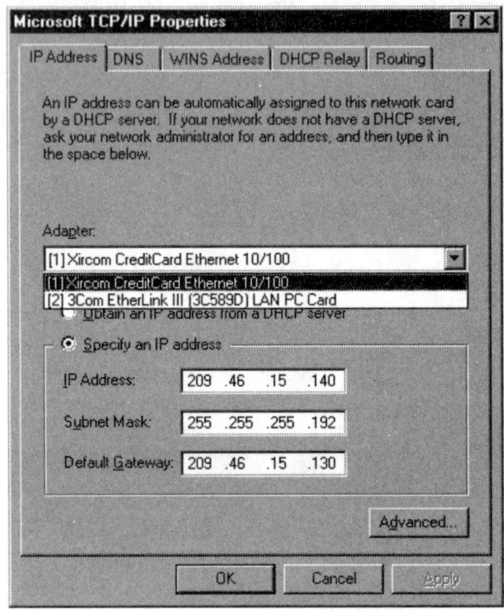

3. To add IP information, from the Microsoft TCP/IP Properties screen, click on the IP address tab and then highlight the adapter you want to configure. Click on the Specify an IP Address radio button. Enter the appropriate IP address, subnet mask, and gateway information.
4. Repeat step 3 for any other adapters that need to be configured.
5. To enable IP forwarding or routing, from the Microsoft TCP/IP Properties screen, click on the Routing tab.
6. Click on the box marked Enable IP Forwarding.
7. Click OK to close the Microsoft TCP/IP Properties window.
8. Click OK to close the Network window.

NOTE Following these instructions exactly may give you an error message. The card has not been configured to recognize a Windows Internet Name Service (WINS) Server. That will be done later in this chapter.

Exam Essentials

This objective deals primarily with background information. You need to know this information to be successful on the test even though there may not be many direct questions.

Know the difference between a multihomed computer and a multihomed system. A multihomed computer is any computer with several IP addresses. A multihomed system is a multihomed computer that houses multiple network cards attached to separate physical networks.

Know the settings necessary to configure TCP/IP addressing for a network card. To configure a network card, you need a unique IP host address and the subnet mask. If there are multiple subnets, you will also need the gateway address.

Key Terms and Concepts

Multihomed computer: A computer with multiple IP addresses assigned to it.

Multihomed system: A multihomed computer with multiple network cards that are each bound to a different subnetwork.

Router: A hardware device designed to route packets between networks.

Sample Questions

1. The NT Server named NTSRV_1 is assigned five IP addresses to its single network card. It is a

   A. Router

   B. Multihomed system

   C. Multihomed computer

   D. DHCP server

   Answer: C. It is a multihomed computer. If it had multiple network cards bound to separate networks, it would be a multihomed system.

2. When configuring a network card to communicate using TCP/IP, which two entries are mandatory?

   A. IP address

   B. Gateway

   C. WINS Server

   D. Subnet mask

   Answer: A and D. You must enter the IP address and the subnet mask. If your network is small, you may not need a gateway or a WINS Server, but if you are communicating using IP, you will need unique IP addresses and a subnet mask.

3. TCP/IP protocol properties are found as part of which Control Panel selection?

   A. Modems

   B. Networks

   C. Devices

   D. TCP/IP protocol

   Answer: B. TCP/IP protocol properties are found as part of the Network selection in the Control Panel.

Configure scopes by using DHCP Manager.

Two of the greatest time-savers for administrators who use TCP/IP have been Microsoft's 32-bit operating systems and DHCP. Prior to Windows NT and Windows 95, configuring a DOS-based computer to run a TCP/IP stack was not a job for the faint of heart. Manually configuring workstations with IP addresses and tracking those addresses to prevent duplication was a nightmare. DHCP has certainly relieved much of that strain.

Critical Information

Any host that wants to communicate using TCP/IP must have a unique IP address. An IP address is made up of 4 bytes and each byte is referred to as an *octet*. Because each byte is 8 bits, an IP address is 32 bits long. To simplify matters, we refer to IP addresses in their decimal equivalency. In the last section, we configured a network card to have the IP address of 210.47.26.33 with a subnet mask of 255.255.255.224.

NOTE A full explanation of subnets is coming later in this chapter as part of the section on configuring subnet masks.

There are two ways of assigning IP addresses: manually, as we did in the last section, and dynamically. Using the dynamic approach, you can configure one server on a subnet to "lease" IP addresses to any host that needs one. You can specify the range of IP address the server can assign and reserve certain addresses for particular computers. You can even make sure the hosts receive other information, such as gateway or WINS Server addresses. When a host is done with an address, it returns the address to the server. The next time the host comes up, it will ask for and receive an IP address. It may not be the same address the host had before shutting down, but in most cases that doesn't matter.

The choice between manual assignments or dynamic assignments is not an either/or type solution. You can, and probably will, do both. Some systems do not do well getting their addresses from a DHCP server. For example, if you want to host an intranet, it will make sense for the host server to have a static IP address, one that will never change.

How does DHCP work? The process is really quite simple. You configure an NT 3.5 server or better to be a DHCP server. You then provide the DHCP server with a "scope" of valid IP addresses. Don't let the word "scope" throw you, a scope is just a list. You also configure the DHCP server to pass out all that other information you want the systems to know about, things such as the IP address of the gateway and the IP address of the WINS Server. You then set the lease period so that it can loan addresses out for a period of time. By default, the IP lease is three days.

Placement of a DHCP server can be important. If your network uses routers, check to make sure the routers comply with Request for Comment (RFC) 1542. If the router complies with RFC 1542, it will pass requests for DHCP assignments from one subnet to another. If the router does not meet those specifications, there should be a DHCP server on each network segment, or you will have to configure systems to act as DHCP relay agents.

TIP DHCP configuration, what a great concept for repeated test questions! You must have a DHCP server on each subnet or there must be a computer configured as a DHCP relay agent. DHCP relay agents will be discussed during the objective on IP routing.

Now that the server is configured, what about the client? When you configure an NT Server, NT Workstation, or Windows 9*x* to use TCP/IP, by default it will go out and look for a DHCP server. What this means to the administrator is simple: configure the OS, select the

TCP/IP protocol, copy the files, and it's a done deal. Now, if the computer is moved from one network segment to another, nothing must be done to reconfigure the machine to continue running TCP/IP.

When a workstation is turned on, it recognizes the need for an IP address. At this point, the workstation broadcasts a lease request, called a DHCPDISCOVER message. The client has no idea about the IP address of the DHCP server. This means the DHCPDISCOVER message is a *broadcast message*, so every client on the subnet will receive the packet. If nothing responds to the request, the workstation will send the lease request four more times, at 9 seconds, 13 seconds, 16 seconds, and then a random number of seconds. If the client still doesn't get an answer, it will continue to issue lease requests every 5 minutes.

When a DHCP server receives a lease request, it answers by sending back an IP lease offer or a DHCPOFFER packet. The offer packet is also sent as a broadcast message because at this point the client does not have an IP address. The DHCP offer will contain an IP address and subnet mask, the hardware address of the DHCP client, the IP address of the DHCP server and the duration of the lease.

Back at the client side, the client receives the DHCPOFFER packet. If you have multiple DHCP servers on a subnet, the client may receive multiple offers. The client accepts the first offer it receives by sending back a packet called the DHCPREQUEST packet. The DHCPREQUEST packet tells the successful DHCP server that the workstation is taking it up on its offer. All the other servers realize the IP address it offered can be returned to the scope to be used by another workstation.

The process has not been completed. The DHCP server still needs to verify the successful lease. The server sends back an acknowledgment in the form of a packet known as a DHCPACK. This confirms the address and other configuration information. Once the client receives the DHCPACK, the client can initialize TCP/IP and the communications begin.

What if the client is unsuccessful in its lease, or it is trying to renew a lease that has expired and the number has been reassigned? In that case, the DHCP server will send out a DHCPNACK. When a client gets a DHCPNACK, it knows it is back to square one, and it starts the process over again.

Once the client has acknowledged the configuration information, it can keep that address until the system shuts down or the address is released manually. Like all leases, this one does have to be renewed. The default lease period is three days. After 50 percent of the time is up, the client will attempt to renew its lease. If the DHCP server is up and working, the client gets a new lease on the address. However, if the DHCP server is down, the client can still keep using the address because the lease will not expire for another 36 hours. DHCP clients also attempt to renew their leases on start-up by broadcasting their last leased IP address. If the address hasn't been given out, it will be reassigned.

DHCP addresses are configured using DHCP Manager. DHCP Manager is installed when DHCP is installed on the server and one installation can manage several DHCP servers. Addresses can be grouped in ranges. Some of the address can be excluded and you can use DHCP Manager to choose the duration of the lease. If network traffic is an issue, you may want the lease to be unlimited in duration.

Taking Care of DHCP

All of these addresses and ranges are stored in database files stuck in the %systemroot%\system32\dhcp directory. Like all database files, these files can become corrupted. Table 2.1 describes the databases and what they are responsible for.

TABLE 2.1: DHCP databases

File Name	Description
DHCP.MDB	An actual DHCP database. Do not even think about trying to open this database and looking inside!

TABLE 2.1: DHCP databases *(continued)*

File Name	Description
DHCP.TMP	Temporary database created while the DHCP service is running
JET.LOG and JET*.LOG	Logs of all the transactions written to the DHCP databases. Logged transactions include active leases, lease releases, and lease renewals. These files are used to reconstruct the database in the time of tragedy.
SYSTEM.MDB	The template file for the DHCP database. It contains the information needed to rebuild the structure of the database, if needed.

By default, these databases are backed up to the %systemroot%\system32\dhcp\backup\jet directory every 60 minutes. If you ever have to restore DHCP from these files, the first try should be simply stopping and restarting the DHCP Server service. When you restart the service, it can detect the files that are corrupted and will automatically restore them.

If that fails, you can stop the DHCP Server service and manually copy the contents of the %systemroot%\system32\dhcp\backup\jet directory to the %systemroot%\system32\dhcp folder and then restart the DHCP Server service.

If the DHCP database gets larger than 30MB, it will have to be compacted. This is done by using the JETPACK.EXE utility.

Necessary Procedures

The installation of DHCP is completed in the stages discussed below.

Installing DHCP

To create a DHCP scope, DHCP must be installed on an NT Server. DHCP requires NT 3.5 or greater. To install DHCP on an NT 4 Server:

1. Select Start ➤ Settings ➤ Control Panel ➤ Network.
2. From the Network window, click on the Services tab.
3. Click Add and the server will build a list of available services.
4. From the Select Network Service window, choose Microsoft DHCP Server and click OK.
5. Provide the NT Setup screen with the location of the NT files and click Continue.
6. Click OK on the nag screen requiring adapters within the server to have a static IP address.
7. Click Close to close the network dialog box.
8. At this point you will be prompted to restart the computer. Click on Yes and when the computer restarts, log on as Administrator or as a member of the Administrator group.

Creating a DHCP Scope

Now that the server is a DHCP server, you can open DHCP Manager from the Administrative Tools menu. DHCP Manager lets you create the IP address scopes on multiple DHCP servers. To configure a scope on a machine running DHCP service:

1. Choose Start ➤ Programs ➤ Administrative Tools ➤ DHCP Manager.
2. Because the configuration will take place on this server, choose the Local Machine from the list of DHCP servers.
3. From the DHCP Manager menu, choose Scope ➤ Create.
4. Enter a Start Address and an End Address as well as the subnet mask for the network.

5. If you have addresses with the range that need to be excluded, enter the address range in the Exclusion Range section. You can have multiple ranges excluded.
6. From the Lease Duration section of the Create Scope (Local) window, make whatever changes are necessary. The default lease is three days. You can choose an unlimited lease duration, although this not recommended.
7. Give the range a name and comment, if appropriate.
8. Click OK.
9. You will be prompted to activate the new scope. Click on Yes.
10. Click on OK to close the DHCP Manager Servers screen.

Configuring NT Workstation

To configure an NT Workstation to get its IP address from a DHCP server:

NOTE In most cases TCP/IP support utilizing DHCP is installed as the default protocol on an NT Workstation computer. This section will show you how to check the default settings.

---

1. Select Start ➢ Settings ➢ Control Panel ➢ Network.
2. From the Network window, choose the Protocols tab.
3. Highlight TCP/IP Protocol and click on Properties.
4. Make sure the Obtain an IP address from a DHCP server option is selected.

Compacting the DHCP Database

The DHCP database needs to be compacted when it reaches a size greater than 30MB. Follow these steps to compact the database:

1. Stop the DHCP Server service.

2. Open a command prompt window and change into the \%system-root%\system32\dhcp\ folder.
3. The syntax for using JETPACK.EXE is: jetpack dhcp.mdb tempfilename.mdb
4. Restart the DHCP Server service.

Exam Essentials

This section of the objectives gets some attention from the test writers. The DCHP questions revolve around the concept of scope as well as configuration of a DHCP relay agent. Relay agents will be covered in more detail during the discussion of IP routing.

Know how to create a DHCP server. Creating a DHCP server is done from the Control Panel Network Services tab.

Know what DHCP can provide. DHCP servers can be configured to provide a dynamic IP address, subnet mask, gateway address, addresses of several DNS servers, and the addresses of a WINS Server. Multiple addresses or several ranges of addresses can be excluded from the DHCP scope.

Know the Administrative Tool added when you install the DHCP server. The installation of the DHCP server adds the DHCP Manager to the Administrative Tools (Common) menu. DHCP Manager is used to configure DHCP scopes.

Know the appropriate placement of a DHCP server. Plan on placing either a DHCP server or a DHCP relay agent on each subnet segment.

Key Terms and Concepts

DHCP (Dynamic Host Configuration Protocol): A service configured on an NT 3.5 Server or better to provide dynamic IP addresses and configuration information to hosts on a subnet.

DHCP lease: The amount of time a workstation can keep an address.

DHCP Manager: Manages DHCP properties.

DHCP scope: The range of addresses the DHCP server can manage.

Sample Questions

1. By default, a DHCP client leases a DHCP address for:

   A. One day

   B. Two days

   C. Three days

   D. Four days

   Answer: C. DHCP addresses are leased for three days by default.

2. If a workstation has leased a DHCP address for three days, when does it try to renew the lease the first time?

   A. After 12 hours

   B. After 24 hours

   C. After 36 hours

   D. After 48 hours

   E. After 72 hours

   Answer: C. A DHCP client will attempt to renew the lease after fifty percent of the lease period has expired, or approximately 36 hours.

3. Which utility is used to configure DHCP scopes?

   A. DHCP Manager

   B. Domain Manager

   C. TCP/IP Manager

   D. User Manager for Domains

   Answer: A. DHCP Manager is used to configure scopes.

4. Your network consists of six subnets. On each subnet, you want IP addresses to be assigned dynamically. You must have either a(n) _____________ or a(n) _________________ on each subnet.

   A. PDC, BDC

   B. DHCP server, DHCP relay agent

   C. NT 3.51 Server, NT 4.0 Server

   D. Windows 98 Workstation, Windows 95 Workstation

   Answer: B. To accomplish this task, you should have either a DHCP server or a DHCP relay agent on each subnet.

Install and Configure a WINS Server.

- Import LMHOSTS files to WINS.
- Run WINS on a multihomed computer.
- Configure WINS replication.
- Configure static mappings in the WINS database.

During the early days of Windows networking, it was knocked for not being extensible to the enterprise. After all, Windows networking revolved around the NetBEUI protocol, and while NetBEUI is a great little protocol, the fact that you can't route it definitely limits its use in a wide area network (WAN) implementation. Windows networking also worked with computer names to find things. This is part of the NetBIOS name resolution, and again, it just wasn't usable on a WAN.

The proper configuration of Windows Internet Name Server or WINS Servers can make name resolution a much faster process and helps gives legitimacy to NT in the enterprise. The discussion of WINS starts the process of address resolution.

Critical Information

In a Windows NT environment running TCP/IP, a computer can be identified in a variety of ways. If you remember all the way back to Chapter 1, the book opened with a discussion of the seven layers of the OSI model or the four layers of the DOD model. The Application layer (the first one in each case) dealt with how information was put onto the wire and how that information was addressed to find its way back to the sending computer. This hardware level address is a unique hexadecimal number assigned by the network card manufacturer. This address, also called the Media Access Control or MAC address, is the final destination for communications destined for a computer. Everything else—IP address, NetBIOS computer name, DNS name—must be resolved to this MAC layer address.

Address Resolution

Resolving an IP address to a MAC address is done by a TCP/IP protocol called the Address Resolution Protocol (ARP). Once a packet ends up at the proper subnet, it is up to the ARP to resolve the IP address to a MAC layer address and get the packet to its final destination.

Other resolution methods, such as WINS and DNS have a variety of ways of resolving computer or host names to an IP address. In this way, if you send a command to www.microsoft.com, DNS will resolve the name www.microsoft.com to an IP address and direct the packet to that IP address. Once the packet arrives on the appropriate subnet, it is up to ARP to get it to the right host. WINS does the same thing, sort of. Instead of taking the global approach of DNS, WINS takes a somewhat smaller approach, resolving computer names to IP addresses. It is up to WINS to resolve the computer name you find in Network Neighborhood to the MAC address that represents the system.

WINS

WINS is a semi-dynamic system. It is semi-dynamic because in a large Windows environment, most of the information in the database will come dynamically from the client. Other information on non-WINS clients, such as UNIX or LAN Manager computers, can be added to the database manually or by importing a copy of an LMHOSTS file. The process starts with the designation of a WINS Server. A WINS Server will maintain a database of all active computer names that it knows about complete with addresses.

Here is the way NetBIOS and WINS work. In a small (non-routed) environment, any time a computer needs to know a resource's NetBIOS it asks by using the broadcast method, meaning every computer on the network gets the message. NetBIOS names are assigned when you install the Windows operating system. The names can be up to 15 characters in length. Now, if you know anything about computers, you know that 15 is a strange number for computers to use; usually, everything is in multiples of eight. The NetBIOS name is no different. You have the ability to assign a name up to 15 characters, but the protocol reserves the sixteenth character to indicate what service will be registering the name. The Computer Browser service or Net Logon are examples of these services.

The problem with NetBIOS arises whenever you decide that you need to route information. Broadcast messages do not get routed. This means that you would be able to resolve NetBIOS names for all computers on your subnet and not see anything else on the network. Because you probably will want to see things such as shares on the other side of the router, this is not acceptable. So, your friends in Redmond came up with WINS.

When computers want something, they have two ways of asking for it: by means of a broadcast request or a directed request. When a computer uses a *broadcast request*, it sends the request out to every other computer on the network. It would be kind of like standing up in the middle of a crowded room and yelling at the top your lungs, "I need to talk to my editor!" That might be effective, unless everyone else in the room started yelling, also.

Given the limitations of NetBIOS, it became obvious that for a computer to access resources on a computer, it had to issue a directed request to that computer. Now, that term, "directed request," sounds a lot fancier than it really is. A *directed request* means that your computer resolves the NetBIOS name to an address and then sends its request directly to that address. In this case, if I needed to talk with my editor, I would resolve the name to an address by looking up her information in the phone directory. Once I had her address, I could direct my message to her, by either calling or sending her snail mail. No one else would be bothered and the system would use a whole lot less cable bandwidth.

So, how does a computer resolve a NetBIOS name to an IP address? Well, first it looks to itself. When computers "hear" about other computers, they put the computer name and IP address in NetBIOS name cache—they simply store the information in memory. Next, the computer will send out a broadcast request looking for the name. Then, the host will use WINS to try and resolve the name. If all of these systems fail, the computer will read (parse) the LMHOSTS file, parse the HOSTS file, and finally ask DNS if it knows where the other computer is.

Bringing this back to human terms, I need to find my editor. I check my memory, do I know her address? Nope, not there. Let's check the room. I stand up and yell out my editor's name to everyone in the room and tell them that I am looking for her address. Does anyone respond? Nope, no one in the room knows where she lives either. Next, just like WINS, I will call information and see if information for my area has information on her. I call 411 and ask if they know where she lives. Nope, this woman is really elusive. Let me think, I may have had her address written down at one time; let me read through my entire LMHOSTS file. Hmmm, still not there. Let me read through my entire HOSTS file; still no luck. My last resort, go out to the Internet and check with the main repository of directory information. If it is there, all is good. If not, I receive an error message. Obviously, if any one of the above procedures returns a positive response, the search is over. After all, a thing is always in the last place you look for it.

Specifically, how does NetBIOS name resolution work over TCP/IP? It would seem to be incompatible. There are two RFCs written that address the subject: RFC1001 and RFC1002 address the four different modes that NetBIOS uses for name resolution. These four modes are defined for the entire world using RFCs. Microsoft has taken one of the modes and "enhanced" it, so Microsoft TCP/IP actually uses five modes for resolution.

Each of the five modes starts out just like our example above. It first checks name cache. If the name and address are stored in memory, why go any farther? Once it has been shown that name cache does not have the answer, then modes begin to take the path less traveled.

The modes include B-mode, P-mode, M-mode, H-mode, and Microsoft Enhanced B-mode. Don't let the funky names scare you off; as you can see, it is pretty easy to remember what each mode does:

- **B-mode** is broadcast mode.
- **H-mode** is hybrid mode.
- **M-mode** is mixed mode.
- **P-mode** is peer mode (ask all your friends).

Using B-mode, Microsoft Enhanced B-mode Methods, and P-mode

The first mode that will be used for name resolution is a B-mode method. A computer using B-mode will try and resolve NetBIOS names to IP addresses using only broadcast methods. As you can tell, this is probably not going to be a very efficient means of name resolution. Microsoft recognized this and enhanced the standard.

In Microsoft Enhanced B-mode, the system will try a broadcast and if that doesn't work, the computer will then parse the LMHOSTS file and the HOSTS file to see if the name is in there. Again, it is an enhancement over B-mode, but somehow I find it difficult to believe that many companies would make sure that every computer in the organization is going to be listed in an LMHOSTS file or a HOSTS file. That just doesn't sound too realistic. If you do not have a WINS Server configured, this is the mode your Windows computer will come back to by default.

P-mode is higher up on the elegant scale. With P-mode, or peer-to-peer mode, the computer sends a directed datagram to a WINS Server for assistance. This would be similar to a person who will call and ask directions every time he or she wants to go somewhere.

In all three cases, the systems configured to use these methods use only one way of finding out the IP address. Not very flexible, are they?

TIP Modes can be manually configured by editing the registry parameter HKEY_LOCAL_MACHINE\SYSTEM\CurrentControlSet\Services\NetBT\Parameters.

M-mode and H-mode

This is the good stuff. H-mode and M-mode are preferable to the B-mode and P-mode types because they can use more than one resolution method. For example, M-mode will try a B-mode (broadcast) method first. If that doesn't work, it will try a P-mode (peer) method, looking for a WINS Server.

H-mode will do the B-mode and P-mode thing, but it reverses the M-mode order. Working with H-mode, the computer will use the P-mode method first. In other words, the host goes directly to the WINS Server and asks if it knows where this resource is before it tries to broadcast a request. If a WINS Server is configured, the system will default to H-mode for NetBIOS name resolution.

In order for this system to work, workstations need to know that a WINS Server is there. For clients running Microsoft's Windows products, this is done by providing the WINS Server's address during the configuration of TCP/IP. During the section on DHCP, it was mentioned that IP addresses can be configured dynamically or manually. The same is true of providing a client with the WINS address. This can be done manually or dynamically as part of the DHCP process.

For those clients that are not running Windows, Microsoft TCP/IP includes WINS proxy agents. The proxy agent acts like a quasi-WINS Server. It will listen for name registration requests or name queries.

When it "hears" one, it checks its cache for the information. If the information is in cache, the proxy agent responds. If the information is not in cache, the proxy agent sends the request on to the WINS Server. The WINS Server will handle any name resolution requests and send the information back to the proxy agent. The proxy agent then sends the information on to the non-WINS client requesting the service. It is important to note that non-WINS clients can send a name registration request to the WINS Server through the proxy agent, but the name will just be verified. The name registration requests will not be added to the WINS Server database.

If you have non-WINS clients on the network and want to install a WINS proxy agent, here are some guidelines:

- A WINS proxy agent can be any computer running NT Server, NT Workstation, Windows 9*x*, or Windows for Workgroups (WFW). The WFW computers must be running the 32-bit version of Microsoft TCP/IP.
- The WINS proxy agent must be configured as a WINS client, not as a WINS Server.
- The proxy agent must be on the same subnet as the non-WINS clients.
- You should have a maximum of two proxy agents per subnet.

WINS Server Installation and Configuration

WINS Server has to be installed on a computer running Windows NT Server, version 3.5*x* or higher. The computer can be a backup domain controller (BDC) or a member server. Microsoft suggests that the WINS Server not be a Primary Domain Controller (PDC) because the PDC may become overworked. Because the WINS client computers will be looking to the WINS Server for guidance, it is important they know where to find the server. The server should be configured with a static IP address.

Theoretically, one WINS Server could provide name resolution for an entire network. This could pose a problem for the network if the only WINS Server were to go down, so it is recommended that you have two WINS Servers. Microsoft recommends that if your network grows to over 10,000 clients you should add a primary and secondary WINS Server for each 10,000 clients.

If you have a large network, and there are a lot of name resolution requests, your WINS Servers will be awfully busy. There may be a time when the load of handling WINS resolutions is all that the server can take, so you can have a server dedicated to nothing but WINS.

WINS is installed through the Network option of the Control Panel. Just like DHCP, installation is done through the Services tab. Once the service has been installed another new icon appears on the Administrative Tools menu, this time it is the WINS Manager. WINS Manager allows you to configure the time lines for maintaining certain lease parameters. For example, you can choose how long a computer can go before renewing its name with the WINS Server. The default is six days.

Import LMHOSTS to WINS

A WINS Server has two ways of gathering information about a network, statically and dynamically. When a WINS *client* (a machine running some form of Windows operating system) begins the boot process, it sends its computer name and address in a direct broadcast to the WINS Server. That is how WINS dynamically learns about its network each time a Windows client starts: it registers its computer name with the WINS Server.

What about those computers on your network that are not WINS clients? These are things such as UNIX computers that have host names but do not use NetBIOS. How can these machines take advantage of the resolution provided by a WINS Server? Because these foreign hosts do not run NetBIOS, they cannot register dynamically on boot up, so the registration has to be done manually.

In Chapter 1, “Planning,” we briefly looked at the role of the LMHOSTS file. We will examine the LMHOSTS file in more depth later in this chapter. For the sake of the WINS Server, it has to import an LMHOSTS file into its database to learn about all the hosts registered with the file.

Each host can have an LMHOSTS file that contains different information. Fortunately, there can be a "master" LMHOSTS file that other systems can refer to; it acts like a clearinghouse of host information. A copy of this LMHOSTS file is imported into the WINS database to provide a comprehensive list of foreign clients on the network. Notice the key word, "copy." The file must be copied and renamed for the process to be truly successful. If you try and import an LMHOSTS file into the WINS database, the system will tell you the file was imported successfully, but nothing shows up in the database. Copying the file and giving it another name solves the problem.

TIP In the LMHOSTS sample file shown in Chapter 1, "Planning," you may have noticed the different tags in the file—things such as #PRE to pre-load the information in the hosts cache. When an LMHOSTS file is imported into a WINS Server, all tags except the domain tag, #DOM, are ignored.

WINS on a Multihomed Computer

Earlier in the chapter, there was a discussion of multihomed computers and multihomed systems. To review, a multihomed computer is a computer with a network card that has up to 25 IP addresses assigned to it. A multihomed system is a multihomed computer with more that one network card and more than one IP address. Why would someone create a multihomed system? Think of an internet service provider that hosts Web sites for each of its clients. Each client may have a different base IP address, but the NT Server computer can only have a finite number of network cards.

A multihomed computer is created by manually adding more than one TCP/IP address to any network card. Once the multihomed computer has been created, if it is to take part in WINS resolution, it should be added to the static addresses on the WINS Server. When you use WINS Manager to configure static addresses in the WINS database, you can choose what type of system they represent. In addition to the multihomed computer there are the following system types:

- *Unique* is a unique name in the WINS database. There can be only one address per name. The unique name is the WINS client's computer name.
- *Group* indicates a normal group for which the IP addresses of the individual clients are not stored. A *normal group* is the name to which broadcasts are sent and is the domain name used for browsing purposes. A normal group name does not have an IP address associated with it and can be valid on multiple networks and registered with multiple WINS Servers. When a WINS Server receives a request for the group name, the WINS Server returns the limited broadcast address 255.255.255.255, which the WINS client will then use to broadcast to the network.
- *Internet Group* is a group that contains the IP addresses for up to 25 primary and backup domain controllers for the domain. The Internet group name is another instance of the domain name being registered; however, this instance is used for the domain controllers in the domain to communicate with each other.

The static addresses will be added to the database, though only one will show up in the Static Mappings – (Local) window; that is all the system needs. If it receives a request for a computer with the name of the multihomed computer, it sends the request to the primary address listed.

NOTE More information on adding static addresses to the WINS database will be provided later in this chapter in the section, "Configure static mappings in the WINS database."

WINS Replication

Why is there a need for replication of the WINS database? Microsoft recommends a WINS Server for each of the 10,000 clients. One of the reasons you will replicate WINS Servers is to cut down on traffic from each of those 10,000 clients to a single server.

Client-to-server communication is a chatty event. When a client starts up, it sends a NetBIOS name registration message for each service that it initializes to its primary WINS Server. For example, the sample server used as part of the preparation for this book is running six services, so when this system comes online, six name registration messages will be sent to the primary WINS Server. These messages are directed packets, meaning that each packet is sent directly to the WINS Server's IP address. If the WINS Server does not answer, the client will then send out the packets to the address 255.255.255.255 or a broadcast. Every host on the network will receive the packet and have to deal with it, even if the host is not a WINS Server.

If the client's name is not registered in the WINS database, the server will respond with a positive name registration response. The positive name registration response contains the Time To Live, or TTL. If the name is already taken, the WINS Server responds by querying the previously registered computer to see if it is still online. If the computer is still online, the client requesting the name gets a negative name registration response. If the previously registered computer does not respond, the WINS Server takes that to mean the system is offline, and issues the name to the system currently making the request.

When a computer shuts down, if it closes properly, it sends a name release request for each of the services to the WINS Server. Again, six services, six different name release requests. When the server receives the request, it will respond with a positive name release response. The WINS Server checks the name as inactive and the name then becomes available.

WINS Renewal

If the computer has been up for awhile, say half the TTL, it will attempt to renew its name. The computer sends a name refresh request to the server, one for each service. If the server is up and working, it will respond with a name refresh response, one for each service. If the client cannot get in touch with the primary WINS Server it will try the secondary WINS Server. If it does not get the name refresh response, it will continue to use the assigned NetBIOS name because its lease has not expired.

WINS Redundancy

As you can see, there is an awful lot of communication going on just to assign, refresh, and release names. Performance may dictate that you have more than one WINS Server on a network, but that would not be the only reason. The primary reason for WINS is to allow computers to browse the network for services by using computer names. If the only WINS Server on the network goes down, computers will be limited in how many computer names can be resolved to IP addresses by the contents of the local LMHOSTS file. To prevent that from becoming a problem, you can configure a secondary WINS Server and have the WINS Servers exchange databases.

Data exchange at the WINS Server level is done through a push and pull relationship. One of the servers must be configured to push its information to its partner while the other system is configured as a pull partner. Either the push partner or the pull partner can be configured to start the replication process.

The replication works something like this. The push partner has a new computer come online and register. Therefore, the WINS database has changed. The push partner sends a message to the pull partner, informing it the database has changed. The pull partner has to ask to have changes sent to it. When the push partner receives the request for changes, it will send information on just the changes or additions.

Push partner replication is usually configured across fast WAN or LAN links. This is done because push replication is triggered by the number of changes that occur to the database. More changes are made during the busy times of day so push replication should take advantage of the links that can handle the traffic.

If the push partner replication should use the faster WAN links, what about pull partner replication? Pull partner replication can be scheduled or it will occur whenever the pull partner starts up, otherwise the Administrator can force a replication. This form of replication can use slower links because it is usually a time-based process. The pull partner can be configured to request updates at certain start times or intervals. This way, the pull partner can request the changes during periods of low traffic.

By default, replication is a one-way process (see Figure 2.1).

FIGURE 2.1: Replication across WAN Links

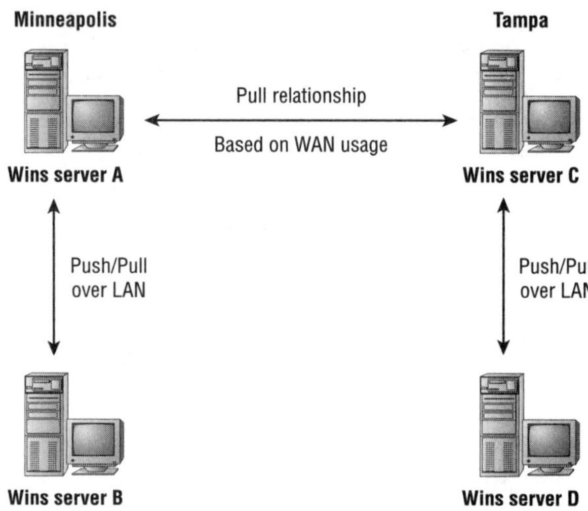

In Figure 2.1 above, WINS Server A is configured as a push partner to WINS Server C. This way, systems in Tampa will have a copy of the Minneapolis database. In order for Minneapolis to have a copy of Tampa's database, each server must be configured to be a push/pull partner of the other. When properly configured, all the systems in Tampa will know about all the systems in Minneapolis and vice versa.

TIP For purposes of the exam, it is important to know that push partners start the process based on the number of changes and pull partners are based on time. There many be several scenario-based questions on the exam, so remember push uses fast links, pull uses slower links.

Backing Up and Restoring a WINS Server Database

Replication is a way to control WAN/LAN traffic. It is also a way of providing fault tolerance for the database. Like it or not, even the most stable database can become corrupted and sometimes restoring from a good backup is the only way to correct a corrupted database. Although it is not specifically covered in the objectives, it is important to know how to compact the WINS database and to configure the WINS databases to get backed up.

The WINS database is named wins.mdb and is located in the %systemroot%\system32\wins directory. Like most databases generated by NT, it is a JET database and occasionally needs some tender loving care before it can be backed up. If the database becomes too large (greater than 30MB), it should be compacted using the JETPACK.EXE utility. To compact the database, you stop the WINS service, execute JETPACK from the same directory the database resides in, and then restart WINS.

NOTE JETPACK.EXE is a command-line utility. The syntax for the command is JETPACK wins.mdb temp name mdb.

In addition, like all databases, the WINS database should be backed up. When we discussed DHCP, we mentioned that the databases were backed up automatically. This is not the case with a WINS database. You have to configure the system to back up the database. Once configured and the first manual backup has been completed, the database will be backed up every 24 hours to a directory you specify. The backup can be a complete backup. If you have a corrupt database, all you have to do to restore from backup is to stop and start the WINS service. When the WINS Server restarts, it will recognize the corruption and immediately restore from backup. You can also restore from choosing a menu option in WINS Manager, or as a last resort, restores can be done manually.

TIP It may be important for you to remember that you can restore the WINS database simply by stopping and starting the WINS service.

Static Mappings in the WINS Database

A static mapping is placed in the WINS database to reserve or hold a computer name for a specific computer. It is used primarily for non-WINS clients, allowing WINS-enabled clients to resolve the IP address to the computer name. Non-WINS clients are computers running UNIX or LAN Manager 2.2c for OS/2.

One of the benefits of adding the non-WINS computers to the database is you will no longer need to maintain an entry in the LMHOSTS file for that computer. WINS clients will be able to resolve computer names to IP addresses for the non-WINS enabled clients. The reverse, however, is not the case. You will still need to have some sort of HOST/LMHOST file to resolve names to addresses at the UNIX host.

NOTE To make maintenance of the static mappings in the WINS database easier, a copy of the LMHOSTS file can be imported into the database.

Static mappings are added to the WINS database using WINS Manager. Before starting WINS Manager, you will need the name of the computer, its IP address, and the type of system you are defining. Types include the following:

- *Unique* is a unique name in the WINS database that permits only one IP address per name. The unique name is the WINS client's computer name.
- *Group* indicates a normal group for which the IP addresses of the individual clients are not stored. A *normal group* is the name to which broadcasts are sent and is the domain name used for browsing purposes. A normal group name has [1Eh] in the 16th byte field at the end of the name in WINS Manager. A normal

group name does not have an IP address associated with it and can be valid on multiple networks and registered with multiple WINS Servers. When a WINS Server receives a request for the group name, the WINS Server returns the limited broadcast address 255.255.255.255, which the WINS client will then use to broadcast to the network.

- *Domain name* allows you to specify a group with NetBIOS names that have 0x1c as the 16th byte. A domain name group stores up to 25 addresses for its members. For registration after the 25th address, WINS overwrites a replica address or the oldest registration. Choosing this option will provide you with additional options to add multiple addresses to the list.
- *Internet group* is a group that contains the IP addresses for up to 25 primary and backup domain controllers for the domain. An Internet group has a 0x1c as its 16th byte, which appears as a [1Ch] at the end of the name WINS Manager. The Internet group name is another instance of the domain name being registered; however, this instance is used for the domain controllers in the domain to communicate with each other.
- *Multihomed* is similar to a unique name in that it is the WINS client's computer name; however, it can have up to 25 addresses and is for use by multihomed systems. A *multihomed system* is a system with more than one network interface and more than one IP address.

NOTE When you open Show Database from the WINS Manager Mappings menu option, you will be presented with a detail screen that shows what computer name has been mapped to which IP address. Immediately following the computer name, there is a hexadecimal identifier, which points to the type service being mapped. This is referred to as the 16th bit.

Necessary Procedures

The proper configuration of Windows Internet Name Service is accomplished through several steps, starting with the installation and configuration. Once the server has been installed and configured, you can decide how the WINS Server will gather information—by a dynamic method, a static method, or both.

Installing and Configuring a WINS Server

1. Select Start ➤ Settings ➤ Control Panel ➤ Network.
2. From the Network window, click on the Services tab.
3. Click Add and the server will build a list of available services.
4. From the Select Network Service window, choose Windows Internet Name Service and click OK.
5. Provide the NT Setup screen with the location of the NT files and click Continue.
6. Click Close to close the network dialog box.
7. At this point you will be prompted to restart the computer. Click on Yes and when the computer restarts, log on as Administrator or as a member of the Administration group.

Once the WINS Server has been installed and the computer restarted, you can check on how hard the service is working by using the WINS Manager.

To start WINS Manager:

1. Select Start ➤ Programs ➤ Administrative Tools.
2. Click on WINS Manager.

To use WINS Manager to configure the WINS Server:

From WINS Manager, select Server ➤ Configuration ➤ Advanced. If you look at the WINS Server Configuration window in the illustration below, you will notice that you can configure the Renewal

Interval, the Extinction Interval, the Extinction Timeout, and the Verify Interval. Each is set in terms of hours.

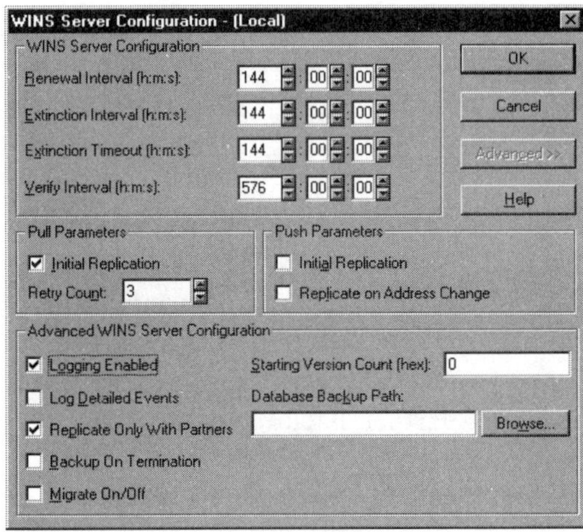

Table 2.2 shows what each of the configuration parameters controls.

TABLE 2.2: WINS Server configuration parameters

Interval	Description
Renewal Interval	The default time period before the WINS Server releases the client name. If the client does not renew within this time period, it will have to register again.
Extinction Interval	The number of hours that a released name or non-renewed name will remain in the database before it is determined to be extinct.
Extinction Timeout	The amount of time an extinct record will remain in the database before it is purged.
Verify Interval	How often this WINS Server waits before verifying the material stored in other WINS databases.

WINS Servers should work in pairs and should trade databases. This is done through the pull parameters and push parameters.

SEE ALSO For more information on this subject, see the section, "Configure WINS Replication," later in this chapter.

Some advanced WINS configuration options allow you to maintain logging and detailed events. You can set up the server to Replicate Only With Partners, Backup on Termination, and set Migrate On/Off. Replicate Only With Partners means that an administrator cannot ask a WINS Server to pull or push replication to an unlisted WINS Server partner. Backup on Termination causes the WINS database to be backed up if the WINS service is stopped unless the system is shutting down. Migrate On/Off specifies that static, unique, and multihomed records in the database are treated as dynamic records when they conflict with a new registration or replica.

Installing a WINS Proxy Agent

Proxy agents are not mentioned in the objectives, but the Microsoft exam writers have an interesting way of bringing other things into the exam. It will help to know about proxy agents.

A WINS proxy agent can be any computer running NT Server, NT Workstation, Windows 9*x*, or Windows for Worksgroups, if the Workgroup computer is running the 32-bit version of TCP/IP. The proxy agent must be configured as a WINS Server and cannot be the WINS Server. The proxy agent must reside on the same subnet as the non-WINS clients. There can be two proxy agents per subnet.

WARNING Beware: Configuring an NT system to be a proxy agent requires you to edit the registry. There have been cases where editing the registry has given Microsoft an excuse not to provide tech support.

To configure an NT system to be a proxy agent, follow these steps:

1. Select Start ➤ Run.
2. Type **Regedt32** in the Open box and click OK.
3. Browse to the registry key HKEY_LOCAL_MACHINE\SYSTEM\CurrentControlSet\Services\NetBT\Parameters.
4. Double-click on the EnableProxy value entry.
5. In the DWORD Editor box Data window type **1**.
6. Click OK and close the Registry Editor.
7. Restart the computer.

Configuring an NT Server to Be a WINS Client

Any Windows-based computer on the network that is not a WINS Server or a WINS proxy agent can be configured to be a WINS client. There are two ways of providing the client information about the location of the WINS Server, either manually or dynamically using DHCP.

To configure the client manually, follow these steps:

1. Select Start ➤ Settings ➤ Control Panel ➤ Network.
2. Choose the Protocols tab ➤ TCP/IP ➤ Properties.

3. From the Microsoft TCP/IP Properties window, click the tab marked WINS address. Opening the WINS Address window will bring up a screen like the one shown below.

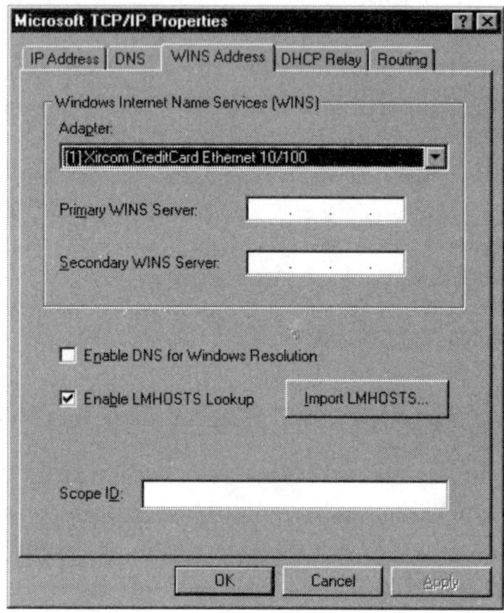

4. In the area marked Primary WINS Server, enter the IP address of the designated WINS Server.

5. In the area marked Secondary WINS Server, enter the IP address of the backup WINS Server.

6. Click OK to close the TCP/IP Properties screen and Network icon.

7. When prompted to restart the computer, click on Yes.

To configure a DHCP server to provide the scope to assign the WINS Server address, follow these steps:

1. Click Start ➤ Programs ➤ Administrative Tools ➤ DHCP Manager.

2. Highlight the appropriate scope under Local Machine in the DHCP server's frame.

3. From the DHCP Manager menu, choose DHCP Options ➤ Scope.

4. From the Unused Options frame, scroll down to 046 WINS/NBT Node Type. Your screen should look like the screen shown below.

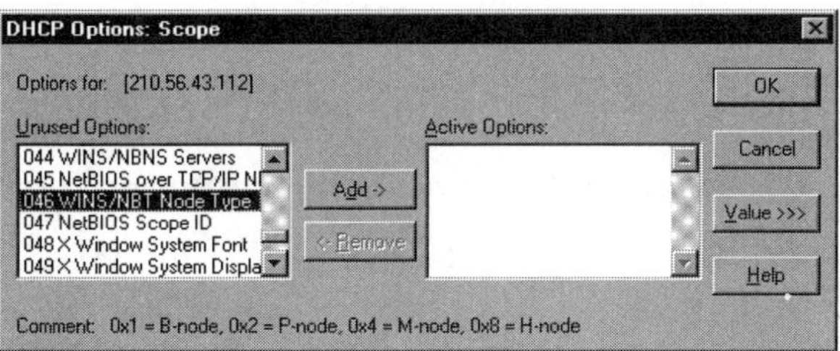

5. Click Add, then select Value.
6. In the Byte text box, type 0x8.

NOTE Using 0x8 will configure the client to use a method of accessing the server called hybrid node or h-node. The different broadcast modes will be explained during the objective on LMHOSTS file and NetBIOS resolution.

---

7. From the Unused Options list box, select 044 WINS/NBNS Server.
8. Click Add.
9. Click Value.
10. Click Edit Array and in the New IP Address box type in the address of the target computer.
11. Click Add.
12. Click OK to close the IP Address Array Editor of the DHCP Options: Scope menu and click OK to close the DHCP Options: Scope menu.
13. Close DHCP Manager – (Local).

Importing LMHOSTS File into WINS

In Chapter 1, “Planning,” there was a copy of the LMHOSTS file on one of the server computers for PSCONSULTING. For simplicity, this will be the file imported into the WINS Server. Before beginning, be sure to copy the LMHOSTS file to a file with another name, something really creative like LMHOSTS.BAK.

To import a file into a WINS database follow these steps:

1. Click Start ➤ Programs ➤ Administrative Tools ➤ WINS Manager.
2. From the menu, choose Mappings ➤ Static Mappings. This will open the Static Mappings – (Local) window shown below.

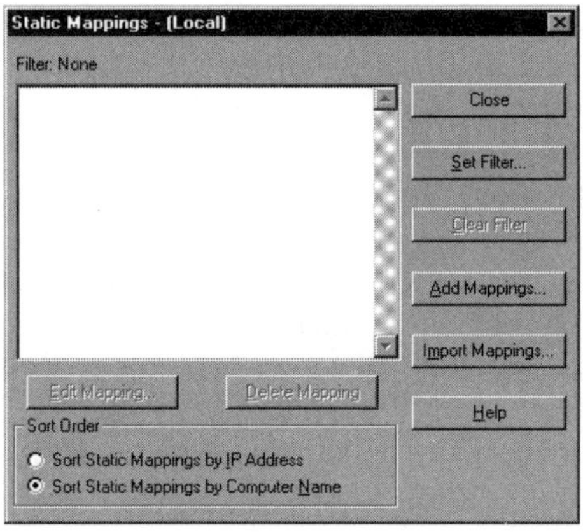

3. From the Static Mappings – (Local) window, click Import Mappings. This opens the Select Static Mapping File browse window. Browse to the path of the file to be imported. In this case, it is D:\winnt\system32\drivers\etc\lmhosts.bak. Click Open.

4. You should receive a message from WINS Manager saying the static mapping file has been successfully imported into the database. The finished product is shown below.

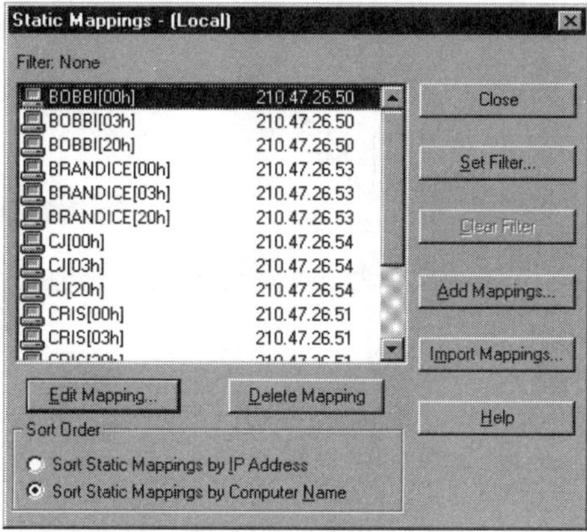

5. Click OK to close the window.

6. Click Close to close the Static Mappings – (Local) window.

Running WINS on a Multihomed Computer

A *multihomed computer* is a computer that has multiple IP addresses added to a network card. To add addresses to an existing network card, follow these steps:

1. Click Start ➢ Settings ➢ Control Panel ➢ double-click Network.

2. Choose the Protocols tab ➢ TCP/IP Protocol and click Properties.

3. Click the Advanced button and you will open the Advanced IP addressing window shown below ➤ Add.

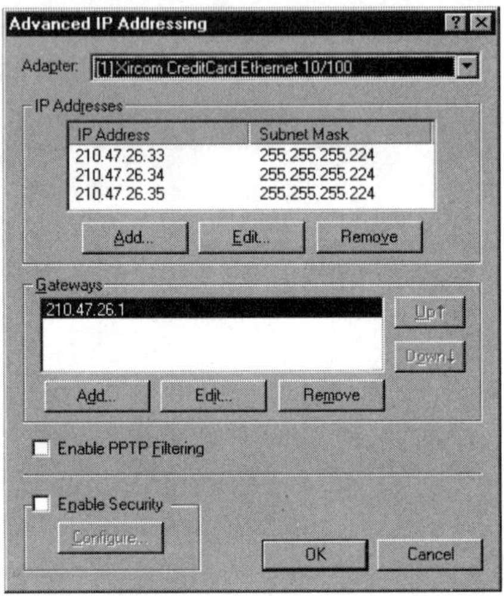

4. Provide the appropriate IP address and subnet mask.

Configuring WINS Replication

To configure a WINS Server as a push/pull partner with another server, complete the following procedures:

1. Click Start ➤ Programs ➤ Administrative Tools (Common) ➤ WINS Manager.
2. To add the IP address of the WINS Server that will be used as a replication partner, choose Server from the menu ➤ Add WINS Server, then enter the computer name or IP address of the WINS Server to be added.
3. To configure replication, highlight a partner in the WINS Server frame, then choose Server from the menu. Choose Replication Partners to open the Replication Partners – (Local) window.
4. Highlight the computer selected for replication and choose Push Partner, Pull Partner, or both in the Replication Options frame.

5. Click on OK to close the window or Replicate Now to force replication.

To customize the push/pull relationship, you can follow these steps:

1. Click Start ➤ Programs ➤ Administrative Tools (Common) ➤ WINS Manager.
2. To add the IP address of the WINS Server that will be used as a replication partner, choose Server from the menu, then choose Add WINS Server. Enter the computer name or IP address of the WINS Server to be added.
3. To configure replication, highlight a partner in the WINS Server frame ➤ Server ➤ Replication Partners to open the Replication Partners – (Local) window.
4. Highlight the computer selected for replication and choose Push Partner, Pull Partner, or both in the Replication Options frame.
5. Click on Configure next to the push partner. For the push partner, you can select the number of changes that will be necessary before a replication is initiated. Click OK to close the window.
6. Click on Configure next to the pull partner and you can configure a start time and a replication interval. Times can be set using either the AM/PM format or the 24-hour military clock. Click OK to close the Window and exit WINS Server Manager.

Backing Up and Restoring the WINS Database

Although this is not specifically covered in the objectives, there are some questions on how to restore a corrupted WINS database. Before you can restore, you have to back up the database. Backups occur once every 24 hours.

To configure the system to back up, start WINS Manager:

1. Select Start ➤ Programs ➤ Administrative Tools (Common) ➤ WINS Manager.
2. Click Mappings from the menu then select Backup Database.

3. Enter a new directory name or choose from the list of directories already present on the drive. Click OK. Notice that a backup is done immediately.

To restore a WINS database using the menu options, you follow these procedures:

1. Select Start ➤ Programs ➤ Administrative Tools (Common) ➤ WINS Manager.
2. Click Mappings ➤ Restore Local Database.

NOTE The option, Restore Local Database, will be grayed out unless the database is corrupted.

To restore a WINS database manually you would follow these steps:

1. Manually stop the WINS service by clicking Start ➤ Settings ➤ Control Panel.
2. Click Services ➤ Windows Internet Name Service ➤ Stop.
3. Delete the JET*.log, WINSTMP.MDB, and the SYSTEM.MDB files from the %systemroot%\system32\wins directory.
4. From the Windows NT Server CD, make a new copy of SYSTEM.MDB to the %systemroot%\system32\wins directory. This is the database template file.
5. After you have located a good copy of the WINS.MDB file, copy it to the %systemroot%\system32\wins directory and restart the WINS service. The WINS.MDB file is the actual WINS Server database file.

Exam Essentials

As you start to allocate your study time, think about this section. WINS is strictly a Microsoft product for the betterment of locating computers running Windows operating systems, using Microsoft's favorite protocol, NetBIOS. So, do you think there are going to be some questions on the exam about WINS?

Know that WINS serves to resolve NetBIOS computer names to IP addresses. NetBIOS computer names are inherent to the installation of Windows, Windows 9*x*, and Windows NT. WINS resolves these unique computer names to IP addresses.

Know that you would need a WINS proxy agent on subnets without a WINS Server if there are non-Windows clients on the subnet. If there is a subnet with UNIX or LAN Manager systems and no WINS Server on the subnet, the subnet must have a system configured as a WINS proxy agent to take advantage of WINS name resolution.

Know that the IP address of the WINS Server can be provided to clients by either a manual installation or through DHCP. The client can have the WINS Server IP address provided as part of the manual configuration of TCP/IP properties or DHCP can be set up to provide the IP address of the WINS Server.

Know the minimum software requirements for a computer to be a WINS Server. WINS Server can run on Windows NT Server 3.5*x* or better.

Know that the WINS Server should be configured with a static IP address. Because all the clients have to be able to find the WINS Server, it must be configured with a static IP address.

Know that your network should have two servers for redundancy. Because WINS is an integral part of the network browsing capabilities, there should be a backup to the primary WINS Server.

Know that a WINS Server's database can be replicated to other servers using a push/pull process. The push/pull replication process is not configured by default. It has to be set up manually. Push/pull replication is a one-way process. You will have to configure each server to ensure that the database is replicated to both systems.

Know when to use push replication. Push replication should be used over fast WAN links.

Know what triggers push replication. Push replication is triggered by changes in the database. The administrator can set how many changes need to occur before the push server notifies its partner that the database needs to be updated. When replication occurs, only the changes are sent to the partner.

Know when to use pull replication. Pull replications should be configured when you are faced with slow network links.

Know what triggers pull replication. Pull replication is triggered by a time event. You can schedule the start time for the replication and then how often after that you want the replication to occur. Pull replication also occurs when the pull partner starts up or it can be forced by the administrator.

Know that a copy of the LMHOSTS file can be imported into the WINS database. A copy of the LMHOSTS file, or a file formatted like the LMHOSTS file, can be imported into the WINS database. All keys in the LMHOSTS file, except the #DOM key, will be ignored.

Know the WINS database can receive entries either statically or dynamically. You can manually enter IP address into the WINS database to make non-WINS clients available on the network. The WINS database will be updated dynamically whenever a WINS client comes online.

Know how to configure the backup and restore of the WINS database. The administrator must use WINS Manager to institute database backups. Backups will occur every 24 hours. The database can be restored by stopping and restarting the WINS service. When WINS recognizes its database has been corrupted, it will automatically try and restore the backup. Restores can also be done from within WINS Manager and can be manually forced.

Know where the WINS database is stored and how to compact it. The WINS database (wins.mdb) is located in the %systemroot%\system32\wins directory and should be compacted when it grows larger than 30MB. To compact the database, use JETPACK.EXE, executed from the %systemroot%\system32\wins directory. The WINS service should be stopped before compacting and restarted afterwards.

Key Terms and Concepts

ARP (Address Resolution Protocol): Resolves an IP address to a local MAC address.

DNS (Domain Name System): Resolves a host name to an IP address.

LMHOSTS file: Provides static resolution of NetBIOS computer names or host names to IP addresses.

MAC address: A Media Access Control layer address is also referred to as the *hardware address*. This is a physical address of the network card, usually hard coded into the card at the manufacturer.

NetBIOS: A communication protocol that allows you to assign each computer a unique name.

Pull replication: A way of configuring WINS database replication. Pull replication is used over slow links, and after initial startup it is triggered by time events.

Push replication: A way of configuring WINS database replication. Push replication is used over fast WAN links and is triggered by the number of changes to the WINS database.

WINS (Windows Internet Name Service): A method of resolving NetBIOS computer names to IP addresses.

WINS proxy agent: A computer configured to provide name caching or request forwarding on a network segment that does not have a resident WINS Server

Sample Questions

1. Your network consists of 10 Windows NT Servers, 100 Windows 9*x* workstations, 37 Windows NT Workstations, and a smattering of Windows for Workgroups workstations. What type of resolution system should you configure?

   A. DHCP

   B. WINS

   C. DNS

   D. ARP

   Answer: B. Because the entire network consists of Windows products, the resolution method of choice is WINS.

2. Non-WINS clients can be added to the WINS database by

   A. The administrator using WINS Manager and entering static entries in the database.

   B. Not taking any action. Because the non-WINS clients still have HOST names, they will be automatically added to the database.

   C. The administrator importing a file that contains all the information about the hosts and is in the format of the LMHOSTS file.

   D. The administrator knowing that if this is an NT 3.51 network, it cannot support non-WINS clients.

   Answer: A and C. Static address can be added to the WINS database either manually using WINS Manager or by importing a file formatted like an LMHOSTS file.

3. The WINS Server database has become corrupt. The database has been configured so it will be backed up. What is the first way to try to restore the database?

   A. From a tape backup.

   B. From the registry backup.

C. From the %systemroot%\system32\backup directory.

D. By stopping and restarting WINS.

Answer: D. The first way to try to restore the database is to stop and restart the WINS service. When WINS senses the corrupt database, it will try and restore the last backup.

4. Which of the following operating systems can host a WINS Server?

A. NetWare 3.12

B. Windows NT 3.5*x* Server

C. Windows 98 Server

D. Windows NT 4.0 Server

Answer: B and D. A WINS Server can run on computers configured with NT Server with a version of 3.5*x* or greater.

Configure subnet masks.

Of all the objectives on the test, the topic of subnets is the topic the exam writers spent the most time with. In one way or another, you will be seeing lots of questions on subnetting, including topics such as:

- How many subnets will you need?
- Given an address and a subnet mask, how many subnets are possible?
- Given an address and a subnet mask, how many hosts can reside on each subnet?
- Given a network address and a subnet mask, what are the network addresses and the range of IP addresses per network?
- Given an address and a subnet mask, what is the host address and what is the network address?

The questions will come up in a variety of formats. As part of this section, we will cover all the basics of subnetting and provide you with some tools that may make the experience of testing a little less stressful.

NOTE Much of the discussion on subnets revolves around conversion of binary numbers into decimal equivalents and decimals back to binary. If you are uncomfortable with doing this manually, the Windows scientific calculator is available during the test.

Critical Information

Communication at any level revolves around a sender and a receiver. For the communication to carry on for any period of time, the sender will become the receiver and the receiver will become the sender. In each case, both parties must have a way of finding each other.

Addressing Basics

Think of the U.S. mail. If you're like me, every day, you go out to the mailbox and bring in the latest load of bills. The people I owe money to certainly know where I live and they make sure that I know how to get in touch with them. I am provided with special envelopes and phone numbers and even toll-free numbers to call if there is a problem.

Computer communication is very similar to the mail service as a familiar means of facilitating communication. For example, when someone sends me a letter, they have my name, home address, city, state, and zip code. When the mail carrier picks up the letter from the sender, it checks the city, state, and zip code to find out if the letter is to be delivered locally or if it out of the local postal zone. If the letter is out of the local postal zone, the letter is forwarded to a regional center, which forwards it to another regional center, which sends it to a local center, which delivers the letter.

In IP communications, the process works this way. Assume that your computer wants to request some information from an FTP server. You enter in the appropriate IP address for the FTP server and press Enter. What happens behind the scenes? The sending computer formats the data to be sent in something called a *packet* or *datagram*. Don't let the fancy terms scare you, just think of it as putting a letter in an envelope. This packet has a source address (the sender) and a destination address (the recipient) as does your envelope. When your computer is ready to send out the packet, it looks at the destination address to determine if the packet is destined for the local network or somewhere else. If the packet is destined for the local network, the computer sends it on its way. If it is destined for somewhere else, the computer sends the packet to the designated gateway and lets the gateway handle it.

The packet addresses are a little more complex than a familiar mailing address. First of all, the packet address is an IP address. Similar to the way your address is made up of several parts, so is an IP address. Your address consists of a street address to identify your house, and a city, state, and zip code. An IP address consists of the network address the host resides on and a host address to identify the computer on the network.

IP Addressing

Network addresses are interesting things. If you have a network that is not connected to the Internet, it really doesn't matter what network address you give each network segment. Just make sure everything is unique and life is good. I like to refer to this approach as the 1.2.3.4 method of network addressing. You start numbering the first machine at 1.2.3.4 and slowly increment by one for each new host you install on the subnet. Things become a little more complicated when you decide to hook your system to the Internet. Every computer on a network must have a unique address. It doesn't matter if the network is the three-workstation configuration at the corner insurance office or the Internet. Everything has to be unique. At the Internet level, you just cannot pick yourself a block of addresses and go. You or your company must be assigned addresses. This assignment is done by the Internet

Network Information Center, affectionately known as the InterNIC. It is up to the InterNIC to determine what address block you can use. There are three ways to apply. You can go to the InterNIC Web site at http://internic.net; you can call Network Solutions at 703-742-4777 or send them an application at the following address:

Network Solutions

InterNIC Registration Services

505 Huntmar Park Drive

Herndon, VA 22070

or you can send e-mail to hostmaster@internic.net.

Applications are available from the Web site.

NOTE Actually, depending on the size of your organization, you can also ask your Internet service provider to cut through the paperwork for you. The ISP may have a block of addresses you can rent. The problem with renting a block of addresses from an ISP is the ISP owns the addresses. If you decide to change ISPs, you have to reconfigure your entire network addressing scheme

---

When you receive your assignment, it will be in the form of an IP address. The typical IP address looks like 205.46.15.198. Funny lookin', huh? Makes you long for the days of 10 Elm Street, Anytown, USA. The funny looking address uniquely identifies a host on a network. The address is actually made up of two parts, a network address and a host address.

This IP address is made up of 4 bytes. Because each byte is made up of 8 bits, each byte is also referred to as an *octet*. Each octet is expressed as the decimal representation of a binary number. To translate a decimal number to a binary number, we need some kind of translation table. The number we are going to translate is the first number of the octet, 205. Look closely at Table 2.3 to see how to translate this number from binary to a decimal.

TABLE 2.3: Binary to decimal translation of 205

	Bit 8	Bit 7	Bit 6	Bit 5	Bit 4	Bit 3	Bit 2	Bit 1
Decimal value	2^7 = 128	2^6= 64	2^5 = 32	2^4 = 16	2^3 = 8	2^2 = 4	2^1 = 2	2^0= 1
Binary value of byte	1	1	0	0	1	1	0	1
Decimal conversion	128	64	0	0	1	1	0	1

If you look at the decimal value of the byte, using the bit binary values, you have 128+64+8+4+1 = 205. To us, it is 205, to your computer it is 11001101. See how it works? Pretty simple, huh?

If all the bits are set to 1, you have a maximum value of 255. There are some rules to IP addressing and one of those rules states that an address cannot have all the bits set to all 1's or all 0's. That means there are no network (or host, for that matter) addresses of 255 or 0. In addition, there is a reserved address, 127.0.0.1, which is called a *loopback address*. A loopback address is an address used for testing the local machine.

The InterNIC has divided IP network addresses into five classes. Microsoft TCP/IP recognizes the first three classes, so those are what we will concentrate on, but you should know about all five. Table 2.4 gives you a breakdown of the classes.

TABLE 2.4: InterNIC address classes

Class	Value of first byte	Binary Range	Decimal Range
A	First bit must be 0.	00000001-01111111 Note: A value of zero for the network address is not permitted.	1 to 127 Note: 127 is reserved for testing.
B	First 2 bits must be 10.	10000000-10111111	128 to 191
C	First 3 bits must be 110.	11000000-11011111	192 to 223
D Note: This range of network addresses is reserved for multicasts and is not available for host addressing.	First 4 bits must be 1110.	11100000-11101111	224-239
E Note: This range of addresses is reserved for experimental purposes and is not available for host addressing.	First 5 bits must be 11110.	11110000-11110111	240-247

Because the Class D and Class E network address are reserved, we will ignore them for the rest of the book.

TIP For the exam, know the class limits. If you can remember the value of the first byte, you will be fine. There can be several questions based on the class of a specific address.

The IP addressing scheme takes into account that some networks are very large, some are medium sized, and some are small. A Class A address uses the first octet to represent the network address and the last three octets to represent hosts. Looking at the chart above, with only 127 numbers available for a Class A address, there aren't many given out. They were designed for a large organization with lots of hosts.

A Class B address fulfills the needs of a medium-sized organization. The first two octets designate the network and the last two octets designate the number of hosts. The Class C address uses the first three octets to designate the network and the last octet to designate the host. There is a formula to determine the number of networks or the number of hosts. The formula is 2 raised to the number of bits for varying minus 2. You subtract 2 to take into account that you cannot use 0 and you cannot use 255. So, in the case of a Class A address, 1 bit is used to designate the network and 7 bits are left for "varying" in the first octet. Given the formula, 2^7-2=126 networks. Now, I like math as much as the next person, but I figure formulas like that are the reason God created calculators. Table 2.5 shows how the addresses break down.

TABLE 2.5: IP addressing scheme

Class	IP Address	Number of Networks	Number of Hosts
A	NET.host.host.host	126 Network = 7 bits 2^7-2 = 126	16,777,214 Hosts =24 bits 2^{24}-2=16,777,214

TABLE 2.5: IP addressing scheme *(continued)*

Class	IP Address	Number of Networks	Number of Hosts
B	NET.NET.host.host	16,384 Network = 14 bits 2^{14}-2=16,384	65,534 Hosts=16 bits 2^{16}-2=65,534
C	NET.NET.NET.host	2,097,152 Network = 21 bits 2^{21}-2 = 2,097,152	254 Hosts=8 bits 2^{8}-2=254

TIP For exam purposes, parts of this chart should be memorized, or at least known cold. You should know which octets are used to designate the network and which octets designate the host for each of the three classes. Memorizing the number of networks and hosts is not necessary, but you should recognize the trend; Class A has few networks and lots of hosts and Class C has lots of networks with a few hosts.

You have heard the old question, "What's in a name?" The 90s' version could be, "What's in an IP address?" When I just pinged Microsoft, I returned an IP address of 207.46.130.17. From the information you have seen so far, you should be able to determine that this is a Class C address because the first octet is greater than 191 and less than 224. Because it is a Class C address, you know that this host is on network number 207.46.130.0 and the unique host number is 0.0.0.17. You also know this is one host out of a possible 254.

Subnets and Subnetting

When you applied to the InterNIC for your IP address, you were returned a number like 207.46.130.0 and a subnet mask of 255.255.255.0. You were told that you could have 254 different hosts on that network. At this point, it is very important we define the term "network." That is one of those terms that gets thrown around and has different meanings depending on its context. I can look in my lab and see an NT Server hooked up to a couple of NT Workstations and that is a network. I can drive down the street to the IS headquarters of a major bank and start talking about the nationwide network. In terms of this section, a network should really be defined as a network segment. Each NT Server that has a network card in it has a network number assigned to that card. Each network card may define its own network segment. Look at Figure 2.2 and you will see that even in this extremely simple design, there are four networks.

FIGURE 2.2: Simple network infrastructure

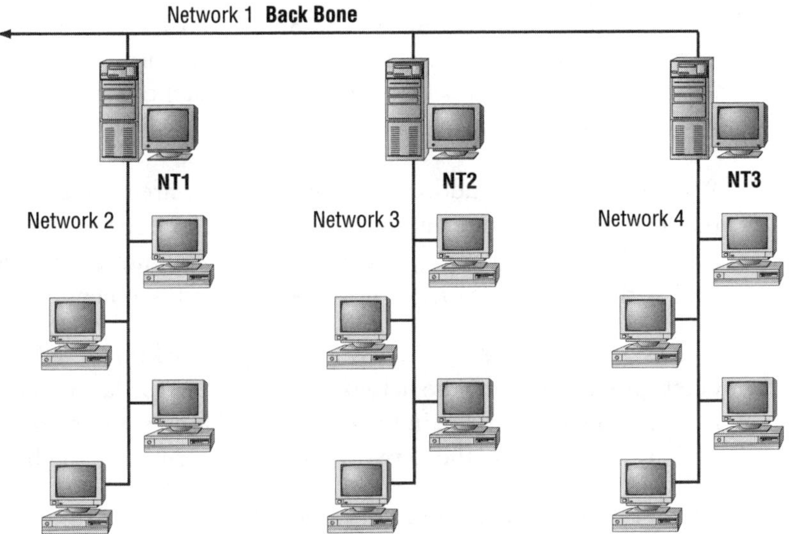

As you look at the structure of your network, you will see that you have multiple network segments. Depending on the type of network you have (Ethernet versus Token Ring), you may only have 50 hosts on any network segment. Does this mean that you will have to apply for a separate IP address for each network segment? After all, each network must have its own unique address. That would be really wasteful. You would have an address that could use up to 254 hosts and you are applying it to a segment that has only 50 hosts, wasting 204 addresses. With the explosive growth of the Internet, everybody wants an IP address, so they are in short supply. Wasting them like that would be criminal. There has got to be a better way. It's called subnetting.

NOTE With the popularity of the Internet, there is a shortage of IP addresses. There is a new IP addressing scheme in the works called IP version 6, or IPv6. In keeping with the current fads, it is also called IPng, for IP Next Generation. The new IP is going to be incompatible with the old IP. In addition, the next generation will have a 128-bit source and destination address. A valid IP address in the future will look something like 1543:B24E:9853:574C:3336:43C7:4B3E:7C36. Rumor has it that given the 128-bit addressing scheme, there will be five IP addresses available for every square meter on earth.

When we take an IP address and subnet it, we are taking an address that is designed for one unique network with 254 hosts (in the case of a Class C network) and giving ourselves more unique network numbers with a fewer number of hosts per network segment.

This is how it works. In a Class C network, we know the first three octets are destined for the network number and the last octet is determined to be the host. So, in binary, it would look something like this, with 1's determining the network and 0's determining the host:

11111111.11111111.11111111.00000000

That would give us the default Class C subnet of 255.255.255.0.

NOTE Each class has its own default subnet; for Class A it is 255.0.0.0, for Class B it is 255.255.0.0, and Class C is 255.255.255.0.

To give us the opportunity to have more networks and fewer hosts, IP will let us "borrow" bits from the host address to use as a network address. We can use the formula of 2^x-2, where x is the number of borrowed bits, to determine the number of networks. Using 2^x-2 with the number of remaining bits will give you the number of hosts per segment.

Before, our subnet in binary was 11111111.11111111.11111111.00000000. Let's change that to 11111111.11111111.11111111.11110000. To figure out what our new custom subnet mask would be, let's take the numbers we used earlier and plug them into the chart. The conversion of this subnet is Table 2.6.

TABLE 2.6: Subnet conversion

	Bit 8	**Bit 7**	**Bit 6**	**Bit 5**	**Bit 4**	**Bit 3**	**Bit 2**	**Bit 1**
Decimal value	2^7 = 128	2^6 = 64	2^5 = 32	2^4 = 16	2^3 = 8	2^2 = 4	2^1 = 2	2^0 = 1
Binary value of byte	1	1	1	1	0	0	0	0
Decimal conversion	128	64	32	16	0	0	0	0

To convert this back to decimal, we add 128+64+32+16=240 so our new subnet mask is 255.255.255.240. Using the formula, we see that we have 2^4-2=14 subnets available and also 14 hosts available per subnet for this Class C address.

If our subnet had been 11111111.11111111.11111111.11100000, our subnet mask would have been 255.255.255.224 and we would have had the ability to have six subnets with 30 hosts each on the subnet. To keep you from having to do the math and conversion each time, look at the tables below to see what the subnet is and how many subnets and hosts you can get for each subnet. Table 2.7 will show Class A addresses.

TABLE 2.7: Summary of subnet mask effects on a Class A address

Number of bits used in the subnet	Subnet Mask	Number of networks	Number of hosts
2	255.192.0.0	2	4,194,302
3	255.224.0.0	6	2,097,150
4	255.240.0.0	14	1,048,574
5	255.248.0.0	30	524,286
6	255.252.0.0	62	262,142
7	255.254.0.0	126	131,070
8	255.255.0.0	254	65,534

Can a Class A network be subnetted down further? Certainly. You can continue to subnet a Class A down to the next to last bit of the last octet. The number of networks will continue to grow and the number of hosts per network will continue to decline.

NOTE Take a close look at the relationship between the number of networks as the numbers of bits used for the subnet increases. In each case the number of networks is doubled plus two. If you look closely at the number of hosts, you will notice that from bottom to top, it increases by the same margin. If you can remember that a subnet of 192 has two networks, and can also recall the formula, you have the rest of the network section figured out. If you can remember a Class A has 65,534 hosts with a subnet mask of 255.255.0.0, you can fill out the rest of the hosts section. For those of you who have math phobia, remember, you do have access to the calculator.

Table 2.8 outlines Class B addresses.

TABLE 2.8: Summary of subnet mask effects on a Class B address

Number of bits used in the subnet	Subnet Mask	Number of networks	Number of hosts
2	255.255.192.0	2	16,382
3	255.255.224.0	6	8,190
4	255.255.240.0	14	4,094
5	255.255.248.0	30	2,046
6	255.255.252.0	62	1,022
7	255.255.254.0	126	510
8	255.255.255.0	254	254

Again, the Class B address can be subnetted down into the next octet. The number of networks will continue to increase and the number of hosts per subnet will continue to decrease.

Finally, Table 2.9 will look at the effects of subnetting a Class C address.

TABLE 2.9: Summary of subnet mask effects on a Class C address

Number of bits used in the subnet	Subnet Mask	Number of networks	Number of hosts
2	255.255.255.192	2	62
3	255.255.255.224	6	30
4	255.255.255.240	14	14
5	255.255.255.248	30	6
6	255.255.255.252	62	2
7	255.255.255.254	Not allowed	Not allowed
8	255.255.255.255	Not allowed	Not allowed

TIP Be sure you know how to use the information in Tables 2.7, 2.8, and 2.9, and how to re-create the tables. In an exam situation, you may be given a question that asks which subnet mask you would apply to a Class C network if you had 11 subnets, each with no more than 12 hosts. In that case, the subnet would be 255.255.255.240 because it has a maximum of 14 subnets with 14 hosts. The majority of questions about subnetting revolve around Class B and Class C addresses.

You will notice in Table 2.9 that there are some "N/As" showing up for bits 7 and 8. If you pay close attention to the number of hosts, every time a bit is added, the number of hosts is reduced by the formula of (x/2-1). Don't let the math frighten you. The first subnet, 255.255.255.192, has a potential total of 62 hosts. The next subnet, 255.255.255.224, has (62/2 – 1) or 30 hosts. When you get to bit 6, 255.255.255.252, there are only two hosts per subnet. The next step would have (2/2-1) or 0 hosts. We have just subnetted the network down as far as it can go.

Determining Network and Host Addresses

If you are given an IP address, we have just shown how to determine the appropriate subnet mask to provide you with the number of network addresses and host addresses. The host addresses must be assigned to the appropriate network address, otherwise, systems on the subnet will not be able to communicate. The next step in the process is to take the network address assigned, with the appropriate subnet mask applied, and break it down into subnets and host addresses.

The sample address from Microsoft was 205.46.15.76. Because this is a Class C address, if the default subnet mask of 255.255.255.0 was used, the network address would be 205.46.15.0 and the host address would be .0.0.0.76. Let's assume when Microsoft was assigned this address, they were going to use this address on a network with four subnets and 25 hosts on each subnet. Looking at Table 2.9, we find that the subnet mask that meets all of those criteria is 255.255.255.224, using the first 3 bits of the last octets for a network address and the remaining 5 bits for host addresses.

Using the 3 bits of the last octet gives us six choices for the network number. These would be the binary choices:

- 00000000 – Invalid address because the network portion contains all 0's
- 00100000 = 32
- 01000000 = 64
- 01100000 = 96
- 10000000 = 128
- 10100000 = 160
- 11000000 = 192
- 11100000 – Invalid address because the network portion contains all 1's

To convert the binary choices to decimal, remember we are dealing with only three places from the octet. The conversion chart shows us the opening three places have values 128, 64, and 32.

Using the original network address of 205.46.15.0 and applying a subnet mask of 255.255.255.224 means these would be our network numbers:

- 205.46.15.32
- 205.46.15.64
- 205.46.15.96
- 205.46.15.128
- 205.46.15.160
- 205.46.15.192

Now that we have determined the network numbers, we must determine the host addresses by applying the last 5 bits of the octet. Using the binary representation for the first network, our range of host addresses would be between 00100001 and 00111110. Converting those binary numbers to decimal we find the network 205.46.15.32 has hosts ranging from 205.46.15.33 to 205.46.15.62. Applying the same principal to the next subnet, we would have addresses ranging from 01000001 to 01011110. Remember, the first three positions are the network address and the last five are the host address. Network number 205.46.15.64 would be made up of hosts 205.46.15.65 to 205.46.15.126. You can use the same procedure to find the host addresses on any subnet, using any subnet mask. Use the binary method to define the network portion of the address and then use the binary method to determine the host portion of the address.

TIP For exam purposes, it is very important you know how to figure out host address ranges. If a host address is on the wrong subnet, it will not be able to communicate with the rest of the subnet. In other words, even though host addresses 205.46.15.62 and 205.46.15.65 are close in proximity, they must be on different subnets to communicate.

You can use the same method to back engineer an IP address. For example, given the sample address of 205.46.15.198 and a subnet mask of 255.255.255.224, what is the network address and what is the host address? In looking at the information above, we know that the highest available network address is 205.46.15.192. This host must reside on that network. If the network address is 192, the host address must be 0.0.0.6.

Case Study Review

The exam writers will pound you with subnet and addressing questions. So, let's start at the beginning with a made-up case study and see how we can apply the principals we discussed in this section.

First of all, remember, the exam writers would concentrate on these questions:

- How many subnets will you need?

- Given an address and a subnet mask, how many subnets are possible?
- Given an address and a subnet mask, how many hosts can reside on each subnet?
- Given a network address and a subnet mask, what are the network addresses and the range of IP addresses per network?
- Given an address and a subnet mask, what is the host address and what is the network address?

We can keep these points in mind as we approach the case study. Let's begin.

For our sample company, Brandice has been named the head of the Information Technology department for the company she works for. Her task is to come up with a TCP/IP addressing scheme for the network based on the following criteria:

1. Brandice's predecessor had applied to the InterNIC for an IP address. The company network received the addresses of 203.45.16.0 with a default subnet mask of 255.255.255.0.
2. When Brandice asked for a map of the computer network, she was told the company currently has the corporate headquarters, with 15 employees. There are two remote offices with 10 employees each.
3. Each employee has a computer. Here are some additional details:
   - At the home office, there is a server with two network interface cards (NICs). There are two laser printers hooked directly into the network, each using a (NIC). Each printer should be assigned an IP address.
   - At each of the remote offices, there is a server with two network cards. There is one laser printer hooked directly into the network with a NIC. Each printer should be assigned an IP address.
   - There is a router that contains three network cards connecting the three offices.

While Brandice was rummaging around her new office, she found the network map that is shown in Figure 2.3.

FIGURE 2.3: A network map

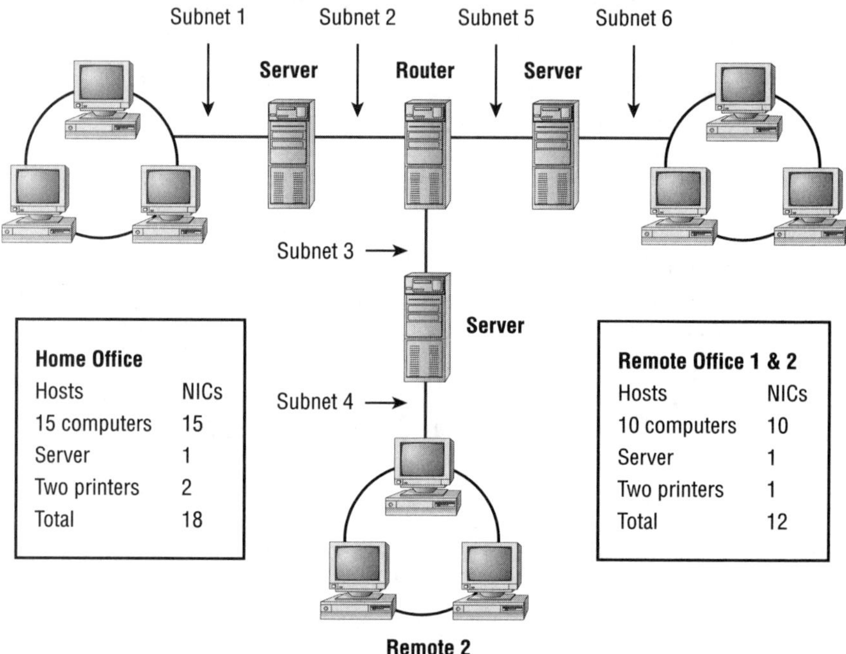

Looking at the network map and using the information above, Brandice devised the chart shown in Table 2.10.

TABLE 2.10: Summary of a network map

Subnet	# of host addresses needed	Comments
1	18	15 computers 1 server NIC 2 printers

TABLE 2.10: Summary of a network map *(continued)*

Subnet	# of host addresses needed	Comments
2	2	1 server NIC 1 router NIC
3	2	1 server NIC 1 router NIC
4	12	10 computers 1 server NIC 1 printer NIC
5	2	1 server NIC 1 router NIC
6	12	10 computers 1 server NIC 1 printer NIC

How many subnets will you need?

Given this information, Brandice is ready to tackle point one: How many subnets will you need? You know that the network address that has been provided; 203.45.16.0 is a Class C address. If a Class C address is a subnet using 255.255.255.224, it can handle six subnets with up to 30 hosts on each subnet. Looking at the table above, that looks like one possible solution. Before running with that solution, Brandice needs to ask about expansion plans. Right now there are six subnets, the largest number of hosts is 18, and the subnet mask of 255.255.255.224 works great. What happens if the company decides to add another branch office? All of a sudden, the network map goes to heck in a hand basket. For the sake of this example, we will say that the company is frozen at current levels and will never expand.

Brandice's other choice was to add another NIC to the servers and subdivide the current networks. Then she could use the 255.255.255.240 subnet mask, giving her 14 subnets with 14 host addresses per subnet.

Given an address and a subnet mask, how many subnets are possible? Given an address and a subnet mask, how many hosts can reside on each subnet?

Let's tackle both of these questions at the same time. If you are curious about how the address can be subnetted, here is a recap in Table 2.11 showing the subnet mask for a Class C address, the number of possible subnets, and the number of possible hosts.

TABLE 2.11: Subnet summary for Class C

Subnet Mask	Number of networks	Number of hosts
255.255.255.192	2	62
255.255.255.224	6	30
255.255.255.240	14	14
255.255.255.248	30	6
255.255.255.252	62	2

Given a network address and a subnet mask, what are the network addresses and the range of IP addresses per network?

We now know our assigned network address and the subnet mask we are going to use, 255.255.255.224. A subnet mask of 224 means we are going to be using the first 3 bits of the last octet for a network number and the last 5 bits of the octet for the host ID. This means our network numbers can be determined by using Table 2.12.

TABLE 2.12: A network conversion

128	64	32	Network ID
0	0	0	Not allowed, all 0's
0	0	1	203.45.16.32
0	1	0	203.45.16.64

TABLE 2.12: A network conversion *(continued)*

128	64	32	Network ID
0	1	1	203.45.16.96
1	0	0	203.45.16.128
1	0	1	203.45.16.160
1	1	0	203.45.16.192
1	1	1	Not allowed, all 1's

What about host addresses? In the case of host addresses, we are using the last five places in the octet. Because there are 30 possible hosts for each, Table 2.13 will demonstrate first address, last address, and the addresses you cannot use. We will use the first network, 203.45.16.32, for the example of host addresses.

TABLE 2.13: Host addressing

16	8	4	2	1	Address	Explanation
0	0	0	0	0	Not allowed, all 0's	
0	0	0	0	1	203.45.16.33	Network address 203.45.16.32 plus the host address of 0.0.0.1 = 203.45.16.33.
1	1	1	1	0	203.45.16.62	Network address 203.45.16.32 plus the host address of 0.0.0.30 = 203.45.16.62.
1	1	1	1	1	Not allowed, all 1's	

Table 2.14 shows the network address, the starting host address, and the ending host address for the six subnets.

TABLE 2.14: Subnet summary

Network Address	Starting Address	Ending Address
203.45.16.32	203.45.16.33	209.45.16.62
203.45.16.64	203.45.16.63	209.45.16.92
203.45.16.96	203.45.16.97	209.45.16.126
203.45.16.128	203.45.16.129	209.45.16.158
203.45.16.160	203.45.16.161	209.45.16.190
203.45.16.192	203.45.16.193	209.45.16.222

Given an address and a subnet mask, what is the host address and what is the network address?

Another aspect of the testing revolves around being able to break down a given IP address into the two components of a network address and a host address. Here is an example.

CJ is working at a computer that has an IP address of 187.26.36.210. The subnet mask is 255.255.240.0. What is the network address and what is host address for this computer?

Actually, this is just reverse engineering of the scenario above. First of all, looking at the address you know it is a Class B address. Class B addresses range from 128 to 191. The default subnet mask for a Class B address is 255.255.0.0. This means that the first 4 bits of the third octet are used for the network address and the last 4 bits of the third octet are used for the host address.

Table 2.15 shows the possible network addresses given this subnet.

TABLE 2.15: Class B subnet addresses

128	64	32	16	Network address
0	0	0	0	Not allowed, all 0's
0	0	0	1	187.26.16.0
0	0	1	0	187.26.32.0
0	0	1	1	187.26.48.0
0	1	0	0	187.26.64.0
0	1	0	1	187.26.80.0
0	1	1	0	187.26.96.0
0	1	1	1	187.26.112.0
1	0	0	0	187.26.128.0
1	0	0	1	187.26.144.0
1	0	1		187.26.160.0
1	0	1	1	187.26.176.0
1	1	0	0	187.26.192.0
1	1	0	1	187.26.208.0
1	1	1	0	187.26.224.0
1	1	1	1	Not allowed, all 1's

If you look at the network address given, you will see it is 187.26.36.210. Looking at the table, you will see the network address must be 187.26.32.0. If that is the network address it means the host address must be 0.0.4.210.

If you have followed the logic of these examples, you shouldn't have any problems with the subnetting portion of the exam.

Supernetting

Another way of handling IP addressing is called supernetting. *Supernetting* actually steals addresses from the network to apply them to hosts.

Supernetting bypasses the concepts of Class A, Class B, and Class C networks, replacing these concepts with the general term, "network prefix." The routers will work with the network prefix to determine where the network address stops and the host address begins.

An example of a supernet address would be something like 208.95.46.32 with a subnet mask of 255.255.240.0. In this case, the supernet borrowed 4 bits from the network number and applied those bits to the host numbers.

TIP For testing purposes, it is not necessary to understand the concept of supernetting, but it is wise to know that it exists.

Exam Essentials

This is a *very* important section. Subnetting and addressing in one form or another will consume a large part of the test. Not only will it consume a large portion of the TCP/IP test, but this is one topic that will come back to haunt you again and again.

Know the three classes of network address and the range of each. A Class A address is anything from 1 to 127. A Class B address goes from 128 to 191 and a Class C address will start at 192 and go to 223. However, 127.x.x.x is not a valid IP address, it is a reserved address.

Know the default subnet masks for each of the address classes. Class A has a default subnet of 255.0.0.0, Class B has a default subnet mask of 255.255.0.0, and Class C has a default subnet mask of 255.255.255.0.

Know how an IP address is made up. Any IP address is made of two parts: a network address and a host address. In a Class A address, with the default subnet mask, the first octet is the network address; the remaining three octets are the host address. In a Class B address, with the default subnet mask, the first two octets are the network address and the last two octets are the host address. In a Class C network address, the first three octets are the network address and the last octet is the host address.

Know how to determine the appropriate subnet mask. To determine the appropriate subnet mask, you must know how many network segments the address will serve and the maximum number of hosts on a segment. Any network may be assigned more than one IP network address by the InterNIC.

Know how to determine the network address and host address. If you are given an IP address with a subnet mask, you should be able to determine the network address and host address.

Know how to determine if two hosts should be on the same subnet together. Given two IP addresses, with a subnet mask, you should be able to determine if the hosts reside on the same subnet.

Know how many networks and hosts are created with each subnet. Know Class A, but concentrate on Class B and Class C. Most of the questions will revolve around those classes.

Key Terms and Concepts

Host address: The portion of an IP address dedicated to the host.

InterNIC: The body that regulates and assigns network addresses.

IP address class: The InterNIC administers five address classes. Class A, Class B, and Class C licenses are most commonly used by computer networks today.

Network address: The portion of an IP address dedicated to identifying the network segment.

Subnet: A network segment.

Subnet mask: A common practice in IP addressing of using bits from the host address to define different network segments.

Sample Questions

1. You find that your workstation has an IP address of 129.16.15.24 with a subnet mask of 255.255.0.0. What is the network portion of that address?

A. 129.0.0.0

B. 129.16.0.0

C. 129.16.15.0

D. 129.16.15.6

Answer: B. Because this is a Class B address, with the default subnet, the network portion of the address would be 129.16.0.0.

2. You are troubleshooting a TCP/IP problem and you find that the IP address is an invalid address. Which address below is the invalid address?

A. 106.34.25.90

B. 128.4.6.224

C. 2.128.224.240

D. 255.23.5.2

Answer: D. 255.23.5.2 is not a valid IP address.

3. How many hosts can you have on a network with the address of 205.46.15.0, with a subnet of 255.255.255.240?

A. 62

B. 30

C. 14

D. 6

Answer: C. A Class C address with a subnet of 255.255.255.240 can have 14 subnets, each with up to 14 hosts.

4. The InterNIC has assigned you an IP address of 205.46.15.0. What is the default subnet mask for this address?

   A. 255.0.0.0

   B. 255.255.0.0

   C. 255.255.255.0

   D. 255.255.255.255

   Answer: C. 205.46.15.0 is a Class C address. The default subnet mask for a Class C address is 255.255.255.0.

Configure a Windows NT Server computer to function as an IP router.

- Install and configure a DHCP relay agent.

One of the main reasons for making TCP/IP the default protocol on an NT Server is because TCP/IP is a routable protocol. NetBIOS helps with computer name resolution; it is easy to install and configure, but it is not routable. That limits the size of the network on which it can be used. Not only is TCP/IP routable, but it is also flexible enough for you to decide how you want it to route. You can create static route tables for security or you can configure a protocol that will update and maintain its route table without any user intervention. You can have it your way!

Critical Information

The more I work with technology, and the more I understand about its inner workings, the more I find subjects I like to call the "gee whiz" stuff. I understand it, I know how it works and why it works, and I can even explain it to folks, but I am still in awe of it. Routing is one of those "gee whiz" topics. Every time I open a browser and type in http:\\something.somewhere.com and a Web page shows up on my machine from somewhere on the Internet, I am awed by the simplicity of the process and the complexity of the action. It is truly cool!

A friend once asked what routers actually do. I am not sure she was pleased with my answer, but in its simplest form, routers route. A router will route a packet from one location to another until it gets to its destination address. It does not matter if the packet is destined for a server on the other side of the building or the host of a Web page on the other side of the world, a router is what gets the packet from one location to another.

If you are used to working on a small network, you may not think you have a router. If you have access to the Internet from your desktop, you have a router. If your file server has more than one network card in it, you have a router. A router can be a very sophisticated (read expensive) piece of equipment dedicated to the task of routing packets or it can be a file server that has two network cards in it. In either case, it is a router. Microsoft also calls routers *gateways* so the terms are synonymous.

Here is how a router works. When a router receives a packet, the packet is kicked up to the Internet layer and handed off to IP. IP looks at the packet, specifically at the Time To Live (TTL) portion of the packet. The Time To Live is a number that represents the number of routers this packet will be allowed to cross. Each time the packet crosses a router, IP will decrement the TTL, usually by a unit of 1. If the TTL hits zero, it is obvious to the router that this little packet has lost its way and the packet is trashed or discarded. The router also looks at the size of packet. Some routers can handle large packets, others can't. If the router is hooked to other routers that can't handle large packets, the router breaks up the packet into fragments, adds new headers to each fragment, and sets a flag. The new packet also acquires a fragment ID and a fragment offset, all so the packets can be put back together in the right order on the other side.

IP now has to calculate a new checksum for each fragment. After the router has done all this, it checks for the hardware address of the next router and sends the packet on its way to the next step in the journey. The next router follows the same routine.

How does the router know where to send the packet? Each router maintains something called a *route table*. This table contains information on everything the router needs to know to do its job. This table can be updated or changed dynamically or statically. In this case, as in most cases, "dynamically" means the router does all the work and "statically" means *you* do all the work.

How does the router get the packet in the first place? When your computer sends out the packet, the computer checks the destination IP address. The computer is looking to see if the IP address is on the same subnet as your computer; that's why proper addressing is so important! If the destination system is on your subnet, the computer sends the packet directly to the destination. If the destination is not on your subnet, the packet goes to a gateway/router.

Determining Local versus Remote Subnets

When a computer wants to send a packet to another host, it puts the remote host's IP address in the destination address area of the packet. The system must then decide where to send the packet. If the destination address is on the same subnet as the sending host, the packet is sent directly to the receiving computer. However, if the host address is on a different subnet, the packet is automatically forwarded to the subnet's gateway for its trip around the network.

How does the computer determine if the destination address is local or remote? It uses a process called ANDing. This process comes from Boolean logic. ANDing takes the destination address and converts it to binary. It then applies the subnet mask and begins to work its magic to see if the two network addresses work.

ANDing works like this. It compares two numbers, a 0 AND any value is always 0. A 1 AND another 1 is always 1.

Let's take a closer look at how this works. Earlier in this chapter, under the subnetting objective, we worked with a network address for a Class B address. We worked with the address of 187.26.36.210. Let's see how the Boolean ANDing process will determine the network address. Table 2.16 shows how the octets are handled in binary.

TABLE 2.16: ANDing 187.26.36.210, subnet of 255.255.240.0

IP Address/ Subnet	1	2	3	4
187.26.36.210	10111011	00011010	00100100	11010010
255.255.240.0	11111111	11111111	11110000	00000000
Result	10111011	00011010	00100000	00000000
	187.	26	32	0

Judging from this, the network address that we arrived at in the earlier example matches, so we must be right.

NOTE Yes, I know, I didn't describe how I converted the IP address to binary. Actually, I used the scientific calculator that is available in Windows. This calculator is available to you during the exam.

Now let's try ANDing another IP address to see if it is on the same subnet. Let's say that the computer at 187.26.36.210 was sending a message to a computer at 187.26.30.16. Judging from the fact both are Class B addresses, it's possible that their hosts could reside on the same subnet. The ANDing process will find out if the target host is on the right network.

Table 2.17 will show the ANDing process for this address, and yes, I am going to use the calculator again!

TABLE 2.17: ANDing 187.26.30.16, subnet mask 255.255.240.0

IP Address/ Subnet	1	2	3	4
187.26.30.16	10111011	00011010	00011110	00010000
255.255.240.0	11111111	11111111	11110000	00000000
ANDing Results	10111011	00011010	00010000	00000000
	187	26	30	0

Through ANDing we have determined that these two computers are on separate subnets. Therefore, the sending computer would send the packet on to the gateway for transport through the network.

NT Server as a Static Router

To be configured as a static router, the NT Server has to have at least two network interface cards (NICs) installed. As you begin to plan the configuration, remember that you have to configure a static router so that its route table contains an entry for the routes to all of the other subnets on your network. A route table entry consists of a destination network address, the subnet mask, and the address of the gateway to reach that network address.

When a static router receives a packet, it has to determine where to forward the packet based on the destination network address. These destination network addresses are found in the route table. The router makes these decisions for the packet:

- If the destination network is listed in the route table, and the router is connected directly to that network, the router forwards the packet directly to the host.
- If the destination network is listed in the route table, and the router is not directly connected to the network, the router forwards the packet to the router specified in the router table.

- If the route table does not have an entry for the destination network, the router gets rid of the packet by forwarding it to the default gateway. The default gateway can handle the problem.

Before you can configure the route table, you have to know how the network is laid out. This is one of those times when you really hope your documentation is up to date.

Planning a Route Table

Figure 2.4 shows a relatively small network with four servers, each with two network cards. Any time a server has more than one network card, it becomes a multihomed computer; it also becomes a router. For the sake of this diagram, don't think of the servers as servers, think of the computers as routers.

FIGURE 2.4: Design of a small network

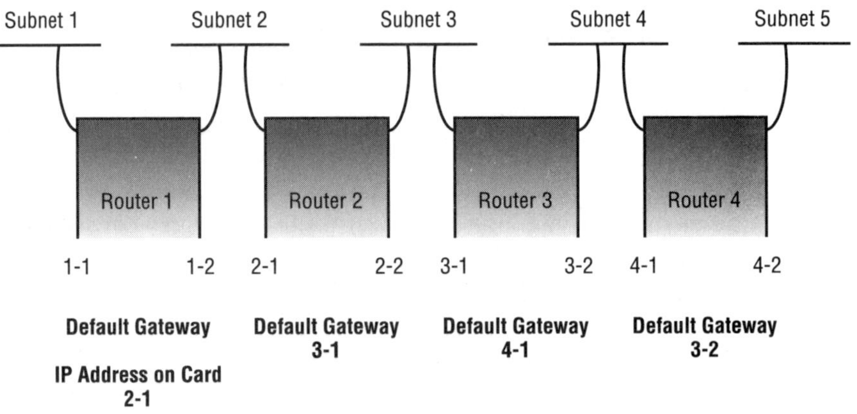

Table 2.18 shows how the route table would have to be configured. Each server knows about the networks it is directly connected to without entries having to be made in the route table. This condition accounts for the N/A settings in Table 2.18.

TABLE 2.18: Route table worksheet

Destination Subnet	**Router 1 forwards the packet to:**	**Router 2 forwards the packet to:**	**Router 3 forwards the packet to:**	**Router 4 forwards the packet to:**
Subnet 1	N/A	Adapter 1-2	Adapter 2-2	Adapter 3-2
Subnet 2	N/A	N/A	Adapter 2-2	Adapter 3-2
Subnet 3	Adapter 2-1	N/A	N/A	Adapter 3-2
Subnet 4	Adapter 2-1	Adapter 3-1	N/A	N/A
Subnet 5	Adapter 2-1	Adapter 3-1	Adapter 4-1	N/A

In the case of the route table worksheet for your company, the adapter number would be replaced by the IP address and subnet mask.

Static Routing Implementation

To utilize your server as a static router, it must have at least two properly configured network cards attached to different network segments or subnets. Each card must have the appropriate IP address and subnet mask, and have IP forwarding enabled from the Routing tab for Microsoft TCP/IP Properties page.

Once that has been accomplished and tested, you can start configuring your route table using the route command. The syntax for the route command is

route [-f] [-p] [*command* [*destination*] [**MASK** *netmask*] [*gateway*] [**METRIC** *metric*]]

-f clears the route tables of all gateway entries. If this parameter is used in conjunction with a command, the tables are cleared before the command is run.

-p enables persistent routes. (Route table changes are carried over automatically after restarting your computer.)

command can be one of the commands shown in Table 2.19.

TABLE 2.19: Commands used with the route command

Command	Purpose
print	Prints a route.
add	Adds a route.
delete	Deletes a route.
change	Modifies an existing route.

destination is the host or network to which you want to route.

mask specifies that the next parameter be interpreted as the *netmask* parameter.

netmask is the subnet mask value to be associated with this route entry. If not present, this parameter defaults to 255.255.255.255.

gateway is the gateway to the destination.

Metric specifies that the next parameter be interpreted as the *metric* parameter.

Metric associates a cost/hop count for the destination specified by the route entry. Generally, this specifies the distance in the number of hops from the destination. If not specified, the metric is set to 1 by default.

The gateway must be on the same logical network as your computer. Otherwise, the route will not be added.

Default Gateways

In a TCP/IP configuration, you can add default gateways for each network card. On a computer on which multiple default gateways are defined, all remote network traffic that does not match an entry in the route table is passed over the first default gateway defined. Because one default gateway is used, you should configure only one card to have a default gateway. This reduces confusion and ensures the results you intended. If you add a second gateway to the same network, the entry is added to the route table and is used if the first gateway goes down.

Example of Adding a Static Route

At the command prompt, type the following:

```
route add 199.199.41.0 mask 255.255.255.0 199.199.40.1
metric 2
```

It is important to note that in the sample above, the entry in the route table would be volatile. It would only last until the computer was restarted. If the computer was restarted, the entry would be lost. To make sure the entry is persistent, this would be the command:

```
Route -p add 199.199.41.0 mask 255.255.255.0
199.199.40.1 metric 2
```

Each router would have to be updated with the appropriate routes. Any time that a new router was added to the network, entries would have to be made in the route table of each router. As you can see, deciding to go with a static route table in a large network would be a considerable task and one that would be ongoing.

NT Server with Dynamic Routing

With dynamic routing, the work involved in building and maintaining a route table is eliminated because the routers automatically exchange information about the known routes. Windows NT uses the Routing Information Protocol for dynamic routing. The only configuration that needs to be done on the host is to point the host to the default gateway, in this case, the network card in the router serving the subnet.

While this may seem like a great solution after imagining the horror of configuring and updating the route tables of 100 different routers, RIP does have some problems. By default, any entry in the route table is given a time-out value of three minutes. If the route is not confirmed every three minutes, it is discarded. If a router goes down, it may be a while (at least three minutes) before anyone knows it.

The biggest problem with RIP in a WAN environment is network traffic. RIP broadcasts the entire contents of its route table to all the other routers on the system, once every 30 seconds. If you have multiple routers and slow WAN links, much of your bandwidth is going to be taken up by RIP broadcasts.

RIP is a service that is installed through the Network icon in Control Panel.

NOTE Windows NT can use other IP routing protocols, such as Open Shortest Path First (OSPF). OSPF is a better solution for a WAN environment because it does not broadcast the entire route table, it just sends out changes. This dramatically cuts down on the amount of WAN traffic. OSPF is not provided with Windows NT by default, which is why it is not covered in this book.

DHCP Relay Agent Installation and Configuration

Earlier in this chapter, DHCP was discussed as a way to dynamically assign IP information to workstations throughout the network. This is a great solution as long as the DHCP server is on the same subnet as the DHCP client. DHCP requests are not routable, so if a client exists on one subnet and the DHCP server resides on another subnet, there has to be some kind of intermediary configured. The intermediary is the DHCP relay agent.

When a client on a subnet that does not contain a DHCP server broadcasts a request for an IP address, the DHCP relay agent gets the request. It forwards the request to the DHCP server on the other subnet. The request to the server contains the address of the client so the DHCP server returns the information back directly to the requesting host.

There is some information that the DHCP relay agent must have. It must have the IP address of the DHCP server so it knows where to forward the requests. The DHCP server must have a scope defined for each subnet that it will service using the relay agent.

Necessary Procedures

In this section, we will perform the following tasks using a sample network:

- Configure IP forwarding.
- Design a static IP route table.
- Write the routing commands for each router.
- Demonstrate how to configure a DHCP relay agent.

After the static routing has been configured, we will install the Routing Information Protocol (RIP) to provide dynamic routing.

The illustration below shows the sample network that will be used as part of this section. It consists of three servers, each with two network cards. As you look at the illustration, pay close attention to the IP addresses of each card. Each server has two cards, each card connects to a different subnet, and the addressing scheme reflects this.

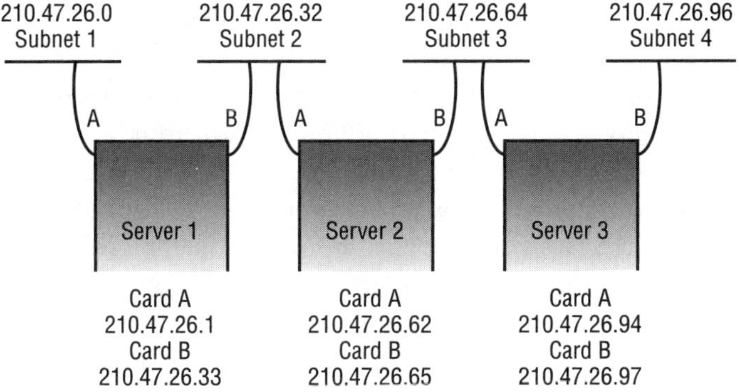

Configuring IP Forwarding

Each network card in our example must be configured to forward IP packets. To accomplish this, follow these steps:

1. Click Start ➤ Settings ➤ Control Panel.
2. From the Control Panel window, double-click on Network.
3. From the Network window, select the Protocols tab ➤ TCP/IP ➤ Properties.
4. From the Microsoft TCP/IP Properties window, click on the Routing tab and click in the box, Enable IP forwarding.
5. Click OK to close the Properties window.
6. Click OK to close the Network window.
7. Agree to restart the computer by clicking Yes.

Designing a Static IP Route Table

The next step in the process is to have an idea of what goes where and how it gets there. You may have a complete set of documentation for your network (yes, there truly are networks out in the real world that are completely documented. At last count, there were at least two), or you may just use a sketch. Whatever form your documentation comes in, some is better than none. Table 2.20 is the route table for our sample network. Because each router knows about the networks it is connected to, you do not have to add the information to the route table. These entries are marked with N/A in the table below.

TABLE 2.20: A routing worksheet for a sample network

Destination Subnet	Server 1 forwards the packet to:	Server 2 forwards the packet to:	Server 3 forwards the packet to:
Subnet 1 (210.47.26.0)	N/A	210.47.26.33	210.47.26.65
Subnet 2 (210.47.26.32)	N/A	N/A	210.47.26.65

TABLE 2.20: A routing worksheet for a sample network *(continued)*

Destination Subnet	Server 1 forwards the packet to:	Server 2 forwards the packet to:	Server 3 forwards the packet to:
Subnet 3 (210.47.26.64)	210.47.26.62	N/A	N/A
Subnet 4 210.47.26.96	210.47.26.62	210.47.26.94	N/A

Routing Commands for Each Server

When you decide to use the static form of routing, you are faced with several ways you can enter data into the route table. If you use the *route add* command, you can configure all the commands to run in a batch file at start-up; you can add the commands manually each time the server starts back up; or you can enter the commands once, using the -p parameter to enable persistent routes. With persistent routes, the route table will reinitialize on start-up. There are pluses and minuses to each approach, even the approach where you enter all the information manually each time the system starts up. This is usually referred to as job security.

I, on the other hand, work for myself. My job is really secure, I wouldn't have the heart to fire me. I also recognize that I am basically a lazy person. So I have immediately ruled out entering the commands each time the server comes up. That leaves a batch file and the persistent switch. If I have to write a batch file, I still have to type in all the commands, plus save them in a batch file format, put the batch file somewhere that it will start every time the server starts up, and test it. The persistent switch means all I have to do is enter the commands once and if the computer gods smile on me, that should be it, unless someone clears the route table. If someone clears the route table, I believe I could make a strong case for torture. So, I will opt for the persistent method.

On server 1, my commands would be:
To get to subnet 3 (210.47.26.64):

route –p add 210.47.26.64 mask 255.255.255.224 gateway 210.47.26.62

To get to subnet 4 (210.47.26.96):

route –p add 210.47.26.96 mask 255.255.255.224 gateway 210.47.26.62 metric 2

On server 2, my commands would be:
To get to subnet 1 (210.47.26.0):

route –p add 210.47.26.0 mask 255.255.255.224 gateway 210.47.26.33

To get to subnet 4 (210.47.26.96)

route –p add 210.47.26.96 mask 255.255.255.224 gateway 210.47.26.94

On server 3, my commands would be:
To get to subnet 2 (210.47.26.32)

route –p add 210.47.26.32 mask 255.255.255.224 gateway 210.47.26.65

To get to subnet 1 (210.47.26.0)

route –p add 210.47.26.0 mask 255.255.255.224 gateway 210.47.26.65 metric 2

TIP The metric parameter is added to indicate that the network is another hop or router away.

Installing and Configuring a DHCP Relay Agent

Configuration of the DHCP relay agent is a two-step process. The first step is to install the DHCP Relay Agent service on the NT Server that will act as the agent. The agents can then be configured, using the Microsoft TCP/IP Protocol Properties dialog box with the IP address of the computer running Windows NT Server DHCP, so the agent will know where to forward requests from clients for available IP addresses. Installing the service and configuring the agents are done using the Network icon in the Control Panel.

1. Click Start ➤ Settings ➤ Control Panel.
2. Select Network ➤ Services tab ➤ Add.
3. Under Network Services, click DHCP Relay Agent, then click OK.
4. In the message that appears, type the full path to the Windows NT Server DHCP files and click Continue. The DHCP service is installed.
5. Click Close. Configuration and binding information is checked.
6. You will get an error message as part of unattended setup. It requires a DHCP server IP address be listed. Click Yes to add the server address. This opens the Microsoft TCP/IP Properties window.
7. Click the DHCP Relay tab, click Add, then type in the address of the DHCP server. Your screen should look something like the one shown below.

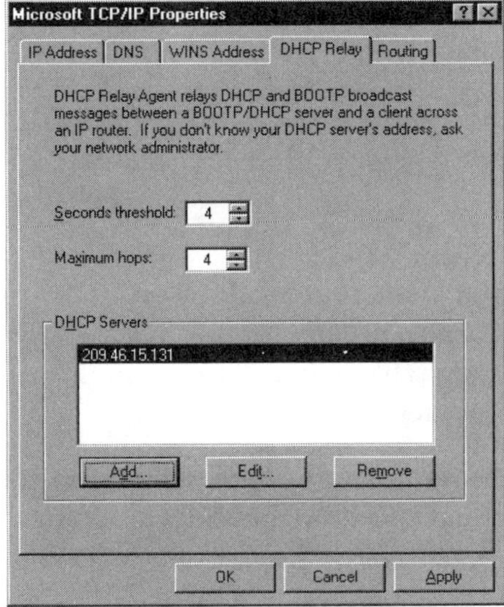

8. Click OK and agree to restart the computer by clicking Yes.

Installing and Configuring Routing Information Protocol

The installation of RIP is done from the same place as the installation of a DHCP relay agent, the Network Services tab.

1. Click Start ➤ Settings ➤ Control Panel.
2. Double-click Network, then click the Services tab and click Add.
3. Under Network Services, select RIP for Internet Protocol, then click OK.
4. Provide a complete path to the NT system files in the dialogue section of the Windows NT Setup window and click Continue.
5. Click Close to shut the Network window and the bindings will be checked.
6. Agree to restart the computer when prompted by clicking Yes.

Exam Essentials

While this section is not covered as extensively as the section on subnetting, it is still addressed. Most of the questions revolve around procedure matters.

Know the syntax of the route command. Specifically, know the route add command. The command syntax is:

route add *network-address* mask *subnet-mask gateway-address*

Know that static routes added using the route add command without the –p parameter are volatile. The route will only remain in the router table until the server is restarted. Then, the commands must be reentered.

Know the name of the dynamic routing protocol. Windows NT Server uses the Routing Information Protocol or RIP.

Know the disadvantages to using RIP. Because RIP broadcasts its entire route table every 30 seconds, it can consume massive amounts of bandwidth.

Know that a DHCP request will not cross a router. Because of this shortcoming a DHCP relay agent must be configured for each subnet without a DHCP server.

Key Terms and Concepts

DHCP relay agent: DHCP requests cannot cross a router. Therefore, a relay agent must be configured on any subnet that does not have a DHCP server, but where hosts are using DHCP.

Dynamic router: A type of routing protocol that will determine the location of other routes and dynamically discover the routes available on the network.

Gateway: A Microsoft synonym for a router. A default gateway is the next address in the trip through the network.

Hops: The number of routers a packet has to cross to get to its destination.

Metric: A parameter of the route command that specifies the number of hops between two network segments.

Route command: Adds static routes to a route table.

Route table: The router's database of how to move packets from one subnet to another.

Router: A hardware device that moves packets from one subnet to another.

Routing Information Protocol (RIP): A dynamic protocol provided with Windows NT.

Static router: A router that requires the manual input of the route table.

Time to Live (TTL): Each packet has a TTL. The default TTL is set to 16 and each time the packet crosses a router, the TTL is decremented by 1. If the TTL reaches 0, the packet is discarded.

Sample Questions

1. The dynamic routing protocol that is provided with Windows NT Server is:

   A. SAP

   B. RIP

   C. IPX

   D. SPX

   E. NetBIOS

   Answer: B. Windows NT Server comes with the Routing Information Protocol or RIP.

2. What happens to the TTL when a packet crosses a router?

   A. The router adds 1 to the TTL.

   B. Nothing happens to the TTL.

   C. The router subtracts 1 from the TTL.

   D. The router adds a number equal to the metric to the TTL.

   Answer: C. The router will decrease the TTL by 1 until it reaches 0. If the TTL is 0, the packet is discarded.

3. What two ways can Windows NT establish and maintain a route table?

   A. Volatile

   B. Dynamic

   C. TTL

   D. Static

   Answer: B and D. NT route tables can be established and maintained either statically or dynamically.

4. How do you add static routes to a router table?
   A. Using the route command-line utility
   B. Using the Server Manager for Domains graphical user interface
   C. Using the Route Manager graphical user interface
   D. Using the table command-line utility

Answer: A. Static routes are added to an NT route table using the Route command-line utility.

Install and configure the Microsoft DNS Server service on a Windows NT Server computer.

- Integrate DNS with other name servers.
- Connect a DNS server to a DNS root server.
- Configure DNS server roles.

Talk about simple yet elegant, the Domain Name System or DNS really fits the bill! When the Internet was young and the number of hosts few, systems connected to the Internet relied on a text file to resolve host names to IP addresses. This text file, called the HOSTS file, will be discussed further in the next objective.

As the Internet continued to grow, and it became more and more obvious that some type of system was needed to regulate and locate host names, DNS was born.

Critical Information

DNS is a static, distributed, hierarchical database system of millions of registered, unique domain names. Each domain name needs to be unique within its section of the database. Some of the top-level domain databases commonly used are included in Table 2.21.

TABLE 2.21: Some of the major domains

Top-level Domain	Description	Examples
.com	Commercial	Microsoft.com Psconsulting.com Compaq.com
.gov	Governmental	Whitehouse.gov Senate.gov
.mil	Military	Army.mil Navy.mil
.edu	Education	Umich.edu UMN.edu
.net	Network services	InterNIC.net
.se	Sweden	www.stockholm.se
.au	Australia	www.smh.com.au

The top level of the domain database hierarchy is <*root*>, which is usually represented by a trailing period in the domain name. The trailing period is so common, it's ignored. The Internet is broken down by domain names. Domains are then broken down to the host level by a fully qualified domain name (FQDN). A FQDN starts at the host level and works its way back all the way through the DNS hierarchy, left to right, smallest to biggest. For example, my registered domain name is psconsulting.com. As part of psconsulting.com, I have an NT Server host that is named mail. The FQDN for that server would be mail.psconsulting.com. As long as all the host names within a domain are unique, all FQDNs are unique.

TIP The InterNIC is also in charge of registering domain names. You can check and see if the domain name you want is already taken by using the WHOIS site at the InterNIC. The URL is http://www.internic.net/cgi-bin/whois. Your ISP can register your name for you. If your network is not connected to the Internet, you can still use DNS, you just don't have to worry about a unique domain name.

At this point in the discussion, I should probably issue a few disclaimers to make sure there is no confusion. There is absolutely no connection between what Microsoft calls a domain and what the InterNIC calls a domain. These are two completely different things. Microsoft calls a grouping of computers in your company a domain. The InterNIC takes a much broader view of things. It groups hosts from multiple companies together by the type of DNS name the company uses. For example, .com would be a domain.

Also, while DNS and WINS serve similar functions, the two should not be confused. WINS resolves NetBIOS computer names and DNS resolves host names. There are some other differences. For example, WINS maintains a single dynamic database while DNS has distributed, static databases. The WINS name space is flat while the DNS name space is hierarchical. WINS operates at your network level. While DNS can be configured to operate at your network level, it was designed to work at the Internet level. When configured to work at the local network level, DNS can also communicate with other DNS servers on the Internet to provide Internet level resolution.

NOTE Throughout this discussion of DNS you will come across the term BIND. It stands for the UNIX-based Berkeley Internet Name Domain servers that provide name resolution at the Internet level. For more information, the definitive tome on DNS is *DNS and BIND* by Paul Albitz and Cricket Liu (O'Reilly and Associates, 1997).

Microsoft DNS Server Service on a Windows NT Server Computer

Before you run right out and install DNS, it would probably be a good thing to figure out where you are going to put it and what you are going to have to do with it after you get it installed.

DNS on NT runs as a server service. Therefore, it must run on an NT Server. DNS is also one of those server services that have been patched a couple of times, so it would probably be a good idea to reapply the latest NT Service Pack (SP #3 or greater) as well as any DNS related patches. If you are running NT on an Intel platform, there is at least one additional patch available at Microsoft's post-SP3 FTP site. The URL is ftp://ftp.microsoft.com/bussys/winnt/winnt-public/fixes/usa/nt40/hotfixes-postsp3/dns-fix. There were two files in this site; one is for the Alpha installation of NT and the other is for an installation on an Intel server. If you are installing on an Intel system, the file name is dnsfix_i.exe.

After the DNS Server service is installed, you will notice there is another new utility on the Administrative Tools (Common) menu, DNS Manager. You start the configuration of DNS by defining the computer as a DNS server in DNS Manager. Once you have defined the server, you will notice that immediately under the server is the word Cache. See Figure 2.5 below.

FIGURE 2.5: Domain Name Service Manager

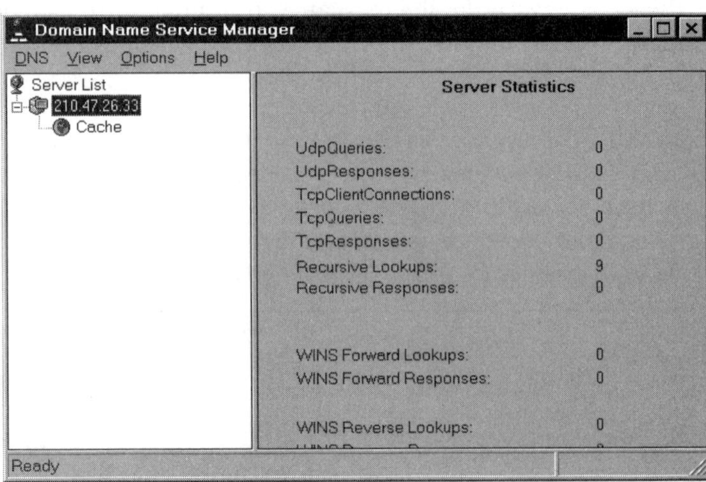

When you first create a DNS server, it is a caching-only server. As a caching-only server, it will not maintain any of the DNS database, it will just help resolve names by contacting other DNS servers. Does this sound like too much middle management? Not really, because once the names have been resolved, the DNS caching server stores the queries in memory as part of cache. Each entry has a TTL (doesn't everything?). If you want to see the entries in your cache, simply go to the Domain Name Service Manager and click Cache. You will be presented with a listing of all the information stored in memory.

Besides the information that the DNS server has been able to ascertain for itself, it also caches entries in a file called cache.dns. This is just a text file that contains information on where DNS should go to find top-level servers to resolve names to IP addresses. Figure 2.6 shows all the Root servers stored in cache for name resolution.

FIGURE 2.6: DNS cache

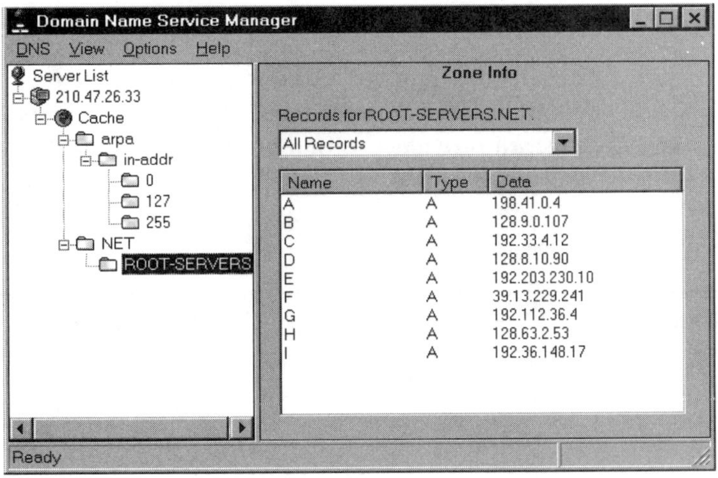

NOTE DNS Manager can manage up to 15 servers.

Earlier in this objective, we mentioned that DNS used a static database. That means you or someone like you is the person responsible for adding information to the database. However, before information can be added to the database, you have to tell DNS just what it controls. This is called a DNS Zone. A DNS Zone is the portion of the DNS name space whose database records exist and are managed in a particular zone file. For example, one server may manage the zone that handles the .com, .edu, and .gov name space while a server on my network will manage the psconsulting.com name space.

When you create the first DNS Zone, it will be the Primary Zone. The Primary Zone is where the zone file is stored. The zone file is nothing more than a text file that contains all the records for the zone the DNS server manages. It is usually named after the zone with an extension of .dns. When you enter information into the zone file, you are creating DNS entries for your network. This can be done using any text editor or a graphical utility. In the case of DNS, you can use DNS Manager to add the information called *resource records* to the DNS database.

There are many different types of resource records that can be added to a DNS database. Each record has a type designator assigned to it and each record provides a different service. Table 2.22 provides a summary of some of these records.

TABLE 2.22: DNS record types

Record Type	Record Name	Description
SOA	Start of Authority	The SOA record is always the first record in the database files. This record indicates the server is an "authority" on host names.

TABLE 2.22: DNS record types *(continued)*

Record Type	Record Name	Description
NS	Name Server	This record points to another DNS name server. If the local DNS name server cannot resolve the name, it will forward the request to other servers.
A	Address	An A record maps the host name to the IP address.
CNAME	Canonical Name (Alias)	An *alias* is just an alternative name to a host.
PTR	Pointer	This record maps the IP address to the host name. It is the reverse of an A record.
MX Record	Mail Exchanger	An MX record dictates where to send e-mail for any specific domain name.
RP	Responsible Person	If you use the InterNIC's WHOIS utility, you will see that each domain name has a responsible person listed. This is where it gets that information.

After you create the zone, you will notice that several records are added for you. Look at Figure 2.7 and you will see that an SOA record and an NS record were created for my server.

After you have created the zone, your DNS server is fully configured. You can now add records to the database or integrate DNS into the network with other name services.

FIGURE 2.7: Domain Name Service Manager with default zone records

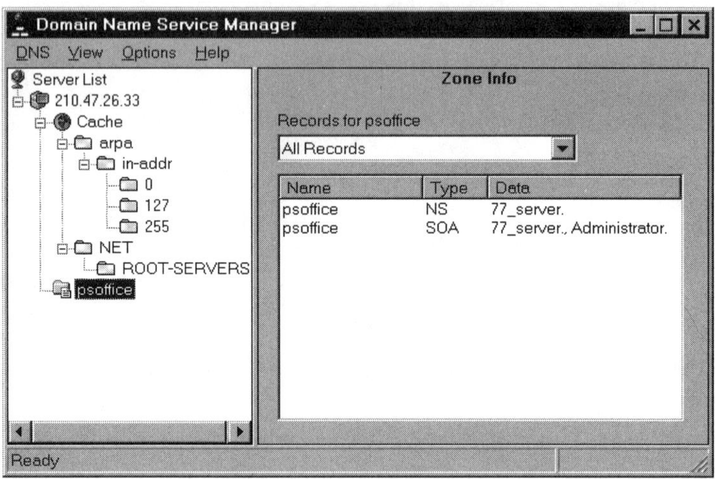

DNS Integration with Other Name Servers

Actually, this section is misnamed. It should be called, "Integrate DNS with WINS," because that's what it's all about.

WINS and DNS are sort of the same, but sort of different. Both services resolve names to IP addresses, but the types of names and the way the resolution occurs is really different. The databases themselves are also very different.

DNS works with host names. On a Windows-based machine, by default, the host name is the computer name. On non-Windows machines, such as those UNIX boxes that are popping up all over the place, there is no such thing as a NetBIOS computer name; there is just the host name. Somehow, it has to be possible to meld the best of both worlds.

You can configure a DNS server to use a WINS Server to resolve just the host name portion of the FQDN. Here is how it would work. Suppose the DNS server for psconsulting.com received a request for ntmail.psconsulting.com and the DNS server did not have an entry for the host name, ntmail. At that point, DNS would ask the WINS Server for the IP address of the WINS client, ntmail. If WINS had the client information, it would pass the information back to the DNS server, which would then forward the information to the client.

One of the benefits of configuring DNS and WINS to work together is making DNS appear to be almost dynamic. Because many companies are now relying on DHCP to assign IP addresses, that means host names will change from one IP address to another. In a DNS environment, where the address table is static, this can lead to chaos. Because WINS is a dynamic system, it will help resolve the host name with the current IP address, whether the client is using DHCP or a permanent address.

TIP The only way DNS and WINS can work together in this manner is if the host name and the NetBIOS computer names are the same throughout the network.

Integrating WINS and DNS is done through the Zone Properties page of the DNS Zone. When completed, the WINS integration creates a WINS resource record in the Primary Zone file. This is a record that cannot be added manually.

DNS Server Connection to a DNS Root Server

Now that a DNS server has been installed, perhaps it's time to look at how these things all work together. Earlier in this section, it was mentioned that the DNS is a distributed database. This is "geek" for there are several databases stored on the Internet that you probably don't know about, nor do you have to. DNS knows about these databases and knows how to find them, that's all that matters.

The structure of the DNS database is very similar to a DOS file system. It starts out at the root and branches out from there. Remember, the root name of this database is a null character or " ", but it is designated by a period. Figure 2.8 gives a simplified view of the structure.

FIGURE 2.8: Representation of the DNS database system

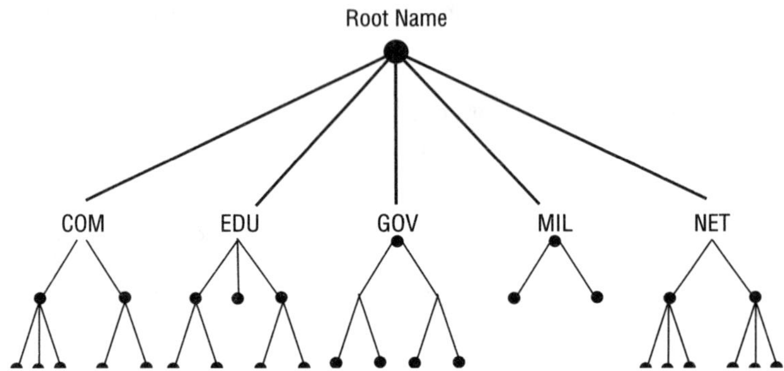

In the DNS system, each root of the domain (for instance the part of the database that handles the commercial or .com domains) is divided into subdomains. Each domain and subdomain has a domain name that shows the position in the domain database. So, for example, psconsulting is my domain name, which resides in the .com database.

Because I now have my "own" domain name, I can divide it up further if I so choose. I may name part of my domain .corp so references to that section of the DNS tree would be corp.psconsulting.com.

In addition to all these domain names, remember that each host has a unique name on the Internet. I may configure a server to handle all my incoming and outgoing Internet mail, so I will call the server something really creative like mail.corp.psconsulting.com. In the course of daily events, you decide to send me an e-mail message. While we are not even going to start getting into the inner workings of e-mail, let's just say your computer wants to send a packet to mail.corp.psconsulting.com. As soon as your computer decides to send that packet, it becomes a *resolver.*

A resolver runs on the client that needs information. It doesn't really know how to find the information, but it does have a starting point. When TCP/IP was configured for that client, someone gave it at least one IP address of a DNS server. The resolver simply asks the DNS server if it knows the location of the host, mail.corp.psconsulting.com.

The DNS name server may not know where this system is located, but it knows where the root name server resides, so it queries the root name server. The root name server provides the IP address of the domain root server in question, in this case the root server for the .com domain. The root server for the .com domain knows where psconsulting is, so it refers the request to psconsulting. Psconsulting knows where corp is, so it refers the request to corp, which finally resolves the request to the mail host.

This system works really well in the world of the Internet and it can also work well for an intranet, even if it is not hooked up to the outside world. When you design your DNS system, you must make sure your DNS servers know about each other. How do you do that?

Actually, that part is a no-brainer. If you remember, earlier in this section when the DNS server was installed, the file cache.dns was discussed. This file comes complete with all the root server's IP addresses already installed. If your DNS server is connected to the Internet, it should be able to help resolve DNS names with the information provided on installation.

What about if your network is not connected to the Internet and you still want to use DNS? How can you link one server to another? In Domain Manager, you start by creating a new host in your primary zone. To do this, you will need the host name of the DNS server that will be asked for help and its IP address. Once the host has been created, create a resource record of type NS pointing to the new DNS host. Then, when your DNS server has a problem resolving names, it will look to the other DNS server for help.

DNS Server Roles

When DNS is originally installed, it is installed as a caching-only computer. When configured as part of a zone, computers can take on different server roles.

Primary Name Server

The primary name server gets all of its zone data from local files. Any changes to a zone are done at the primary name server level.

Secondary Name Server

A secondary name server gets its information from another name server across the network. This provides for DNS redundancy. If you position the servers carefully, you can also speed up DNS access for remote locations and reduce the load on the primary name server.

Master Name Server

A secondary name server must receive its information from another name server. The information source can be a primary name server or a secondary name server. When you designate a source name server, that server becomes the master name server for the receiving secondary name server.

When a secondary name server starts up, it contacts the master name server and initiates a zone transfer of information for that server.

Necessary Procedures

Several installations and configurations are part of this chapter.

Installing and Configuring the Microsoft DNS Server Service on a Windows NT Server Computer

To install the DNS Server service, follow these procedures:

1. Select Start ➢ Settings ➢ Control Panel.
2. Double-click Network, then click the Services tab and click Add.
3. Choose Microsoft DNS Server from the Select Network Services window. Click OK
4. If prompted, provide a complete path to the setup files in the dialogue window of the Windows NT setup screen and ➢ click Continue.
5. Click Close to exit the Network window and begin the check of the bindings.
6. Agree to shut down and restart the computer when prompted by clicking Yes.

To reapply Service Pack 3 to patch DNS Server service, follow these procedures:

1. Locate where the file NT4sp3_I is stored and click on the file name to begin the extraction and installation process.

NOTE The file name may change. This was the latest NT 4.0 Service Pack at the time this book was written.

---

2. From the Welcome screen, click Next to install the Service Pack.
3. Click Yes to agree to the license and this will take you to the Service Pack Setup menu.
4. Make sure the radio button that will allow you to install the Service Pack is selected. Click Next.
5. Choose whether you want to create an uninstall directory or not, then ➢ click Next.
6. Click Finish to complete the installation.
7. After the Service Pack setup is complete, you will be prompted to restart the computer. Click OK.

To install the DNS Service Pack, follow these steps:

1. Browse to the location where you stored the file dnsfix_i.exe.
2. Double-click on the file to install the patch.
3. Remove any diskettes from the drive and click OK to restart your computer.

Once the DNS Server service has been installed, you must define a new server. To define a new DNS server, follow these steps:

1. Click Start ➢ Programs ➢ Administrative Tools (Common) ➢ click on DNS Manager
2. From the Domain Name Service Manager, click DNS ➢ New Server.
3. Enter the name or IP address of the new DNS server.

Before you can enter records into the DNS database, you must also configure a DNS Zone. To create the Primary DNS Zone, follow these procedures:

1. Click Start ➤ Programs ➤ Administrative Tools (Common), then click on DNS Manager.
2. From the Domain Name Service Manager, click DNS.
3. Click New Zone. This will open a dialogue window called Creating new zone for IP Address.
4. Choose whether this zone will be a Primary or Secondary Zone type by clicking the radio button next to Primary. Click next.
5. Enter in the zone name. If you look at the illustration below, you will notice that the zone name is the default name for the zone file. Click Next after entering the name.

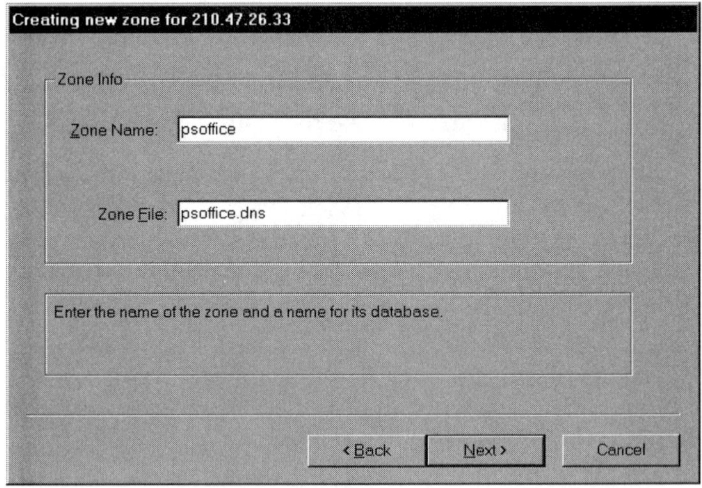

6. Click Finish to create the new zone.

Integrating DNS with Other Name Servers

To integrate DNS with WINS, follow these steps:

1. Click Start ➤ Programs ➤ Administrative Tools (Common) ➤ DNS Manager.

2. Click on the server that houses the Primary Zone.
3. Highlight the zone name ➤ right mouse button ➤ properties.
4. Click on the WINS Lookup tab.
5. Fill the check box next to Use WINS Resolution and add the IP address of the WINS server.
6. There is another check box available, Settings only affect local server. If this box is not checked, all secondary servers will use the WINS server as well. If any secondary DNS servers are non-Windows servers, this box should be checked.

NOTE NetBIOS names and host names must be the same throughout the network.

Connecting a DNS Server to a DNS Root Server

When DNS is installed, the addresses of all the DNS root servers are placed in the cache.dns file. If your DNS server is connected to the Internet, the system will take care of the rest.

Configuring DNS Server Roles

The primary name server was created as part of the integration process with other name services. To create a secondary name server, follow these steps:

1. Click Start ➤ Programs ➤ Administrative Tools (Common) ➤ DNS Manager.
2. Highlight the name of the primary domain and click with the right mouse button. Select Properties to bring up the Zone Properties window.
3. Click on the Notify tab.
4. Add in the IP address of the secondary server in the dialog box and click Add. See the illustration below. Notice that you can add more

than one system to the Notify list. This allows the server to service more than one secondary server.

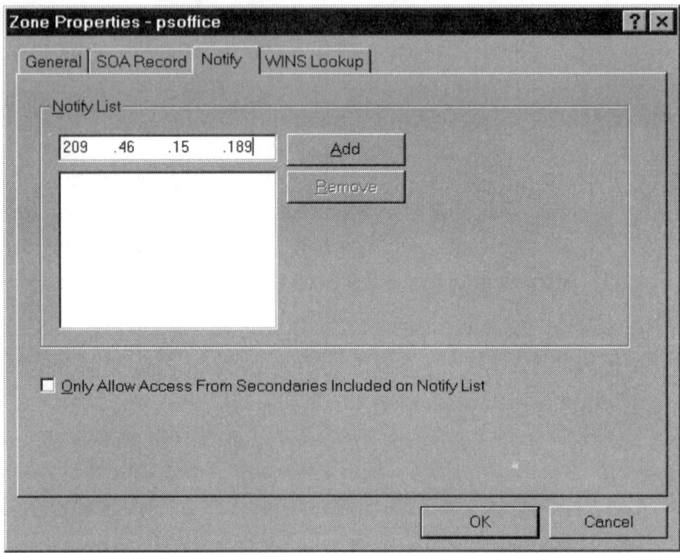

5. Clicking the box, Only Allow Access From Secondaries Included on Notify List, means that only DNS servers on the notify list can replicate this Zone file.
6. Click OK to close Zone Properties and close Domain Name Service Manager.

Exam Essentials

This is a section that is chock full of stuff, all of that little minutiae that exam writers just love!

Know the characteristics of the Domain Name System. DNS is a static, distributed, hierarchical database that keeps track of millions of host names.

Know the differences between WINS and DNS. WINS is a single, dynamic database that keeps track of NetBIOS computer names. WINS uses flat naming. DNS is a static, distributed database that keeps track of host names. DNS uses hierarchical naming.

Know how to integrate WINS with DNS. WINS integration is done with DNS Manager from the Zone Properties Page.

Know how WINS works with DNS. If DNS cannot resolve a host name, it will query the WINS database to see if there is an entry. Because WINS is a dynamic database, this gives DNS the appearance of being dynamic.

Know what FQDN stands for. An FQDN is a fully qualified domain name.

Know how to administer a DNS server. DNS is administered using Domain Name Server Manager from the Administrative Tools (Common) menu.

Know the role of the primary name server. The primary name server is the first DNS server created. It gets all of its zone data from local files. Any changes to a zone are done at the primary name server level.

Know the role of the secondary name server. A secondary name server gets its information from another name server across the network. This provides for DNS redundancy. If you position the servers carefully, you can also speed up DNS access for remote locations and reduce the load on the primary name server.

Know the role of the master name server. A secondary name server must receive its information from another name server. The information source can be a primary name server or a secondary name server. When you designate a source name server, that server becomes the master name server for the receiving secondary name server.

When a secondary name server starts up, it contacts the master name server and initiates a zone transfer of information for that server.

Know how a DNS server is originally configured. A DNS server is originally a caching-only server. It does not pass information to any other server, it just requests information from other DNS servers. When it gets the information, it caches it in a file.

Know where DNS information is cached. DNS information is cached in a text file named cache.dns, stored in the %systemroot%\winnt\system32\dns folder.

Know the definition of a resource record. A resource record is an entry in a DNS database.

Know the common types of resource records and their characteristics. These are some of the common types of resource records:

- **SOA** (Start of Authority) is the first record in a DNS database.
- **CNAME** (Canonical name) is the alias for another host name.
- **A** (Address Record) maps the host name to the IP address.
- **PTR** (Pointer) is the reverse of an A record; it maps the IP address to a host name.
- **NS** (Name Server) is the record indicating another DNS name server.

Key Terms and Concepts

Berkeley Internet Name Domain (BIND): The most popular implementation of DNS used today.

Caching only server: When a DNS server is first configured, it only caches information it receives from other servers. It does not pass information to other servers. When a caching server receives information, it maintains that information in memory for use at a later time. This is a dynamic process and also a volatile process. If the server should come down for any reason, all the information stored in cache will be lost.

FQDN (Fully Qualified Domain Name): The full name of a host computer, complete with the full DNS name, for example, ntmail.corp.psconsulting.com.

Master name server: A DNS server that passes its information off to a secondary name server. A master name server can either be a primary name server or a secondary name server.

Primary name server: The server that hosts information for the Primary Zone.

Primary Zone: The first zone created in a DNS system, a management area.

Resolver: Usually a client asking for a DNS name to be resolved to an IP address.

Resource record: Added to a DNS database to indicate the function of the host or the purpose of the record.

Secondary name server: Provides DNS redundancy, load balancing, and faster client access. The secondary name server gets its information from the master name server. A **Secondary name server** cannot be used to manipulate the DNS database.

Zone: An area of the DNS database that a particular server manages.

Zone properties: These are aspects of a zone that can be managed, including WINS integration. The zone properties that can be managed include the Time To Live feature of the WINS lookup. When a host name gets resolved via WINS, the address is cached for the WINS Cache Time-out Value. If this address is ever forwarded to another DNS, the WINS Cache Time-out Value TTL is sent.

Sample Questions

1. The first record created in a DNS database is a:

A. SOA

B. PTR

C. A

D. NDS

Answer: A. The first record created in a DNS database is a Start of Authority record or SOA.

2. In the DNS database a "zone" is:

A. Another name for the root of the database

B. The way the database is divided. COM and EDU are DNS Zones.

C. The part of the database this server manages

D. A scope of IP addresses

Answer: C. A DNS Zone is the part of the database managed by a particular server.

3. Which term(s) would describe a DNS database?

A. Distributed

B. Dynamic

C. Manually configured

D. Hierarchical

Answer: A, C, and D. The DNS database is distributed over many sites; it is manually configured, even at the highest levels; and it is hierarchical.

4. Which listing is not a DNS resource record?

A. SOA

B. A

C. PTR

D. ADS

Answer: D. ADS is not a DNS resource record. SOA is Start of Authority, A is address, and PTR is a pointer.

Configure HOSTS and LMHOSTS files.

Throughout this section, the HOSTS and LMHOSTS files have been mentioned over and over. Just to do a high-level overview, when you think of HOSTS, think of resolving the UNIX or non-Windows–based host names to an IP address. When you think of LMHOSTS, think of manually resolving WINS computer names to IP addresses.

Critical Information

While we have cleared up some of the mysteries of TCP/IP addressing, there seems to be much discussion about these computer names or host names. UNIX host names were put in place to simplify the life of the end user. It is much easier to remember a host named microsoft.com than it is to remember the appropriate IP address.

HOSTS File Configuration

Host names are much more convenient to use than IP addresses, but somehow that host name needs to be resolved to the appropriate IP address. We have already discussed one method of host-to-address resolution in the section on Domain Name System or DNS. Like most things in computing, there is more than one way to approach any task.

The HOSTS file is a simple text file that sits on the local machine. It contains line after line of entries mapping IP addresses to host names. If DNS does the same thing, what is the advantage of a HOSTS file? In a word, speed. The name to address resolution process on your average UNIX computer starts out with the computer checking to see if the requested host name is the host name of the local computer. Kind of a "Check to see if it's me first" kind of thing. If the computer is not requesting local resources, it checks the local HOSTS file to see if the information is there. If the information is not in the HOSTS file, the system then starts the DNS process.

How to Be a Good HOSTS File

The HOSTS file is very similar to the LMHOSTS file in many ways. It is created using any text editor. It is saved in the %systemroot%\system32\drivers\etc subdirectory with a file name of HOSTS and no extension. The syntax for each entry is

```
IP address <tab> Host Name <tab> Alias Names <tab>
#Comment
```

Alias names are alternate names assigned to any host, so they are optional. Comments are also optional.

These are the rules of the HOSTS file:

- Case doesn't matter, the entries can be all uppercase, all lowercase, or any combination of the two.
- Each entry can contain up to 255 characters.
- HOSTS files are parsed (read) from the top down. Put the hosts you will use the most toward the top of the file.
- HOSTS files do not support any of the tags that the LMHOSTS file uses. The only special characters you can use are the # (pound sign) or the ; (semicolon) to signal a comment.
- LOCALHOST is an entry created by default; it must be in each HOSTS file.
- If you create a HOSTS file using WordPad or Notepad, you will probably have to go in and rename the file after you save it. WordPad and Notepad have a bad habit of adding unwanted extensions to file names.
- The HOSTS file must be created in the %systemroot%\system32\drivers\etc folder.
- Because the HOSTS file does not use the #INCLUDE statement like the LMHOSTS file, it is difficult to have a central copy of the file. Users would have to copy the central file down to the workstation every time there was a change and any local entries would be lost.

Troubleshooting a HOSTS File

After you create a HOSTS file, if you have problems, the easiest way of troubleshooting is to look in a mirror. Sorry, but because this is a manually configured file, the only way something can go wrong is if the carbon-unit interface between the chair and the keyboard screws it up. Of course, this makes it somewhat simpler to troubleshoot because you will be intimately familiar with the ways you manage to make those little typos. You know, if it weren't for a spelling checker and a great editor, every time you saw the word "receive" in this book, it would be spelled wrong!

Common things to check:

- Is the host name spelled right?
- Is the IP address correct?
- Is the file named HOSTS? Does it have an extension? (Hint: Type the DIR command at the command line to check. Explorer doesn't show extensions unless asked!)
- Is the HOSTS file stored in the right place?
- Is the HOSTS file in the right format? Word is a great tool, but not for creating text files. This is why the computer gods created the Edit command.
- Do you have duplicate entries in the file?
- Is the LOCALHOST listing there?

LMHOSTS File Configuration

An LMHOSTS file has all the charm of a HOSTS file, but it also has an attitude. With an LMHOSTS file, you are resolving NetBIOS computer names to IP addresses rather than host names with the HOSTS file. The LMHOSTS file is parsed from top to bottom, just like the HOSTS file. The LMHOSTS file is maintained using a text editor, just like the HOSTS file. The LMHOSTS file is saved in the %systemroot%\system32\drivers\etc directory and should be saved without an extension. The LMHOSTS file does have some special tags that can be embedded to provide advanced functions.

This is the syntax of the LMHOSTS file:

```
IP_address<tab>computer_name<tab>#PRE<tab>#DOM:Domain_
name<tab>#Comments.
```

In the LMHOSTS file the pound sign (#) does double duty. It not only serves as a flag that a special tag is coming, but also as a mark that a comment will follow. Only the IP address and the computer name are required.

How to Be a Good LMHOSTS File

The LMHOSTS file can be tweaked to a greater extent than the HOSTS file. For example, let's look at the use of the #PRE tag. Normally, when the system gets a request for name resolution, the first place it will check in the operating system will be memory. If it does not find the information in name cache, the operating system will then parse the LMHOSTS file line by line until it comes to the right computer name.

When the computer first comes up, the operating system checks the LMHOSTS file. When the #PRE tag is found during start-up, the system immediately loads the entry into name cache. Name cache is always better than the LMHOSTS file because the response from memory is always quicker.

You can also share an LMHOSTS file. This definitely simplifies management. Instead of having to maintain several hundred LMHOSTS files, you can create a corporate standard to roll out to all the desktops on installation and then include the commands necessary to refer to a file in a central location. Any changes just have to be made to the shared file and everyone gets the benefit.

The tags and their meanings are covered in Table 2.23.

TABLE 2.23: LMHOSTS file tags

Keyword	Meaning
#PRE	This keyword is added after an entry so the information will be pre-loaded into name cache. #PRE must be appended for any entries also appearing in the #INCLUDE statements. If #PRE is not present, the #INCLUDE statement will be ignored.
#DOM:*domain*	This keyword is put in after an entry to refer to a group name for the domain. This keyword impacts how the Browser and Logon services work. The #DOM entry must be proceeded by #PRE.
#INCLUDE *filename*	This keyword causes the system to go out and look for a file that may not reside on the host computer. Once this file is located, it will be treated as if it were local. A UNC mapping to the server must be provided before the #INCLUDE section and the #INCLUDE section must be proceeded by #PRE.
#BEGIN-ALTERNATE	This keyword starts a section of multiple #INCLUDE statements. It provides for fault tolerance.
#END-ALTERNATE	This keyword ends a section of multiple #INCLUDE statements. It provides for fault tolerance.

What happens if the server that hosts the shared file is not available? LMHOSTS files also have the ability to provide for fault tolerance. If the primary server that hosts the shared file is not available, the system will look to the tags between #BEGIN-ALTERNATE and #END-ALTERNATE.

The computers that host the master LMHOSTS file need to have the registry edited. The registry parameter, HKEY_LOCAL_MACHINE\SYSTEM\CurrentControlSet\Services\LanmanServer\Parameters\NullSessionShares, needs to be edited with the name of the share to which you want to grant null logon privileges. After this has been done, other Windows NT machines can access the LMHOSTS file without authenticating to the computer.

Troubleshooting an LMHOSTS File

Once again, when troubleshooting an LMHOSTS file problem, remember the adage "To err is human." I have also heard that adding a computer changes the adage to a physical law, kind of like gravity, but I have never been able to prove that. Basic troubleshooting skills involve checking the following items:

- Is the computer name spelled right?
- Is the IP address correct?
- Is the file named correctly? It is LMHOSTS without an extension. It is saved in the %systemroot%\system32\drivers\etc directory.
- Are the #PRE and #DOM tags entered correctly? All tags must be entered in capital letters.
- If you cannot access the LMHOSTS file on a remote machine, has its registry been properly updated?
- Is the UNC path in the #INCLUDE statement correct?
- Are there duplicate entries?

Necessary Procedures

If you have made it this far in the MCSE track, you can probably handle firing up the Edit command, so I will just show you samples of the HOSTS file and the LMHOSTS file.

Sample of the HOSTS File

```
# Host file for portable PC
#Manually configured IP address 210.47.26.34

127.0.0.1 localhost
210.47.26.50bobbi
207.46.130.16 microsoft
137.65.2.9 novell
192.9.9.100sun
## end of file
```

Sample of an LMHOSTS File

```
#LMHOSTS file for PSCONSULTING. Created 4/16/98
210.47.26.50 Bobbi
210.47.26.51 Cris
210.47.26.52 Denise
210.47.26.53 Brandice
210.47.26.54 CJ
210.47.26.55 PSCONSULT#PRE#DOM:PSDOM
210.47.26.56 PSService#PRE
#BEGIN_ALTERNATE
#INCLUDE \\PSCONSULT\SYSTEM32\DRIVERS\ETC\LMHOSTS
#INCLUDE \\PSSERVICE\SYSTEM32\DRIVERS\ETC\LMHOSTS
#END_ALTERNATE
```

Key Terms and Concepts

Carbon-unit interface: The end user.

HOSTS: A text-based file used to resolve host names to IP addresses.

LMHOSTS: A text-based file used to resolve NetBIOS computer names to IP addresses.

Tag: A special feature of the LMHOSTS file to pre-load information into cache, designate a domain, or reference an external LMHOSTS file. Tags include the following:

#PRE: Pre-loads the entry into name cache.

#DOM: Associates the entry with a domain.

#INCLUDE: Forces NetBIOS to seek the specified file name and parse it as if it were local.

#BEGIN_ALTERNATE, #END_ALTERNATE: Allows multiple #INCLUDE statements to be grouped together. Any successful #INCLUDE will cause the group to succeed. This is provided for redundancy.

Sample Questions

1. An LMHOSTS file can be created with the following utilities:

   A. DNS Manager

   B. DHCP Manager

   C. User Manager for Domains

   D. WordPad

   Answer: D. An LMHOSTS file can be created using any text editor, so WordPad works. Make sure the file is saved without an extension.

2. You need to edit the HOSTS file. Where is it stored?

   A. %systemroot%\windows\system\drivers

   B. %systemroot%\etc

   C. %systemroot%\system32\drivers\etc

   D. %systemroot%\windows\drivers\system32\etc

   Answer: C. The HOSTS file is stored in the %systemroot%\system32\drivers\etc folder.

3. What is the # (pound sign) used for in the LMHOSTS file?

   A. To designate a comment line

   B. To designate the end of a line

   C. To designate the end of page

   D. To designate a special tag

   Answer: A and D. In an LMHOSTS file, the # (pound sign) is used for a comment and to start a tag.

4. What is the (#) pound sign used for in the HOSTS file?

   A. To designate a comment line

   B. To designate the end of a line

   C. To designate the end of page

   D. To designate a special tag

   Answer: A. In a HOSTS file, the # (pound sign) is used for a comment.

Configure a Windows NT Server computer to support TCP/IP printing.

There are printers and then there are PRINTERS. There are the printers that can be hooked directly to a PC and do a pretty nice job of printing your average letter, and then there are printers that hook directly into the network and can do everything but start the morning coffee.

Critical Information

When you start talking about printing in a TCP/IP environment, you can have only so many kinds of printers. You can have a printer that is hooked directly into the network and comes complete with its own IP address. You can have a printer hooked to a UNIX-based host that needs to be shared with computers running Windows NT, and you can have printers hooked to an NT-based system that the UNIX folks want to access.

Three different printing choices offer three different ways to configure the printer. Three different configuration options offer three different utilities. First, for the UNIX user who wants to access a printer on the NT network, you would have the LPDSVC utility. For the Windows NT system that needs to use the printer attached to the UNIX computer, there is the LPRMON utility. Finally, there is the Add Printer Wizard for that printer, which is hooked directly to the network.

NOTE You will be seeing the terms LPD and LPR in the discussion of UNIX printing. LPD is the Line Printer Daemon, or software piece that makes the TCP/IP printer shareable. LPR is the Line Printer utility that sends information to the printer.

To support TCP/IP printing, the Microsoft TCP/IP printing service must first be installed and the TCP/IP print server has to be started. Beware, some of the management of the print server has to be done through the registry.

Once the print server is up, the TCP/IP printers need to be configured. This is done through the Add Printer Wizard, just as you would configure any other printer. Well, almost like any other printer, with the exception of the printer port; here you have to configure an LPR port.

SEE ALSO Configuring an LPR port will be covered in the "Necessary Procedures" section of this objective.

Accessing Printers with an IP Address

NT can use the Add Printer Wizard to install or connect to a TCP/IP printer that is either hooked directly to the network or connected directly to an NT Server. To attach to a printer hooked to a UNIX host, the LPR command-line utility will allow users to print to the printer. The LPQ utility can be used to view the status of jobs.

LRP and LPQ can both be used to print to printers running on Windows NT.

Necessary Procedures

The first step involved in making printers available to workstations using TCP/IP is to add the TCP/IP Print Service to the NT Server.

Installing Microsoft TCP/IP Printing

To install TCP/IP printing, follow these steps:

1. Click Start ➢ Settings ➢ Control Panel.
2. Double-click Network to open the Network window.
3. From the Network window, click the Services tab.
4. Click Add.
5. From the Select Network Service window, highlight Microsoft TCP/IP Printing and click OK.
6. Provide the path to the Windows NT Setup files and click Continue.
7. Windows NT will copy some files and add the service. Click Close to shut the Network dialog box, and agree to shutting down and restarting the computer by clicking Yes.

Configure the TCP/IP Print Server to Start Automatically

In order for TCP/IP print services to be available every time the NT Server restarts, the TCP/IP Print Server has to be configured to start automatically. To do this, follow these steps:

1. Click Start ➢ Settings ➢ Control Panel.
2. Double-click Services to open the Services window.
3. Scroll down through the Service window until you see TCP/IP Print Server. As you can see in the illustration below, by default, the Print Server requires a manual start.

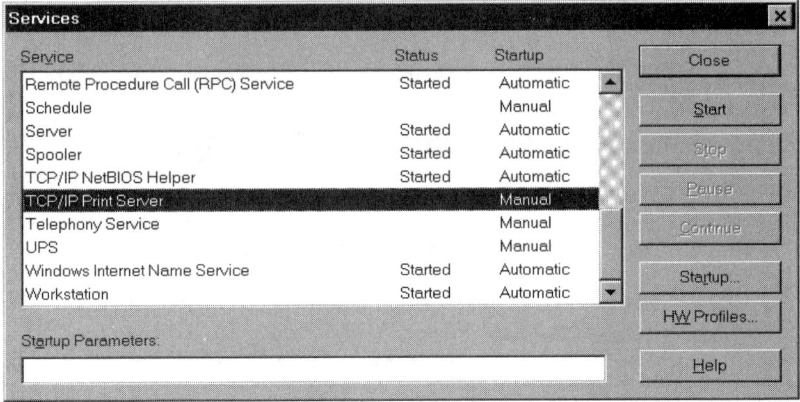

4. With TCP/IP Print Server highlighted, click on Startup.
5. In the Startup Type box, click the Automatic radio button and click OK.
6. Click Close to shut the Services window.
7. Restart the system to test the results.

Some TCP/IP parameters can be configured from the registry. The settings, located in the HKEY_LOCAL_MACHINE\SYSTEM\CurrentControlSet\Services\LPDSVC\Parameters, include settings such as the AllowJobRemoval setting that will allow a user using the LPR command to remove a print job from the printer. The Allow-PrintResume lets a user send the resume printer command to the

Print Server and finally, the MaxConcurrentUsers parameter sets the maximum number of users that can connect to the printer at any one time.

Now that the print server has started, all that is left is to configure the printer and then attach to it.

Configuring a TCP/IP Printer

To create a TCP/IP-based printer, start the Add Printer Wizard.

1. Click Start ➢ Settings ➢ Control Panel.
2. Double-click on Printers to open the Printers window.
3. From the Printers window, double-click Add Printer.
4. Verify that My Computer is checked and click Next.
5. In the Add Printer Wizard box, click Add Port. This will bring up the Printer Ports window shown below.

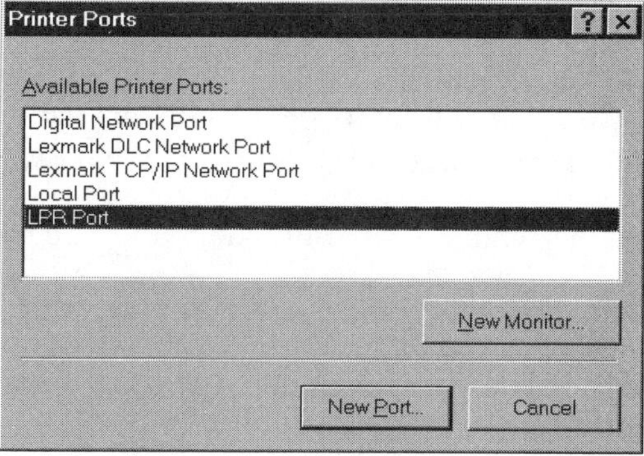

6. Check to make sure LPR Port is highlighted and click on New Port. This brings up the dialog box shown below.

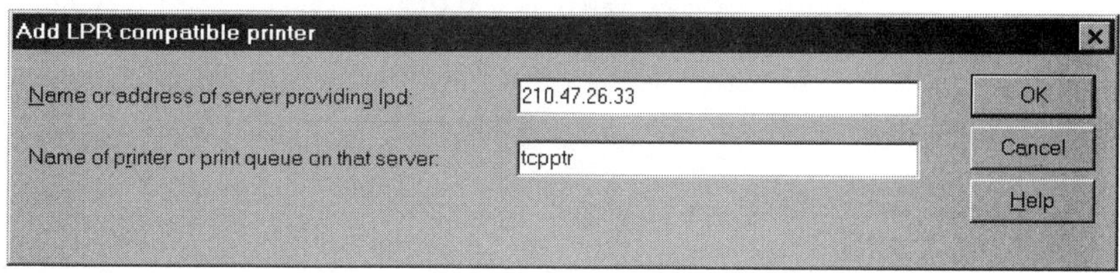

7. Add Name or address of the server providing lpd:. This should be a host name or an IP address. Then add the Name of the printer or printer queue on that server. Click OK to continue.
8. Click close to shut the New Port window, bringing you back to the Available ports window of the Add Printer Wizard. Make sure the port you just added is checked and click Next.
9. From the Manufacturers window, choose the Manufacturer of your printer. From the Printers window, highlight the model of your printer and click Next
10. Type in the Printers Name and click Next. This will bring up the window to share the printer. Click on Shared, accept the default shared name, and click Next.
11. If you would like to print a test page, now is the time to do it. Make your choice and click Finish.

Printing to TCP/IP-Based Printers

The Add Printer Wizard can be used to access a TCP/IP-based printer or connect to a printer configured with NT. Users can use the LPR utility to print to printers on a UNIX host and the LPQ utility to check the status of print jobs on a UNIX host.

This is the syntax of the LPR command-line utility:

lpr –S *ipaddress* –P *printername* –o 1 filename

The options for the lpr command are case sensitive. The –S *ipaddress* is the IP address of the server, the –P is the name of the print queue, and the –o 1 indicates the type of file, if the file is not a text file. In this case the 1 sends a binary file.

The LPQ utility displays the state of the remote print queue. This is the syntax for the LPQ command-line utility:

lpq -S*servername* –P*printer* –l

-l is for verbose output.

In place of the Server name or printer name, you can substitute the IP address.

Exam Essentials

The exam writers don't put much emphasis on this section.

Know the TCP commands used to manage printing. The LPQ utility displays the state of the remote print queue and the LPR utility sends a job to a network computer.

Know a job sent using the LPR utility is expected to be a text file. If you wish to send a binary file, such as a PostScript job, be sure to add the –o 1 parameter.

Know that the TCP/IP print server has to be configured to start automatically. By default, the service is started manually. Configuring it to start automatically ensures the print server will be restarted every time the NT Server is restarted.

Key Terms and Concepts

LPQ: A command-line utility to check the status of a remote print queue.

LPR: A command-line utility to send a text file to a printer.

Sample Questions

1. The utility used to create a TCP/IP Print Server is:

   A. LPQ

   B. LPR

   C. Add Printer Wizard

   D. The Services tab in the Network dialog

   Answer: D. The print server is created when Microsoft TCP/IP Printing is installed from the Services tab of the Network dialog box in the Control Panel.

2. To check on the status of a remote TCP/IP print queue, you would use which command-line utility?

   A. LPQ

   B. LPR

   C. Add Printer Wizard

   D. The Services tab in the Network dialog

   Answer: A. To check the status of a remote TCP/IP print queue, you would use the LPQ command-line utility.

3. To send a job to a remote TCP/IP printer, you would use which command-line utility?

   A. LPQ

   B. LPR

   C. Add Printer Wizard

   D. The Services tab in the Network dialog

   Answer: B. To send a job to a remote TCP/IP printer, you would use the LPR command-line utility.

4. The LPR utility sends print jobs in what format, by default?

   A. Text

   B. PCL

   C. PostScript

   D. Binary

   Answer: A. By default, the jobs are sent in a text format.

Configure SNMP.

One of the really powerful aspects of TCP/IP is the inclusion of SNMP (Simple Network Management Protocol). It is designed to help the network manager be proactive rather than reactive. It helps to show you areas of concern or bottlenecks in your network.

Critical Information

SNMP is made up of two pieces, an SNMP manager and an SNMP agent. It is up to the SNMP manager to request information from an SNMP agent and it is up to the agent to send the information directly to the SNMP manager. Windows NT comes complete with the SNMP agent piece of the puzzle. For the management piece, you will have to look at something such as Microsoft's System Management Server, HP's OpenView, or Intel's LanDesk Manager.

SNMP Basics

SNMP managers get information from SNMP agents using three types of calls or commands. The first is the get operation. In this case the SNMP manager can request or get specific information from the SNMP agent. An example of a get call would be a command sent to a router to get the latest number of TCP/IP packets routed in the last 10 minutes.

The next call is the get-next operation. This procedure does exactly what the name implies. I have set up a prescribed number of values that an agent will keep. My SNMP manager will send out a get call to receive the first value and get-next calls to go through the rest of the list. The final operation is a set call. In this case, the SNMP manager can set a parameter for a particular agent. An example of this would be to reset the number of packets routed over a set period of time to 0.

SNMP Communities

Given the information in SNMP basics, you have an SNMP manager asking all these SNMP agents for information about the network. What is to stop an SNMP manager from another network querying your agents and getting information about the network? In some cases, not much.

One way to combat that problem is by creating SNMP communities. In a community, an SNMP agent can only send information to the SNMP manager in the same community. For the sake of diversity, an SNMP agent can be a member of more than one community. By default, SNMP agents belong to the community, public.

MIBs

SNMP agents collect statistics on a set of defined objects. These objects are defined in Management Information Bases, or MIBs. Several types of MIBs are defined, including the Internet MIB II, which defines over 150 objects that are essential to analyze the health and well-being of a computer network. The Microsoft SNMP agents also support the LAN Manager MIB II. This MIB supports 90 different objects including statistics, shares, session information, user information, and logon information. The DHCP MIB monitors DHCP activity and the WINS MIB monitors WINS activity.

MIB objects are organized in a tree similar to the Windows NT registry. Each object has a unique name that consists of its location in the tree and the object name. The InterNIC handles the assignment. Individual organizations can apply for authority over their part of the name space. This means they can design MIBs especially for their products.

How Does SNMP Work?

How does an SNMP manager get information from an SNMP agent?

1. The SNMP manager starts out by sending a request to the SNMP agent by using either the agent's host name or its IP address. The request is either a get, get-next, or set packet for information on an

object or a set of objects. Because there is some security in place, the request must also have the SNMP manager's community name.

2. The agent receives the manager's request. It checks the community name to make sure that it is valid and then checks the source SNMP manager's host name or IP address. The agent is *very* particular; it will only accept requests from authorized managers.
3. The agent passes the request off to the DLL (dynamic link library) based on the information requested. If the request is for information from the Internet MIB II object, it will be directed to the TCP.DLL. When the DLL returns the information, the SNMP agent sends it back to the SNMP manager.

Even if you do not have an SNMP manager, it might be a good idea to install the SNMP agent. Performance Monitor uses the SNMP agent to monitor TCP/IP statistics.

NOTE There is also a quasi-SNMP manager provided with the Windows NT Resource Kit. It's called SNMPUTIL.

Necessary Procedures

SNMP is a Windows NT Server service.

Installing SNMP

To install SNMP on a computer, follow these steps:

1. Click Start ➤ Settings ➤ Control Panel.
2. Double-click Network to open the Network window.
3. From the Network window, click the Services tab. Click Add.
4. Scroll down through the Network Service screen until you can highlight SNMP Service. Once it has been highlighted, click OK.
5. Provide the path to set up files and click Continue.

6. At this point, the Microsoft SNMP Properties Agent screen will be brought up. It is shown below.

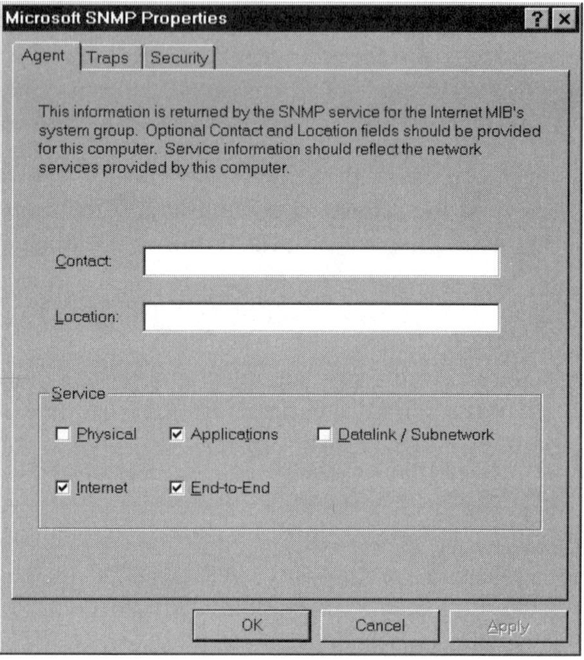

7. The Contact and Location information shown above are optional and for informational use only. The Services include the following:

   - **Physical:** This option is selected if the agent manages a physical device, such as a concentrator or repeater.
   - **Applications:** This option would be selected if the SNMP agent uses any TCP/IP applications. This selection should always be checked.
   - **Datalink/Subnetwork:** This option should be selected if the agent manages a bridge.
   - **Internet:** Select this option if the agent manages an IP router or gateway.
   - **End-to-End:** Select this option if the agent functions as an IP host.

8. Errors that occur with the SNMP Service will be logged automatically and can be viewed in the System Log in the Event Viewer.

WARNING After installing SNMP services, it is very important that you reapply the latest Service Pack patches. Several older files are copied during the SNMP installation.

---

9. After configuring the SNMP Agent screen, you can click on the Traps tab. The result is shown below.

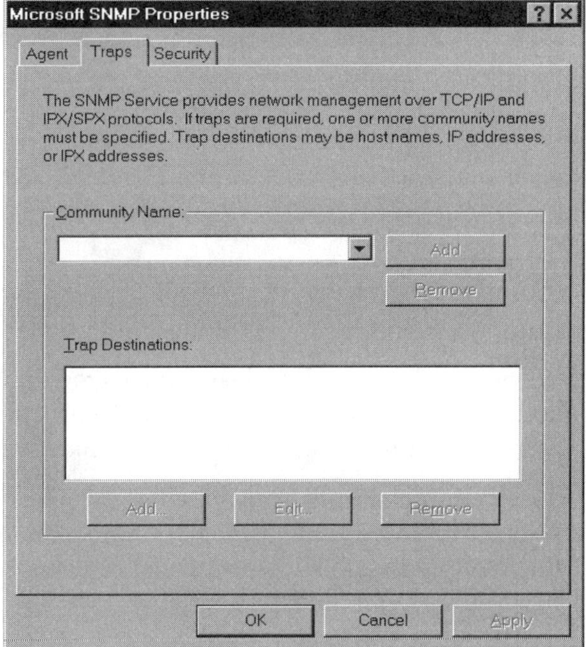

10. Traps may or may not be required. If you enter and add a community name, it will be sent with the trap message. You must then define a management system for the community you defined. The default community name is public. Trap destinations are the IP address of the SNMP manager.

11. Clicking on the Security tab will bring up the following window.

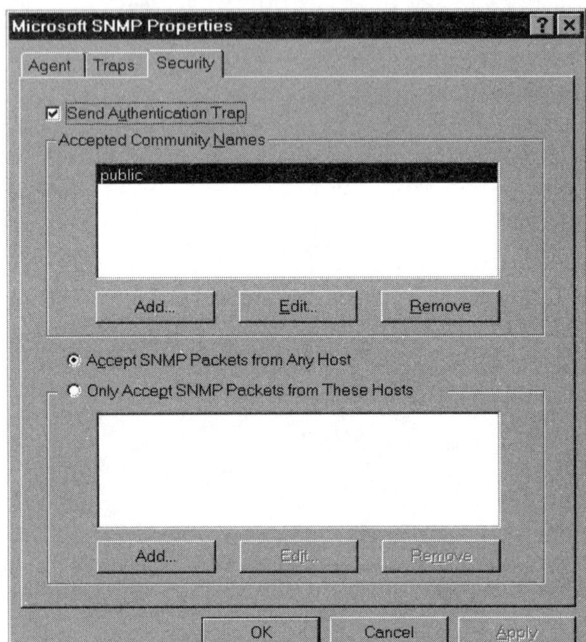

12. When you check Send Authentication Trap, it allows the SNMP agent to send a failed request trap to the SNMP manager when it gets a request for information from an unknown host or manager.

13. Accepted Community Names are the communities the agent belongs to. An agent can belong to multiple communities. Clicking the Add button will allow you to define different communities. Public is the default.

14. Checking the box Accept SNMP Packets from Any Host allows the Agent to accept a request from any SNMP manager in its community.

15. Only Accept SNMP Packets from These Hosts specifies which managers can request information from the agent. To add a manager, click the Add button and provide the IP host or IPX address in the Security Configuration window. Click Add to close the window.

Exam Essentials

There is some good information in this section and the exam writers did manage to come up with a few questions from this group.

Know what two parts make up an SNMP system. There must be an SNMP manager and an SNMP agent.

Know which part of the SNMP system includes Windows NT. Windows NT Server comes with the SNMP agent software. The SNMP manager is available through SMS or through a third-party vendor.

Know about MIBs. MIBs are Management Information Bases. MIBs define the objects that the SNMP system monitors or manages.

Key Terms and Concepts

MIB (Management Information Base): A collection of objects that have been defined for SNMP management. These are the things such as printers, servers, print servers, concentrators, routers, PCs, and more that can be managed or polled for information.

SNMP (Simple Network Management Protocol): The part of the TCP/IP protocol suite that allows users to manage the network. With SNMP you can keep track of what is being used on the network and how the object is behaving. SNMP is made up of two components, an SNMP agent and an SNMP manager.

SNMP agent: A software piece running on the network to gather performance statistics. The SNMP agent is provided with Windows NT.

SNMP community: A grouping of SNMP agents and SNMP managers for security purposes. SNMP agents can be configured to talk only to SNMP managers in the same community.

SNMP manager: The software piece that can manage the network. It can request information from an SNMP agent.

SNMP trap: Where the software agents send the information that has been gathered. Once the information has been trapped, the SNMP Manager can manage it.

Sample Questions

1. SNMP is made up of two key components. These components are:

   A. DHCP

   B. WINS Server

   C. An SNMP manager

   D. An SNMP agent

   Answer: C and D. SNMP is made up of SNMP managers and SNMP agents.

2. A SNMP agent may belong to how many communities?

   A. At least one

   B. Only one

   C. Two

   D. 15

   Answer: A. An SNMP agent must belong to at least one community.

3. The SNMP manager and the SNMP agent must belong to ____________communities.

   A. the same

   B. different

   C. multiple

   D. at least three

   Answer: A. An SNMP manager and an SNMP agent must belong to the same community.

4. The default community name is:

A. Private

B. Domain

C. Corp

D. Public

Answer: D. The default community name is public.

CHAPTER 3

Connectivity

Microsoft Exam Objectives Covered in This Chapter:

- **Given a scenario, identify which utility to use to connect to a TCP/IP-based UNIX host.** *(pages 176 – 195)*
- **Configure a RAS server and dial-up networking for use on a TCP/IP network.** *(pages 195 – 221)*
- **Configure and support browsing in a multiple-domain routed network.** *(pages 221 – 233)*

This chapter could be subtitled, "What if?" That is what connectivity is all about, isn't it? Consider the following scenarios:

- What if you needed to access resources from a UNIX host and could not do it through "normal" channels?
- What if your network suddenly had an outbreak of laptop computers or work-at-home employees who needed to dial in and access the network?
- What if your network was so big that it spanned the continent and you had domains everywhere; would it still be possible to access resources from one end of the network to another? What if your users needed to use stuff that was on that network, but not readily available? Would you be able to provide them with the access they needed?

This section will show you several ways to make sure these various connections can happen.

If you are trying to communicate with a UNIX host, there are several ways you can access resources. FTP (File Transfer Protocol), TFTP (Trivial File Transfer Protocol), and RCP (Remote Copy) will allow you to transfer (copy) files between hosts, and Telnet will let you take over a host and establish a terminal session. Command-line utilities, such as REXEC (Remote Execution), will let you remotely execute programs with a semblance of security. RSH (Remote Shell) will let you start processes on remote hosts without having to worry about security. Finally, there are some utilities, such as your favorite browser and HTTP (Hypertext Transfer Protocol), that you probably use so often you don't even think about them using part of the TCP/IP suite. There are even some printer utilities, such as LPR (Line Printer) and LPQ (Line Printer Queue). These various types of utilities will be discussed later in this chapter.

For the user who is trying to establish access with the network from a distant location, Remote Access Service (RAS) can be a blessing. If RAS is installed on the network, the user can access the network from the workstation with dial-up networking. Parts of the TCP/IP suite come into play in this scenario also. PPP or the Point-to-Point Protocol and Serial Line Internet Protocol (SLIP) will allow users to get onto the network using a simple modem connection. SLIP and PPP have really proven to be a boon to the Internet. Most dial-up connections to the Internet use PPP as the transport protocol of choice. When you see someone dialing in to get Internet mail, or checking into the office using an Internet connection, you are seeing PPP at work.

For the large network, the way to access resources is to see the resource. This is done through Windows NT browsing services. NT servers can accept a variety of roles in the browsing process, all designed to make services and resources more accessible to the network user. In the final part of this section, we will show how browsing works and how to optimize the service.

While the information in this chapter is not covered as extensively as the information in Chapter 2, "Installation and Configuration," it is still covered thoroughly. Be especially aware of knowing when to use each of the utilities. Because some of this section is based on the "scenario" concept, I will show where each utility can be used to its best advantage.

Given a scenario, identify which utility to use to connect to a TCP/IP-based UNIX host.

The utilities listed in the first part of this chapter can be broken down into several areas. REXEC, RSH, and Telnet are used to execute commands; RCP, FTP, and TFTP are used to transfer files; and finally, LPR and LPQ are the printing utilities.

Critical Information

The first group of utilities allows a user to take over another host and execute applications. For the sake of simplicity, let's call these the execution utilities.

Execution Utilities

When you operate in the UNIX world, security can sometimes be unreliable. UNIX was originally written as an open standard, making it easy to share information. All of the source code for the original operating system was put out on the Internet and anyone who wanted to make a change was free to do so. If there was something about the UNIX version you were using that you didn't like, all you had to do was change it. This was especially appealing when it came to utilities. If you wanted a utility, you simply wrote it or rewrote a current utility to increase the functionality. This led to some really interesting utilities—for example, Vi, which is used to edit files.

Given the open history of UNIX, and the fact that the source code is floating around, securing a UNIX network is a challenge that should not be accepted by the faint of heart. Some of the utilities included with Microsoft TCP/IP have this attitude: basically, let anyone do whatever they want. Others provide for some minor security and even then it is not much. In the case of the execution utilities, REXEC has a security piece, RSH doesn't, and Telnet requires an account. Each of these is discussed below.

Remote Execution (REXEC)

REXEC will run a process on a remote system that is equipped with the REXEC server service. REXEC is password protected so the request for the process will not be handled until the password is verified. If you are familiar with NetWare, this would be similar to the RCONSOLE command. Using RCONSOLE, you can sit at a workstation anywhere on the network, and take over the file server console. You can issue commands that will be run on the server, use any utilities that must be run on the server, and edit files on the server. This is done using a secure password protected connection.

SEE ALSO A complete description of the syntax for REXEC is covered in the "Necessary Procedures" section.

An example of REXEC is shown in Figure 3.1.

FIGURE 3.1: REXEC at work

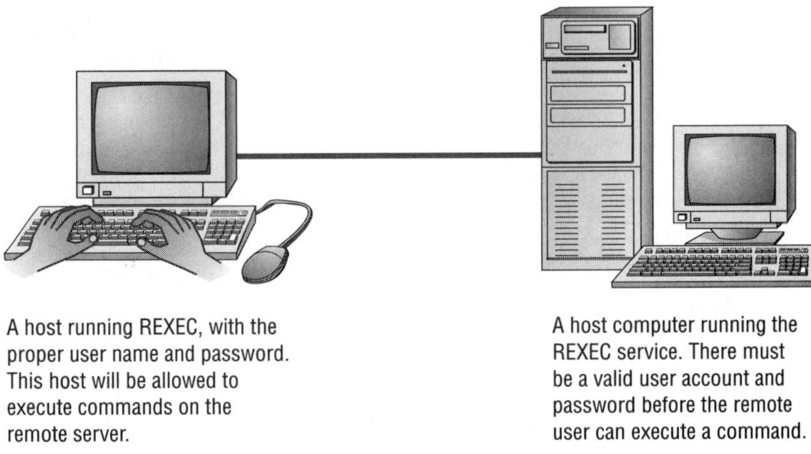

Remote Shell (RSH)

The Remote Shell utility lets a user issue a command to a remote host without logging onto that host. While the system does not require a password, it does require a designated username to exist in the .rhosts file on a UNIX host running the RSH daemon. This command is usually used to execute a program compiler.

SEE ALSO A complete description of the syntax for RSH is covered in the "Necessary Procedures" section.

An example of RSH is shown in Figure 3.2.

FIGURE 3.2: RSH at work

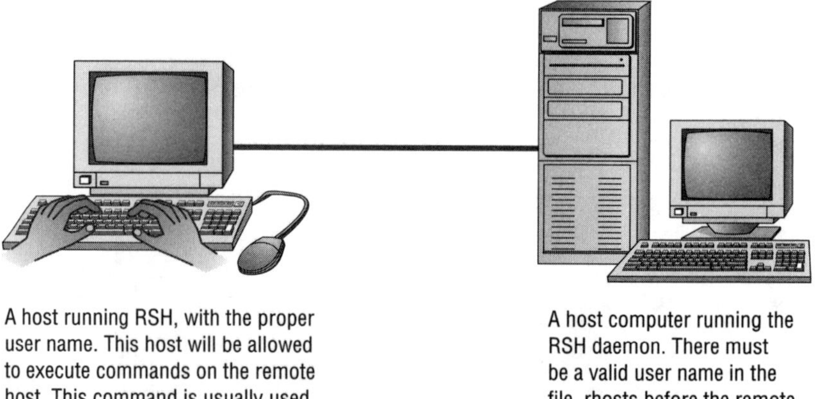

Telnet

Of the execution utilities, Telnet is probably the best recognized and most used. It is used to establish a terminal emulation session with a system running the Telnet service. Telnet, which requires a dependable connection, utilizes TCP.

If you are unfamiliar with Telnet, think of any tool that will let you take over another workstation and operate it like you were sitting at the remote keyboard. There are a couple of examples that jump to mind, such as PC Anywhere from Symantec and even RCONSOLE from Novell. Just like these two utilities, in order for you to take over the remote host, the remote host must know you are coming. There must be a program running on the host that will allow you to take command of the processor. In this case, the remote system must be running the Telnet Server program. If it does, you can Telnet into the host and execute commands that will run on that computer.

TIP The Microsoft Windows NT installation CD does not provide for the Telnet Server program. If you check the NT Resource Kit CD, you will find it provides Telnet Server software.

If TCP/IP is installed on the NT computer, the computer has the capabilities of running Telnet. To establish a Telnet session, use the TELNET command with the IP address or host name. Security is provided by having a username and password identical to those used when logging onto the remote system directly. Figure 3.3 shows how you may use Telnet.

SEE ALSO The syntax for TELNET is covered in the "Necessary Procedures" section.

For the execution utilities portion of the exam, the scenarios may include viewing a document stored on a UNIX computer. In this scenario, look at the utilities presented carefully, but the choice would usually be Telnet. Because Telnet is a TCP/IP utility, your host would use DNS or a HOSTS file to resolve host names. That may also have a bearing on the way you answer the question.

FIGURE 3.3: Working with Telnet

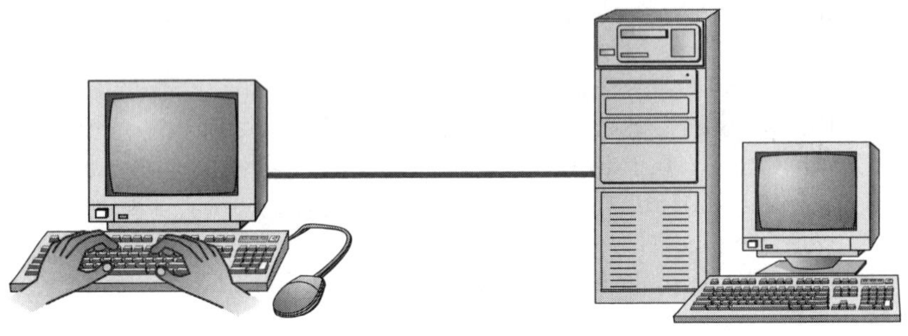

A host running TELNET, with the proper user name and password. Host can use a variety of terminal emulations including VT100, VT 52 or TTY. Telnet can be used to connect to libraries to access card catalogs. You can even TELNET into the InterNIC and access the DNS lookup information from the menu options. The command would be TELNET internic.net.

A host computer running the TELNET. There must be a valid user name and password created before the remote user can establish a session. Once the user establishes a session, it is as if the user is sitting at this machine. Many hosts will offer menu-driven options to allow users to access information or even place orders.

SEE ALSO Syntax and options for each of these utilities are discussed in the "Necessary Procedures" section of this chapter.

File Transfer Utilities

When it comes to choosing a file transfer utility, you must be aware of the strengths and weakness of each one. Some of these utilities provide more security than others. Some also come with more overhead than others. The utilities that we will be looking at include FTP, TFTP, and RCP.

File Transfer Protocol (FTP)

As is the case in most of the utilities we will be discussing, FTP is a two-sided process. Before you can FTP to a server and download files, the server must be running some kind of FTP server. FTP operates over TCP. TCP, if you remember, is the connection-oriented part of the TCP/IP suite and that brings with it extra overhead, but a more secure transmission.

FTP is a remarkably flexible process. You can require users to authenticate to certain folders using a username and a password. On the same server, you can allow anonymous access, basically letting anyone and everyone have access to the files stored in the public folders. Anonymous access is provided by using "anonymous" as a username and an e-mail address as a password.

FTP can be used to copy single files or multiple files. You can either download files to your system, or, if you have the rights, upload files to the remote host.

An example of how FTP would be used is shown in Figure 3.4

FIGURE 3.4: FTP at work

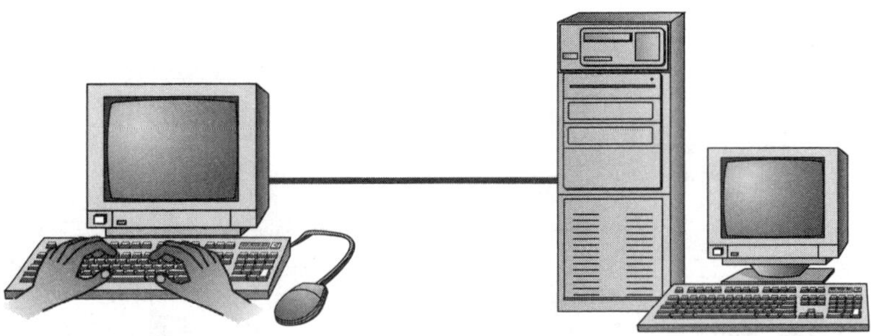

A host connecting to the remote server using FTP, with a user name and password. The host can use a variety of methods to connect to the remote host, including a variety of browsers. FTP can be used to connect to another host to upload or download files.

A host computer running the FTP server service. There may be a variety of user names and passwords created to specify who gets access to which folders. By default an anonymous account is created. The password would be the remote user's e-mail address. FTP is used to provide access to files. An example would be a hardware or software manufacturer that needs to provide patches to their customers.

SEE ALSO FTP has a bunch of commands that are covered in greater detail in the "Necessary Procedures" part of the chapter.

Trivial File Transfer Protocol (TFTP)

TFTP is FTP without the overhead. Because TFTP uses UDP (User Datagram Protocol) instead of TCP, the inherent overhead in a connection-oriented protocol is removed. This means file transfer will be quicker, though the transfer may not be as reliable.

TFTP requires the TFTP server to be running on the target computer. The TFTP server piece is not provided with Windows NT and must come from a third-party vendor or from an alternate operating system, such as UNIX.

An example of TFTP is shown in Figure 3.5.

FIGURE 3.5: TFTP at work

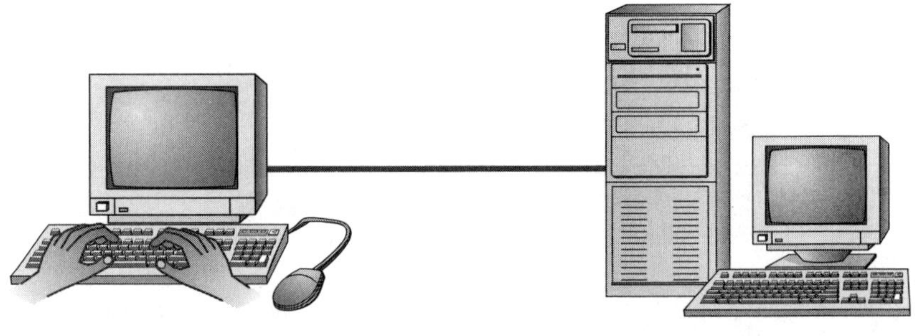

A host connecting to the remote server using TFTP. The host can use a variety of methods to connect to the remote host to upload or download files.

A UNIX host computer running the TFTP daemon. TFTP is used to provide access to files. Since TFTP uses EDP instead of TCP, it is usually faster than an FTP transfer. An example would be a company that needs to provide information or files to the others.

SEE ALSO The syntax for TFTP is covered in the "Necessary Procedures" section.

For the file transfer utilities, scenarios on the exam would include copying several files to/from a UNIX computer. In this scenario, look at the utilities presented carefully, but the choice would usually be FTP. Because FTP is a TCP/IP utility, your host would use DNS or a HOSTS file to resolve host names.

Remote Copy (RCP)

RCP is the "simplest" of the file transfer utilities. It is a command-line utility used to copy files to or from a remote host. Syntax for the command is covered in the "Necessary Procedures" part of this section.

Printer Utilities

Printer utilities are command-line utilities that will allow a non-UNIX computer to print to a UNIX server. There are two basic utilities: LPQ and LPR.

Line Printer Queue (LPQ)

The LPQ command allows a user to see what jobs are in a print queue on an LPD (Line Printer Daemon) server. It shows the state of the remote queue and also allows the user to manage some of the print jobs in the queue. Figure 3.6 shows how you would use LPQ.

SEE ALSO The syntax for LPQ is covered in the "Necessary Procedures" section.

FIGURE 3.6: Using LPQ

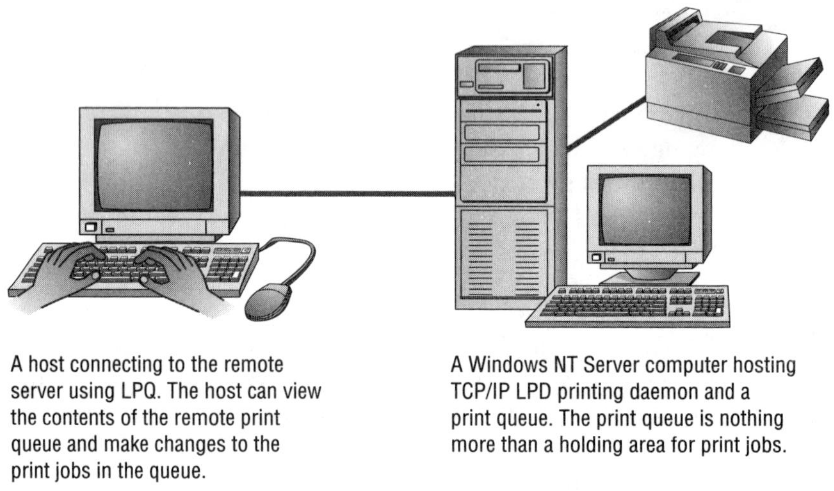

A host connecting to the remote server using LPQ. The host can view the contents of the remote print queue and make changes to the print jobs in the queue.

A Windows NT Server computer hosting TCP/IP LPD printing daemon and a print queue. The print queue is nothing more than a holding area for print jobs.

Line Printer (LPR)

The LPR utility allows jobs to be sent to a printer that is serviced by a host running an LPD server. You can send text-based files to the printer or jobs that must be sent to a PostScript printer.

Figure 3.7 shows how the LPR utility would be used.

The syntax for LPR is covered in the "Necessary Procedures" section. For the printing utilities, scenarios on the exam would include viewing a list of documents sent to a UNIX-based print server. In this scenario, look at the utilities presented carefully, but the choice would usually be LPQ. LPQ has command-line parameters in place to provide an IP address of the target computer. If this is not available, LPQ is a TCP/IP utility, so you would use DNS or a HOSTS file to resolve host names.

FIGURE 3.7: Using LPR

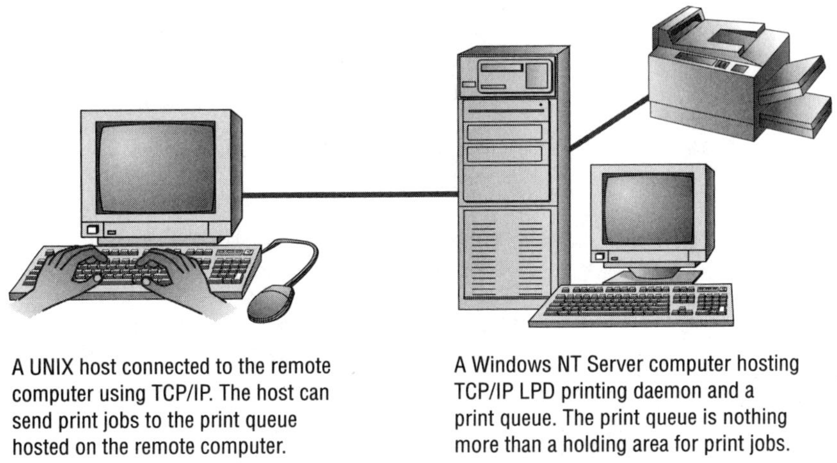

Necessary Procedures

All of the commands and utilities discussed in this chapter come with options that enhance their functionality. For testing purposes, it is not necessary to memorize syntax, but looking over the following examples will give you a better idea of how to use each command.

Using Execution Utilities

Execution utilities let you execute a command or procedure on a remote host.

Remote Execution (REXEC)

Before using REXEC, have the valid password handy. This is a TCP/IP password-protected utility. This is the syntax for REXEC:

```
REXEC host [-l username][-n] command
```

Table 3.1 lists the options available for the REXEC command.

TABLE 3.1: REXEC options

Option	Description
Host	Host specifies the host name or IP address of the target computer.
-l username	This option specifies a valid username on the remote system.
-n	-n redirects the input for REXEC to NULL if you don't need to provide input.
Command	Command specifies the command you want to execute on the remote host.

Remote Shell (RSH)

Remote Shell does not require the user to log into the remote host nor does it require a password. This is the syntax for Remote Shell:

```
RSH host [-l username] command
```

Table 3.2 lists the options available for the RSH command.

TABLE 3.2: RSH options

Option	Description
Host	Host is the host name or IP address of the target system.
-l username	-l username requires a valid username on the target system. The username must appear in the .rhosts file located in the user's home directory .
Command	Command specifies the UNIX command that is to be run on the target computer.

Telnet

To establish a Telnet session with a target computer running the Telnet service, the command is TELNET hostname. Host name specifies the IP address or DNS name of the target computer. The user must have a valid username and password configured on the target computer.

Using File Transfer Utilities

File transfer utilities will allow the copying of files from the local host computer or a remote target computer. Some of these utilities require user validation while others do not.

Remote Copy (RCP)

Remote Copy does not require user validation, per se. It does require the username to be contained in the .rhosts file located on the UNIX server running the RCP daemon. This is the command syntax:

```
RCP [-abhr][localhost.][localuser:]source
[remotehost.][remoteuser:]path/destination
```

Table 3.3 lists the options available for the RCP command.

TABLE 3.3: Remote copy options

Options	Description
-a	-a is the default. It sets the method of transfer to ASCII (as opposed to binary) and specifies the translation of certain characters, including carriage return/linefeed and linefeed.
-b	-b sets the transfer mode to binary.
-h	-h sets the transfer of hidden files.
-r	-r recursively copies the contents of all subdirectories of the source to the destination. Both source and destination must be directories. This option is similar to the DOS XCOPY command with the /s parameter.

TABLE 3.3: Remote copy options *(continued)*

Options	Description
Localhost	Localhost is the host name or IP address of the source system.
Localuser	Localuser specifies valid usernames on the source system. The localuser name is stored in the .rhosts file.
Remotehost	Remotehost is the host name or IP address of the target system.
Remoteuser	Remoteuser specifies valid usernames on the target system. The remoteuser name is stored in the .rhosts file.
Path/destination	Path/destination is the path where the files are going to be copied.

File Transfer Protocol (FTP)

FTP is probably the best known of all the file transfer protocols. It is common when looking for the latest version of drivers or utilities to be referred to a company's FTP site. This is the syntax for FTP:

```
ftp host command
```

When you establish an FTP session with a remote host, you will be prompted for a username and a password. Once the FTP session has been established, there are a plethora of FTP commands that can be used. A sampling of these commands is listed in Table 3.4.

TABLE 3.4: FTP options

Options	Description
Host	Host is the DNS name or IP address of the FTP server.
Append	Append allows you to add information to a file.
Ascii	ASCII sets the transfer mode to ASCII rather than binary.
Bye	Bye closes an FTP session and exits the FTP program.
Binary	Binary sets the transfer file type to binary as opposed to ASCII.
Cd	Cd changes directory on the FTP server.
Close	Close closes the FTP session.
Delete	Delete removes a remote file.
Dir	Dir lists the directory of files.
Get	Get retrieves a file.
Help	Help displays the command description.
Lcd	Lcd changes the local directory.
Ls	Ls lists a directory of files.
Mdelete	Mdelete removes multiple remote files.
Mdir	Mdir provides a directory of multiple remote directories.
Mget	Mget downloads multiple files from a remote system.
Mkdir	Mkdir makes a directory on the remote system.
Mls	Mls provides a directory of multiple remote directories.
Mput	Mput puts multiple files in a remote directory.
Open	Open begins an FTP session.

TABLE 3.4: FTP options *(continued)*

Options	Description
Put	Put uploads a file.
Pwd	Pwd prints a working directory.
Quit	Quit exits the FTP session.
Recv	Recv downloads a file.
Rename	Rename renames a file.
Rmdir	Rmdir removes a remote directory.
Send	Send uploads a file.
Trace	Trace toggles packet tracing.
Type	Type sets the transfer type.
User	User sends new user information.
Verbose	Verbose toggles the verbose mode.

Trivial File Transfer Protocol (TFTP)

This is the syntax for the TFTP command:

```
TFTP [-I] host [GET | PUT] source [destination]
```

The options available for TFTP are listed in Table 3.5.

TABLE 3.5: TFTP options

Options	Description
-l	-l specifies binary image transfer mode. If –l is not present, the file transfer mode is set to ASCII.
Host	Host is the IP address or DNS name of the host computer.
get	The get command transfers a file from a remote host to the local host.
Put	The put command transfers a file from a local host to a remote host.
Source	Source is the path where the file is copied from.
Destination	Destination is the path where the file is copied to.

NOTE Having problems running TCP/IP - UNIX commands? UNIX is a very case-sensitive operating system. When it doubt, try help by typing command /?.

Using Printer Utilities

The two printer command-line utilities are LPQ and LPR.

Line Printer Queue (LPQ)

This is the syntax for the LPQ command:

```
Lpq -Sserver -Pprinter [-l]
```

The options available for the LPQ command are listed in Table 3.6.

TABLE 3.6: LPQ options

Options	Description
-Sserver	-Sserver is the DNS host name or IP address of the host providing the LPD service.
-Pprinter	-Pprinter is the name of the print queue.
-l	-l specifies that a detailed status should be given.

Line Printer (LPR)

This is the syntax for the LPR utility:

```
Lpr -Sserver -Pprinter [-Cclass][-Jjobname][-oOption][-
x][-d]filename
```

Table 3.7 lists the options available for the LPR command.

TABLE 3.7: LPR options

Options	Description
-Sserver	-Sserver is the DNS host name or the IP address of the host providing the LPD service.
-Pprinter	-Pprinter is the name of print queue.
-Cclass	-Cclass is the job classification for the banner or cover page.
-Jjob	-Jjob is the job name to be printed on the banner or cover page.
-oOption	-oOption specifies the type of file. By default, it is a text file.
-x	-x is a compatibility switch for SunOS 4.1.*x* or a prior version.
-d	-d is for sending a data file first.

Exam Essentials

There is a lot of minutiae in this section. Luckily, you don't have to memorize all of the command-line options, though it would probably be a good bet to be familiar with them.

Know when to use Telnet. Telnet is used to establish a terminal session with a remote host. It is used to execute programs or procedures on the remote host.

Know when to use FTP. FTP is used to transfer files to or from a remote host.

Know when to use LPQ. LPQ is used to view the documents currently waiting to be printed in a UNIX-based print queue.

Know the command-line options for FTP. Understand what the options do and when you would use each of them.

Key Terms and Concepts

File Transfer Protocol (FTP): Attaches to a server and downloads files. FTP can require users to authenticate to certain folders using a username and a password. On the same server, you can allow anonymous access. FTP can be used to copy single files or multiple files.

Line Printer (LPR): Allows jobs to be sent to a printer that is serviced by a host running an LPD server.

Line Printer Queue (LPQ): Allows a user to see what jobs are in a print queue on an LPD (Line Printer Daemon) server. It shows the state of the remote queue.

Remote Execution (REXEC): Used to run a process on a remote host equipped with the REXEC server service. REXEC is password protected.

Remote Shell (RSH): Lets a user issue a command to a remote host without logging onto that host. A designated username must exist in the .rhosts file on a UNIX host running the RSH daemon.

Telnet: Establishes a terminal emulation session with a UNIX-based host running the Telnet service. Telnet, which requires a dependable connection, utilizes TCP.

Trivial File Transfer Protocol (TFTP): FTP without the overhead. Because TFTP uses UDP instead of TCP, the inherent overhead in a connection-oriented protocol is removed. This means file transfer will be quicker, though the transfer may not be as reliable.

Sample Questions

1. You want to view a college catalog stored on a remote UNIX host. You want to use a program stored on the host to view the catalog. Which utility would you use?

   A. FTP

   B. TFTP

   C. Telnet

   D. LPQ

   Answer: C. The only utility mentioned that will allow you to remotely execute a program or procedure on a remote host is Telnet.

2. You want to transfer multiple files to a remote host. Which utility would you use?

   A. FTP

   B. Telnet

   C. RPC

   D. LPQ

   Answer: A. FTP is the only utility mentioned that can transfer files.

3. Which methods can FTP use for address resolution?

   A. WINS

   B. LMHOSTS

   C. DNS

   D. DHCP

   E. HOSTS

   Answer: C and E. FTP is a TCP/IP-based utility. It will use either DNS or a HOSTS file for address resolution.

4. You want to ensure that a print job you sent to a UNIX-based print server actually arrived. Which utility will you use to verify that the print job arrived?

   A. LPD

   B. LPR

   C. LPQ

   D. LQP

   Answer C. You can view a remote print server using the LPQ utility.

Configure a RAS server and dial-up networking for use on a TCP/IP network.

One of the things that is nice about the Microsoft exams is there is always some overlap. By this time in the MCSE testing process, you have probably already taken some of the tests, so you have probably noticed some of the material presented on the Server test shows up on the Enterprise test and vice versa. This is another of those topics. RAS is a popular topic with Microsoft, so you will see questions on the Server exam, Enterprise exam, Workstation exam, and here on the TCP/IP exam. Some of the material here has been covered in other Sybex books, but it is always good to review.

SEE ALSO For more information on RAS, check out *MCSE Exam Notes: NT Server 4* or *MCSE Exam Notes: NT Server 4 in the Enterprise* by Gary Govanus and Robert King (both Sybex, 1998).

Sometimes, I really feel like network administrators should just learn to say "no." Now, be honest, haven't you ever wanted to tell the latest "suit" with an idea, "No, we can't do that?"

Ever since networking came out, things have just gotten worse and worse. First, the suits wanted to connect to the mainframe, then they wanted Macs on the network. Then we had to let the UNIX bit-heads on the system, not to mention contending with those people who still insist everything runs better on NetWare.

It is not bad enough that you have to deal with all those different types of systems, but now, laptops are the vogue and everyone wants to dial into the network and connect as if they were sitting right at their desks. Do these people have any clue about the work they are causing?

NT and RAS to the rescue. Remote Access Service or RAS will allow a workstation computer configured to use Microsoft TCP/IP while running Windows NT or Windows 95 to connect to remote systems using the POTS (Plain Old Telephone System). When the client connects, the workstation is treated just like any other client. So users can access the network, check e-mail, get documents; just about anything they would do from their desks they can do from their laptops. This is something you can really use on your network and there is also a lot of testable material here. If you have already taken your NT Server and NT Workstation tests, you already know that RAS is a popular subject with the exam writers. If you have taken previous exams, some of this information may be a review, but we can all use a review at times.

Critical Information

The purpose of RAS is to allow for communications between remote locations, usually utilizing nothing more than telephone lines. However, RAS can be configured to work with ISDN (Integrated Services Digital Network) and X.25 connections. The purpose of this book is not to describe the multiple ways to use RAS, but it is designed to give you a broad overview of the product and get you through the test. So, we will stick to client-to-network communication using Microsoft TCP/IP over a dial-up connection.

In order for RAS to work, you need to create a mini-network. A network is nothing more than the following:

- Two systems with some information to share
- A physical communication medium over which to share the information
- Rules to govern the transmittal of the information

To create the network, we look at the first part of this objective. It discusses the server piece of RAS, how to configure the server so it can "answer" the call when it comes. Once the server is configured, we have one of the two parties to the communication. We know that we will be using the telephone lines so our physical medium already exists. The second party to the conversation joins the network when it calls the server. That leaves just the rules. When the server answers the call, it must "talk" with the client using that specific set of rules, so we will discuss the part Microsoft TCP/IP plays and how to configure it to work with a dial-up client. In order to hold any kind of discussion, we must have two parties, so we will also show how to configure dial-up networking clients.

RAS Communications

The best place to start is always at the beginning. If you are going to configure a system where your workstations can call in and get information, then there had better be something there to answer the phone. In this case, it will be our NT Server. There are communication products that would allow you up to 256 dial-up connections from a single expansion card. RAS will take advantage of systems like that, as well as a plain old modem hooked off a COM port.

The first question to ask yourself is, "What is the main goal of this communication channel?" In some cases, your main goal may be to provide dial-up service to all those salespeople and executives out there traveling around the countryside. If your company is small, you may not have a lot of salespeople or high-powered executives traveling all over the country selling your company's wares. However, you may have a remote site that needs to communicate with the home office and doesn't need all the power of a T1 line. In that case, an ISDN line may be just the ticket. ISDN stands for Integrated Services Digital Network. ISDN is a faster, better version of what you normally think of as a modem connection. A modem connection is provided by the Public Switched Telephone Network or PSTN, generally referred to as the phone company.

NOTE Any time you say faster and better, that usually translates into more expensive. Costs vary on ISDN service around the world, but it is safe to say it is more expensive then a standard dial-up line.

Modems modulate and demodulate the signals between two computers, sending the signal over the phone line. Your computer speaks digital. The phone company uses analog. A modem turns a digital signal into an analog signal on the sending end and turns the same signal from analog to digital at the receiving end. Lots of translations are going on in that process, aren't they?

The key word in the definition of ISDN is *digital*. You are now using a phone line that speaks digital so no translation is necessary. The ISDN modem or router just sends digital signals over a line that understands how to deal with 1's and 0's. You have a cleaner, faster communication link. If you are planning on connecting two sites, you may look at installing ISDN service. In some places it may not even be available. In others, it may be prohibitively expensive. In some areas, it may be just the solution you are looking for. When judging cost, keep in mind that ISDN service is really like two phone lines; therefore, you would expect it to cost twice as much as a single phone line. Because there are two channels, you get twice the speed. Because it is digital, and analog modems rarely give you their rated speed, it is usually faster than twice as fast.

You have now gotten over the first hump, but should you use ISDN or a regular phone line? Assuming you are going to be using the dial-up capabilities of the phone company, the phone line has to be dedicated to RAS communications. RAS is very selfish, it doesn't want to share. So, if your system is configured to dial out and notify you if you the power goes out, or if you are running a fax server solution using a modem and phone line, you need to add more hardware. RAS requires its own phone line with its own modem.

If you are installing an ISDN device, follow the manufacturer's directions. The ISDN device is slightly more challenging to install than a modem. Make sure you have somewhere to connect to (another ISDN connection) and make sure you have all the paperwork the phone company left for you when they installed the ISDN line. There are some interesting parameters that you will need to configure, things like SPIDs or Service Profile IDs. A SPID identifies the services the ISDN line is providing. The SPID itself looks like a normal 10-digit phone number, except there are two of them.

After all these decisions have been made and all the hardware is installed, the installation of RAS is really anticlimactic. Because RAS is a service, it is installed through the network icon in the Control Panel. It is just a matter of copying some files off the installation CD and linking the RAS with the modem or communication device you already have configured. Part way through the installation process, the system will begin asking you questions about protocols, which is what this section is all about.

SEE ALSO For a step-by-step discussion of the installation of RAS, see the "Necessary Procedures" section of this objective.

RAS Protocols

As far as protocol support, RAS supports the big three—TCP/IP, NetBEUI, and NWLink. However, it does require some explanation. The explanation even requires some explanation because you are about to be buried in a flow of acronyms.

Transport Driver Interface (TDI)

The first acronym is Transport Driver Interface or TDI. The TDI is a specification to which all Windows NT transport protocols must be written in order to be used by higher-level services, such as RAS.

Point-to-Point Protocol (PPP) and Serial Line Internet Protocol (SLIP)

The next two acronyms deal with *communication framing protocols*, or the set of rules that allows communication devices to negotiate how information will be "framed" or blocked as it is sent over the network. The two framing protocols that RAS can use are Point-to-Point Protocol or PPP and Serial Line Internet Protocol or SLIP. Because SLIP is the grand ol' daddy of framing protocols, it is just an implementation of Internet Protocol (IP) over a serial line. By and large, SLIP has been replaced by PPP.

PPP is a Data Link layer protocol that performs over point-to-point network connections, such as serial or modem lines. PPP can negotiate with any transport protocol used by both systems involved in the link and can automatically assign IP, Domain Name Service (DNS), and gateway addresses when used with Transmission Control Protocol/Internet Protocol (TCP/IP). Cool, huh? This is one protocol that can do DHCP (Dynamic Host Configuration Protocol) as well as communicate.

An Overview of Protocols

Now that terms are defined, we can look at an overview of protocols. When a dial-in client accesses a RAS server, it will use PPP as its Network layer protocol. Think of PPP as the Ethernet or Token Ring of the dial-up world.

NOTE SLIP is an older version of PPP, and while you can configure a RAS server to dial out using SLIP, in most environments SLIP has gone the way of CP/M.

Once connected to the RAS, PPP supports TCP/IP, NWLink, and NetBEUI. Each protocol can be bound to a modem, or a modem may have more than one protocol bound to it. Because we are concentrating on TCP/IP, we will look at its pluses and minuses, depending on the job you are configuring the system to do.

TCP/IP Strengths and Weaknesses

Transmission Control Protocol/Internet Protocol is the standard protocol suite of the Internet. TCP/IP is a mature, stable, robust protocol suite that brings a lot to the table, including routing capabilities and the ability to handle less than perfect phone connections. While it is robust, it is not necessarily the fastest protocol out of the gate.

RAS using TCP/IP will allow the administrator to configure whether the client computer can access just the RAS server or the entire network. In addition, the RAS server controls how the client receives its TCP/IP address.

RAS Security

Once the client computer has called the RAS server and has connected, how do you protect your network against intruders? RAS does have some built-in security features. You can configure the RAS connection security using permissions, encrypted passwords, Point-to-Point Tunneling Protocol (PPTP), and call back. Once you have installed RAS, you can take a look at the Administrative Tools menu and you will see a new utility listed, Remote Access Admin. The Remote Access Admin utility is used to configure communication ports, start and stop the RAS service, and configure user access. This utility also allows you to grant user permissions, which are discussed next.

Permissions

When a user dials in and authenticates to RAS, permissions are the first line of defense for the network. Permissions in RAS are different from other sets of permissions. RAS permissions can only be granted to individual users and cannot be granted to Global Groups or Local Groups. Permissions are granted using the Remote Access Admin utility.

Call Back

One of the ways RAS enforces security is to call back the initiating system before finalizing communication. This way, RAS is sure that the system calling is really what it says it is. Call back features can be set for each user with dial-in access. You cannot set call back authentication for groups of users or for certain modems.

Call back can be configured to be initiated by the caller or it can be preset.

Passwords and Data Encryption

By now, just about everyone in the free world has heard the trials and travails of passing passwords and other information over phone lines and even over the Internet! There are several ways of protecting information sent over phone lines, the most common is some form of encryption.

When the client and the server begin to communicate, they use PPP. To authenticate over PPP, RAS supports three authentication protocols:

- Password Authentication Protocol (PAP)
- Challenge Handshake Authentication Protocol (CHAP)
- Microsoft extensions of CHAP (MS-CHAP)

The default selection is MS-CHAP. When you configure a client to call the RAS, it must encrypt its password via MS-CHAP. Using MS-CHAP ensures that the system on the other end of the phone is at least using Windows 95 or above for an operating system. If the Require Data Encryption button is selected, not only is MS-CHAP used, but the data that is sent over the phone lines is further encrypted.

Suppose you have a diverse environment that is not Microsoft centric. That is the politically correct way of saying you may have some bit-head that wants to dial in from a UNIX box. Because that system cannot use MS-CHAP, something else needs to be provided. You can require encrypted authentication. This option sets up the system to run CHAP as well as MS-CHAP.

The final selection you can make involves those systems that do not support encrypted password authentication. In that case, you can check Allow Any Authentication Including Clear Text. This is the free-for-all method of system access.

PPTP

Another security feature mentioned above is PPTP. PPTP is a new NT 4.0 feature. It is Internet-centered and uses a two-step approach to connecting the client to the server. Here are the two steps:

1. Connect the client to the Internet.
2. Use the Internet to create an encrypted link to the RAS server. In some areas, this is called creating a Virtual Private Network or VPN.

NOTE Using this approach, obviously the RAS server must be attached to the Internet.

If you have a question on the exam where the terms RAS and security are used in the same sentence, start looking for the Point-to-Point Tunneling Protocol. PPTP supports Virtual Private Networks (VPNs) over a variety of different networks, including ISDN, PSTN, and X.25 networks. If you work within a major company that makes use of IBM systems, VPNs can be configured to work over IBM's System Network Architecture protocol (SNA) and other intranet backbones.

Think of PPTP as the leech of the protocol family. PPTP can leech onto a variety of protocols on a variety of public and private networks to create a secure connection between two hosts. An example of this would be if your network was using NetBEUI or IPX (Internet Packet Exchange Protocol). Either type of packet can be encapsulated or hidden in a Point-to-Point Protocol packet and transported over TCP/IP. When the PPTP session is established, security is negotiated using data encryption and the VPN is established.

RAS and the Internet

With the Internet becoming more and more a part of daily life, one of the big decisions companies have to make is how to connect to an Internet service provider (ISP). If you work for a multimillion-dollar-a-year company with hundreds of employees, a T1 or T3 connection is in your future. Suppose you work for a small company and the company cannot afford a 7-by-24 connection to the Internet. Is there a way that RAS can help you connect to a local ISP using dial-up capabilities? Absolutely!

Let's look at this scenario. You have a small network, where access to the Internet is very limited. You want to be able to provide users logging onto the network the ability to connect to the Internet, but you do not want to provide each workstation with dial-up capabilities of modems and phone lines. You can configure your RAS server to dial up the ISP log onto the ISP system and open an Internet connection for the workstation. There are a couple of "gotchas," though. In order to accomplish this, the RAS server is configured with a blank gateway address. The server is then configured to connect to the ISP using a dial-up connection and you will also have to make some changes to the registry. For the exact settings to the exact keys, be sure to check the Microsoft TechNet CD for the latest information. The article I found on TechNet was entitled, "Configuring Dial-up Networking for ISP DNS."

While the RAS server has a blank gateway address, the RAS client (a Windows 95 or Windows NT Workstation computer) will have the gateway address configured to point to the RAS server network interface card that connects to the local network.

Dial-up Networking

Reaching out and touching someone has never been more popular than it is with computer people. We are constantly hitting dial-up connections to the Internet, dialing in to the office to pick up e-mail or voice mail, or connecting to bulletin boards to download the latest in patches and drivers. Now, regular people are even getting into the act; the Internet isn't just for geeks anymore! Salespeople want to transmit their orders electronically and management types want to be in contact with the office for more than 24 hours a day. What is a tech-type to do?

Dial-up networking (DUN), combined with Remote Access Service (RAS), lets you be the star in everyone's eye. You can configure the CEO's laptop to dial up and access the network from anywhere in the world. Road-warrior salespeople can download orders and upload e-mail as easily as plugging in an RJ11 connector to the wall. If these people work from home, rather than from hotel rooms, ISDN lines can be installed for even faster connections. Installation instructions for DUN are covered later in this section.

Windows NT Workstation supports two of the most common telephone line protocols, Serial Line Internet Protocol (SLIP) and Point-to-Point Protocol (PPP). Each of these line protocols takes the standard LAN protocols (TCP/IP, NetBEUI, and NWLink) and hides or *encapsulates* them within the telephone protocol. SLIP is the older of the two protocols and is rarely used anymore. PPP is the most popular because it supports Dynamic Host Control Protocol (DHCP) as well as static IP addressing.

Windows NT Workstation also supports a procedure called *multilink*. With multilink, multiple lines can call the same destination at the same time for faster throughput.

In addition to the standard line protocols, NT supports Point-to-Point Tunneling Protocol (PPTP). This protocol allows you to "steal" a part of the Internet to create a Virtual Private Network (VPN) between your remote location and the office.

Necessary Procedures

There is a lot to do in this section. This objective is all about configuring, and while the first part gave an overview of the decisions to be made and things to be ordered, this is where the meat of the process lies—actually doing the work.

The test developers approached this section in a logical fashion. The first three areas talk about how to install RAS on the server, how to configure the protocols that the systems will use, and finally, how to lock down security.

The last section takes you away from the server and onto the workstation. The client side configuration is a dial-up configuration, similar to configuring the system to dial into AOL or CompuServe.

Configuring RAS Communications

RAS is a network service and is installed like most of the other network services—from the network icon in the Control Panel. Before beginning to install RAS or any network service be sure to have the NT Installation CD handy, or at least have access to the files it contains. Follow these steps to install and configure RAS:

1. Log onto the computer as Administrator.
2. Open the Control Panel by choosing Start ➢ Settings ➢ Control Panel.
3. Next, double-click the Network icon.
4. Next, open the Services tab by single-clicking it.
5. Because RAS is not installed, click Add.
6. Clicking Add will open the Select Network Service window. This is a selection of all the services available, but not currently installed on your server. Scroll down to Remote Access Service, highlight it with a single click, and then click OK.

7. By clicking OK, you have opened the Windows NT setup screen. This Window is looking for the location of the NT setup files. Provide the appropriate location and click the Continue button. At this point, the Installation Wizard copies the files it needs to the places it needs to put them.

8. The next window you are presented lists all the RAS-capable devices attached to the server. If you have more than one modem attached to the server, the drop-down menu will allow you to select the device for RAS communications. If you haven't installed a modem, you can choose Install Modem or Install X.25 pad from this screen. Once you have chosen your RAS capable device, click OK.

NOTE RAS is selfish. The communication channel must be dedicated to RAS. If you want to use the channel for something else, you will have to stop RAS and restart it when you are finished.

---

9. At this juncture, you should see the Remote Access Setup screen shown below. Instead of continuing at this time, click Configure.

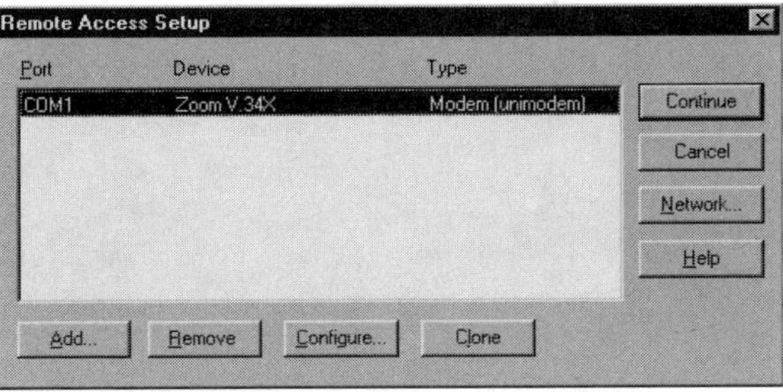

10. Clicking Configure opens the Configure Port Usage screen. This allows you to specify how you want the port to be used. Make your selection from the choices below:

    - **Dial Out Only**: If you are configuring this server to dial into another RAS connection and you only want this machine to dial out, this would be the appropriate selection.

- **Receive Calls Only:** This is the default selection. If your RAS connection will not be going out looking for work and dialing into other servers, this would be the appropriate selection.
- **Dial Out and Receive Calls:** This selection provides two-way communication.

11. Click OK to return to the Remote Access Setup screen.
12. You should now be back at the Remote Access Setup screen. Click Continue to open the RAS Server NetBEUI Configuration window.

NOTE The first protocol that is configured is for the simplest and most basic of network protocols—NetBEUI. We are not interested in NetBEUI here, but it is one of the ways of configuring RAS protocols.

---

13. The next screen is the RAS Server TCP/IP Configuration screen. As you look at the screen below, you will see there are several decisions you will have to make before continuing.

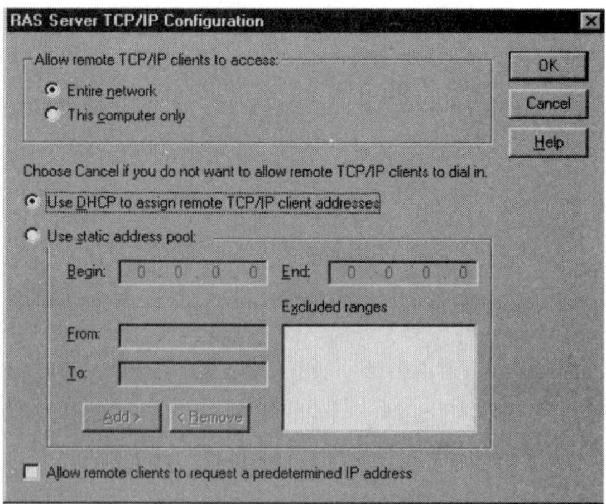

- The first set of radio buttons will allow you to decide how far the TCP/IP client will be allowed to go. The choices are Entire Network or This Computer Only.

- You will also have to make some decisions about TCP/IP addressing. Selecting Use DHCP to Assign Remote TCP/IP Client Addresses causes the server to pass the buck to a DHCP server to provide the IP address. Choosing Use Static Address Pool will let this service decide which of the IP addresses to assign to each connecting device.
- You can also check the box at the bottom of the screen, which allows the remote client to request a predetermined IP address. After making the appropriate selections, click OK.

SEE ALSO Notice there is a Begin and End selection as well as excluded ranges in the Use Static Address Pool area. For a more complete discussion on TCP/IP addressing, read Chapter 2, "Installation and Configuration."

---

14. Next, click OK and close the RAS Installation Wizard.
15. Click Close to close the Network Configuration window.
16. Finally, select Yes to restart the computer.

Installing Dial-up Networking (DUN)

All that stuff up above did the job of getting the server ready to accept phone calls. Some additional work is necessary to configure the client. There are some differences between the way DUN is configured on an NT Workstation, an NT Server, and a Windows 95 client. In this example, DUN will be configured on the Windows NT Workstation. The installation consists of following these steps:

1. Start the installation of dial-up networking by double-clicking on the My Computer icon on the desktop. Then click the Dial-Up Networking icon. This will start the Installation Wizard.
2. The first screen that appears is an information-only kind of screen. It tells you how you can use either a modem or an ISDN line to use dial-up networking. Click Install to get to work.

3. Once you click Install, NT goes out and starts to copy files. It will locate the Remote Access Service device installed in your computer (your modem or ISDN adapter). If you don't like the modem it found, there are choices to install a modem or install an X.25 pad. Click OK to add the RAS device we installed back in Chapter 1, "Planning."

4. This brings up the Remote Access Setup screen. The RAS setup screen shows the modem installed and allows you to add or remove components, configure or clone (copy) a component, or click Continue. Click Continue.

NOTE We will come back to this screen in the "Configuring Dial-up Networking" portion of this chapter.

---

5. Windows NT Workstation installs RAS and binds the appropriate protocols. You finally get a message that says DUN has been installed and you need to restart your computer for the changes to take effect. Click Restart.

Configuring Dial-up Networking

The configuration of the dial-up networking client really begins with the configuration of Remote Access Services and the modem. These steps are outlined below:

1. To access the modem configuration options, go into the Control Panel, then double-click Modems.

2. Highlight the modem and then click Properties. Depending on the modem, there may not be much to configure, as you can see below.

You can configure default line speed, the volume of the modem speaker, and the way the modem connects.

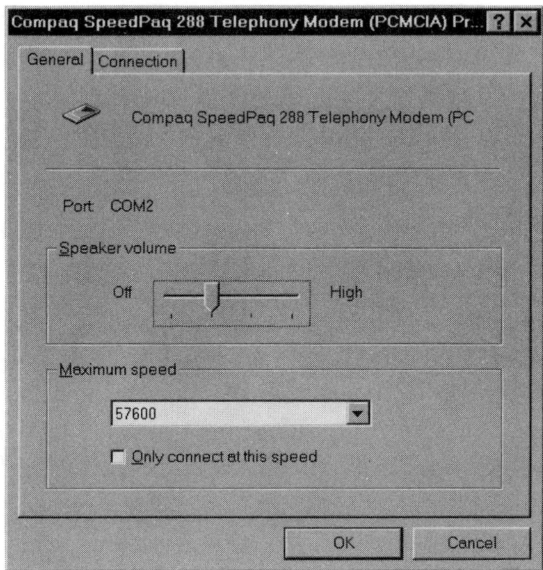

3. From the Modem General page, you can configure your dialing properties. This specifies how your calls are to be dialed. The Modem Properties – General tab gathers some information, such as the following:

   - Clicking on the Dialing Properties button will bring you to the screen shown below. Using the appropriate check boxes, you can set your location depending on the area code you are calling from. You will notice that you can create multiple configurations. If you are working with a laptop and travel to different cities, you can configure one dial-up session for each city.

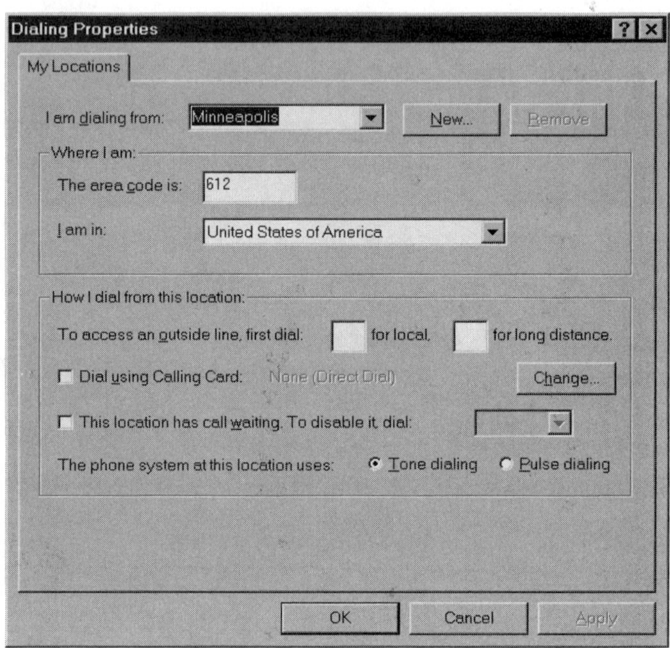

- You can specify if you need to dial an access code to get an outside line for either local or long distance.
- You can set up the system to use a calling card. For the road warrior, this is an especially nice feature. Hotels, motels, and airports tend to add a surcharge to long-distance calls. This surcharge can take the form of arms and legs. Using a calling card to dial the home office bypasses the motel/hotel/airport long-distance profit center and brings the charges back down to a reasonable price.
- You can disable call waiting. There is nothing more frustrating than being in the middle of a large download and having someone call you and activate call waiting. It is usually just enough to disrupt the entire download and cause you to restart it.

- You can tell the system to use tone or pulse dialing. While it has been some time since pulse dialing systems were common, this setting still comes in handy on occasion. As most people who travel with laptops can tell you, hotels/motels/airports tend to have less than top-of-the-line phone systems. There are some occasions where the laptop dials faster than the phone system can handle. The best way around the issue is to slow things way down using pulse dialing.

4. Once the modem configuration has been completed, you can configure RAS. To start the RAS configuration, go to the Control Panel, then double-click the Network icon.
5. Click on the Services tab.
6. Click on Remote Access Service and then click Properties. This returns us to the Remote Access Setup screen shown below.

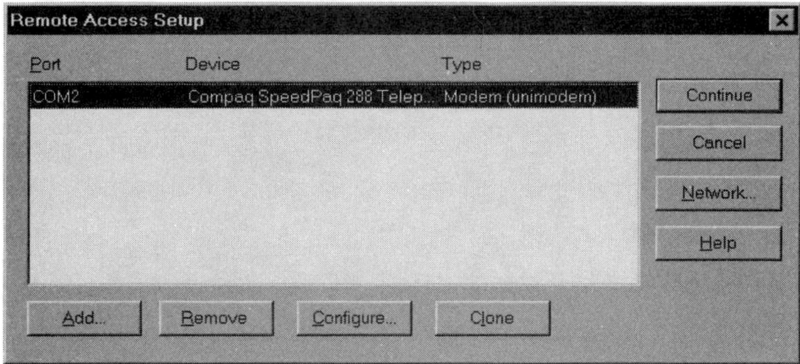

7. Click Configure. As you can see from the screen shown below, this gives you the opportunity to specify how to use the port the modem is attached to. You can tell the system to use the port to dial out only, receive calls only, or dial out and receive calls. The default is Dial Out Only. Make your selections and click OK.

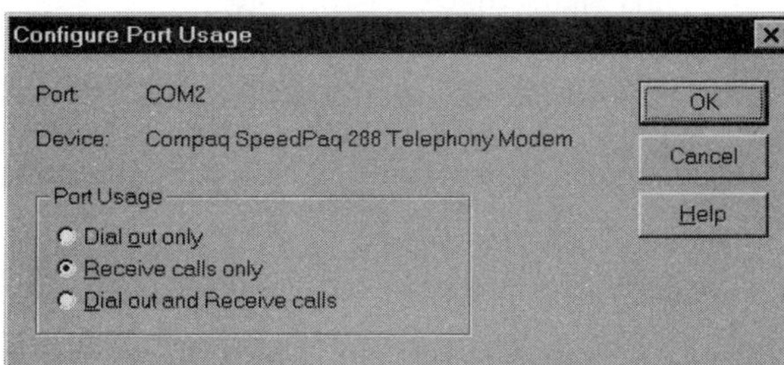

8. Click Network. The Network Configuration screen is shown below. This network selection lets you choose which network protocols will be used on dial out. Your choices are NetBEUI, TCP/IP, and IPX. TCP/IP and IPX are selected by default. If you opted to receive calls also, you can decide how to handle remote clients dialing in. You can allow clients to use NetBEUI, TCP/IP, and IPX. Each of these protocols has its own configuration screen.

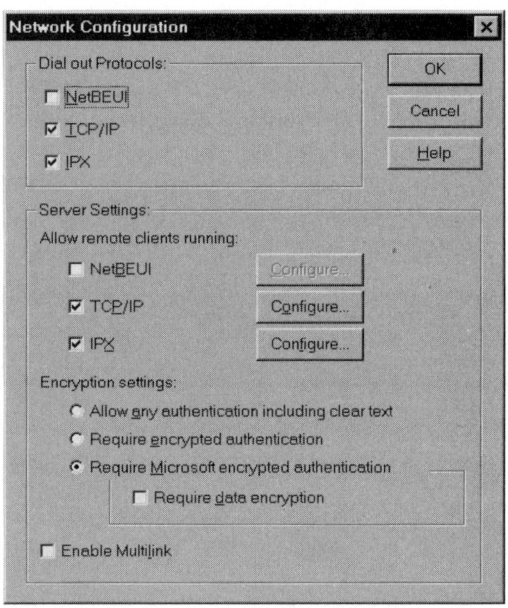

9. Because this book is about TCP/IP, let's take another look at the configuration screen to receive calls made from clients running TCP/IP protocol. From the RAS Server TCP/IP Configuration screen shown again below, you can opt to let clients dialing in access the entire network or just the host computer. You can set up this computer to assign addresses from the manually configured static address pool or let the subnet's DHCP server provide the address. By checking the box at the bottom of the screen, clients can request a predetermined IP address. Setting dial-up clients to use predetermined IP addresses would allow for auditing of calls and connections. Click OK to close the RAS Server TCP/IP Configuration screen.

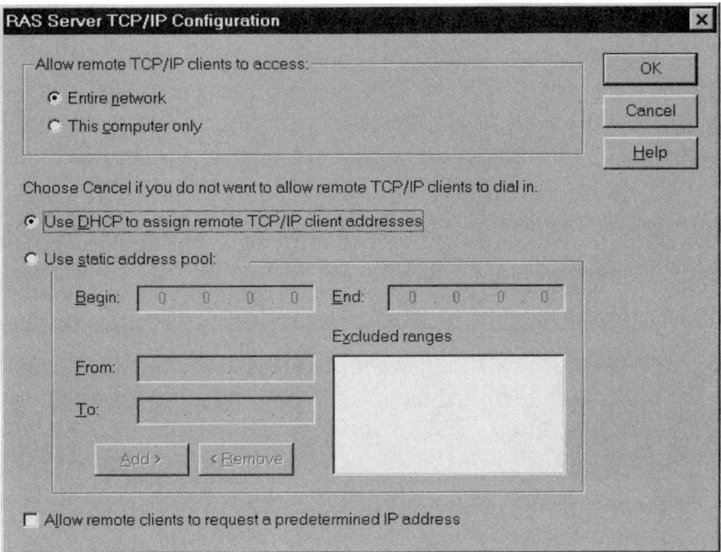

10. Let's take another look at the Network Configuration screen shown above in step 8. You will notice Encryption settings at the bottom of the page. The level of encryption you choose will affect the security of the dial-up session. Allowing any authentication including clear text means everything is out there—there is no encryption at all. Choosing to Require Microsoft Encrypted Authentication and Require Data Encryption means that any communication across the telephone lines will be Encrypted. You can also choose to Enable Multilink, allowing several modems to handle the same phone calls. Make your selections and click OK. If you made changes to the RAS configuration, you must restart the computer. Don't you just hate that?

Creating a Phone Book Entry

At this point DUN is configured and RAS is configured, we just don't have anywhere to call. Now, we must create a phone book entry. Phone book entries are important, not just because they give us somewhere to call, but because this is where RAS security is configured.

Phone book entries are part of the configuration information for the user so the other people who use your NT Workstation won't know where you are calling.

To create a new phone book entry, do the following:

1. Double-click My Computer on your desktop, then double-click Dial-Up Networking and click New. This starts the New Phonebook Entry Wizard.
2. You will be asked to name the new phone book entry. Provide a name and click Next.

NOTE If you know all about phone books, you can check the box that says you would rather edit the properties directly.

---

3. The Server screen shown below now appears and you can check any or all of the three available options:
   - I am calling the Internet.
   - Send a plain text password if that's the only way to connect.
   - The non–Windows NT Server I am calling expects me to type login information after connecting or to know TCP/IP addresses before dialing.

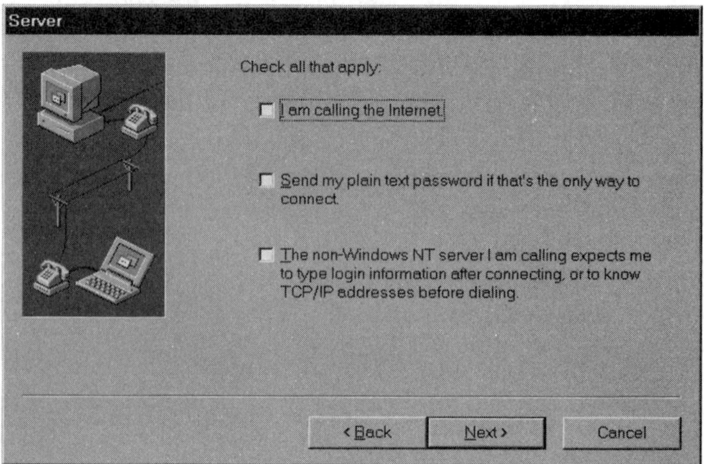

4. Make any and all choices and click Next.
5. Enter the phone number and choose to use telephony dialing properties. One slick feature allows you to add alternate phone numbers, so if your ISP has three local access numbers, NT will try each number. Click Next.
6. Now you can choose your serial line protocol. When in doubt, stay with PPP. It's newer and more widely accepted. Click Next.
7. You are now prompted to enter a login script for after the connection. If in doubt, go with the default of None. Again, click Next.
8. Now you are prompted to enter a static IP address. If you are planning on using a DHCP assigned address, leave the entry to all zeros. Click Next. Again, you are asked for some IP addresses, this time for Domain Name Service servers or Windows Internet Name Service servers. When in doubt, leave it to zeros. Click Next.
9. Click Finish.
10. To test the connection, click Dial. This brings up the Connect screen. Here you can add your username, password, domain (if required), and check the box to save your password. Click OK to dial.

Exam Essentials

This is one of the favorite sections of the exam writers. They just love the protocols and like PPTP and VPNs. Be sure to look over this information carefully. You might even want to review it just before the exam.

Know the two dial-up services offered by Windows NT. The two services are Remote Access Service and dial-up networking (DUN).

Know the differences between SLIP, PPP, and PPTP. SLIP (Serial Line Internet Protocol) is IP over a modem. This is an outdated protocol. PPP (Point-to-Point Protocol) is used with serial or modem communications to provide IP communications, and it can provide additional features such as data compression and DNS and gateway addressing. PPP has largely replaced SLIP. Windows NT Servers can establish SLIP connections only when dialing out or originating a SLIP session. PPTP (Point-to-Point Tunneling Protocol) is PPP with security and is used with the Internet to create an encrypted link to the RAS server. In some areas, this is called creating a Virtual Private Network (VPN).

Know which types of connections PPTP can use to create a VPN. PPTP can use PSTN connections, ISDN connections, and X.25 connections to create a Virtual Private Network.

Know which protocols PPTP can use. PPTP can connect using IP, IPX, and NetBEUI.

Know that PPTP provides security for dial-up connections. Of the major dial-up protocols, PPTP is the most secure. If you see an exam question where the words dial-up and security are mentioned, look for PPTP.

Know how to use a RAS server to connect to an ISP. When you use a RAS server to connect to an ISP, there are several changes that need to be made to the registry, but the gateway address needs to be left blank.

Know how to configure a workstation to connect to the Internet using a RAS server. The workstation can use a RAS server to connect to the Internet. This is done by specifying the IP address of the network interface that connects the RAS server to the local network as the client's gateway address.

Key Terms and Concepts

IPX (Internet Packet Exchange Protocol): A connectionless-oriented protocol; a Novell Netware standard.

ISDN (Integrated Services Digital Network): Provides communications over special phone lines using digital communications.

Modem (from modulate/demodulate): Computer hardware that will turn a computer's digital signal into an analog signal that can be sent over a phone line. The modem at the receiving end will then turn the analog signal into a digital signal that the computer can understand.

Multilink: The ability of RAS to combine several serial signals into one, using either ISDN or modems.

POTS (Plain Old Telephone System): The POTS is otherwise known as the phone company, expletives should be deleted!

PPP (Point-to-Point Protocol): A Data Link layer transport that performs over point-to-point network connections, such as serial or modem lines. PPP can negotiate with any transport protocol used by both systems involved in the link. It can also realize data transfer efficiencies—such as software compression—and automatically assign IP, domain name service (DNS), and gateway addresses when used with Transmission Control Protocol/Internet Protocol (TCP/IP).

PSTN (Public Switched Telephone Network): Another name for the phone company.

RAS (Remote Access Service): Allows other users to dial up the host computer and use the computer's resources, or use the computer as a gateway into the entire network.

SLIP (Serial Line Internet Protocol): An implementation of Internet protocol (IP) over a serial line. SLIP has been replaced, by and large, by PPP.

TCP/IP (Transmission Control Protocol/Internet Protocol): The standard protocol suite of the Internet.

TDI (Transport Driver Interface): A specification to which all Windows NT transport protocols must be written in order to be used by higher-level services, such as RAS.

Sample Questions

1. Which dial-up line protocols does RAS support?

   A. PPP

   B. TCP

   C. SLIP

   D. IPX/SPX

   E. UDP

   Answer: A and C. PPP and SLIP are the only two dial-up line protocols listed above.

2. What is multilink?

   A. The ability to have two or more modems handling different calls at the same time

   B. The ability of two or more modems to call out at the same time

   C. The ability to use more than one communication channel for the same connection

   D. The ability to have two network interface cards in the same system at the same time

   Answer: C. The ability to use more than one communication channel for the same connection.

3. Your company has experienced a sudden growth in the use of laptop computers. Users now want to dial up the company RAS server and access services using encryption. Which protocol(s) should you enable?

   A. PPP

   B. ISDN

   C. SLIP

   D. PPTP

   Answer: D. The Point-to-Point Tunneling Protocol (PPTP) provides for encryption.

4. You have configured your RAS server to dial up your ISP to establish a connection. What gateway address should you put in the server's TCP/IP configuration for the dial-up connection?

A. None, it should be left blank

B. The IP address of the network interface connecting the server to the local network

C. The IP address of the router that hooks into the ISP

D. The IP address of the ISP server

Answer: A. The gateway address should be left blank

Configure and support browsing in a multiple-domain routed network.

You know that when you add a computer to a domain, people can use Network Neighborhood or Explorer to browse for shares or services that are offered to the entire network, even if the network spans multiple domains. What keeps track of where all those computers are located and ways to find the services that are offered? That is what Computer Browser Services provides.

Computer Browser Services maintains something called a *browser list*, which is kind of like the yellow pages. When you need something and you don't know where to find it, you can look in the yellow pages. Around our house, that usually means trying to *find* the yellow pages. This browser list is made available to any client that asks for it.

Critical Information

The term browser seems to be all-inclusive. That is not the case. There are different types of browsers, which are discussed below.

Domain Master Browser

The computer on your desk is part of a massive computer network. Your WAN could have hundreds or thousands of servers, services, and shares available to users. What keeps track of all that information? The Primary Domain Controller (PDC) is not just for authentication and management. It has several other responsibilities, including maintaining a master list of services available for the entire domain. That makes it the Domain Master Browser. Does that sound like a really big job? It can be, which is why the PDC delegates some of its chores. The first delegation goes to the Master Browser.

Master Browser

In any network, there is at least one workgroup. If you have a larger network, you may have several workgroups. If you have several network cards in your file server and you are using the TCP/IP protocol, you will have several subnets in your network. Each of these workgroups or subnets must have a Master Browser. If there are other NT Servers on the subnet or in the workgroup, when that server comes up, it will check in with the Master Browser and tell it what services the newcomer has to offer. Then, when you open your Network Neighborhood, the new server and its services will magically appear. What does the Master Browser do with the list of all services available in its workgroups or on its subnet? It passes that list up to the Domain Master Browser so something knows where everything is in the domain.

Backup Browser

You will never guess what the Backup Browser does. It acts as kind of a backstop for the Master Browser. If you remember, the Master Browser is always trying to keep track of all the services on the subnet or in the workgroup. While the Master Browser is gathering and sorting all that information, the Backup Browser is answering all those "where is" requests floating around the network. The Backup Browser gets its list from the Master Browser.

Potential Browser

The Potential Browser is otherwise known as the Browser Wannabe. This computer is just hanging out waiting to become a browser.

Non-Browser

The name says it all, a non-browser, a true slacker—a computer that cannot act as a browser. Actually, it is probably too busy doing other things to be bothered with answering browser requests.

Browser Elections

How does a Master Browser get to be a Master Browser while a Potential Browser is waiting around with all that potential going to waste? Computer networking is really much more democratic than you may have thought. The systems can actually call for an election.

Here is what happens. You boot your workstation and go into Network Neighborhood looking for the Joke Repository Share. Your computer first looks to the Master Browser and asks for a list of Backup Browsers. Once your computer has the list of Backup Browsers, it will then ask the Backup Browser for the location of the share. What happens if the Master Browser fails? A browser election is held. The election is somewhat weighted. For example, if a computer is running NT Server, it gets more votes than a computer running NT Workstation. If a computer is "just" running Windows 95 it gets fewer votes; you get the picture.

Now that all the computers with NT Server have checked in, there is still a deadlock. NT 4 is higher than NT 3.51, so it gets more votes. If there is still a tie, the Backup Browser will get a higher vote than the Potential Browser. Do you want to feel powerful? You can rig the election. By tweaking the HKEY_Local_Machine\system\CurrentControlSet\Services\Browser\Parameter setting, you can be a political boss. Setting the parameter to Yes means the system will always try to become a browser. No tells the system to sit on the sidelines and watch the elections go by. Auto (which is the default) makes sure the server is at least a potential browser.

Browser elections is one of those behind-the-scenes services that you probably don't think about very often. It just works. Browser services does more than provide information on resources available to your network. It also helps to "load balance" the network by making sure a list of network resources is available on different cable segments and subnets. For your user, this means packets don't have to fly all over the network causing traffic jams at key points. Less traffic usually means quicker response time.

Browsing and Subnets

Every subnet is its own browsing area. That means for each subnet there must be some type of browser hierarchy and at least one NT controller to register the information from the subnet with the Domain Master Browser. This would normally be done with broadcast messages, but there is a problem. If you have multiple subnets, you have routers, and routers do not like broadcast messages at all! A router will usually not allow a broadcast message to pass through the system.

Because broadcasting a message is out, the subnet's Master Browser will use a directed datagram called a MasterBrowserAnnouncement to tell the Domain Master Browser which system rules the roost for the subnet. This announcement is sent out every 15 minutes by default. That way, the Domain Master Browser knows where to send out all the browser lists.

When a Master Browser first boots up, it sends out something called a DomainAnnouncement once a minute for the first five minutes, and then once every 15 minutes after that. If a domain does not respond by sending out a DomainAnnouncement for three consecutive periods, the domain is removed from the Master Browser list. If each period is 15 minutes, and it takes three periods to remove a domain from the Master Browser list, a Domain may be off the network for 45 minutes before the resources are removed from the browser list.

If the Domain Master Browser fails for any reason, the users on the entire network are limited to finding resources on their own subnet if the subnet has a Master Browser. Without a Master Browser, there is no browsing on the subnet at all. To prevent a total meltdown of browsing capabilities, make sure your Domain Master Browser is restored within the three announcement periods or promote the Backup Domain Controller (BDC) to the role of Domain Master Browser.

Windows Browsing and IP Networks—a Match Not Made in Heaven

The problem with browsing is that it is basically a NetBIOS kind of task. While NetBIOS is a great little protocol, it does not necessarily work and play well with the big networks. On the other hand, TCP/IP was made to work and play on a big network and it already has in place a very elegant way of finding host names anywhere on the network. Unfortunately, the way TCP/IP and the way NetBIOS resolve names is *very* different.

Broadcast versus Directed

NetBIOS starts out the resolution process with a broadcast message. A *broadcast message* means that all computers on the network will receive and have to act on that message. In a small network, broadcast messages do not cause a problem. You can imagine the problem that would be caused if 10 percent of the hosts on the Microsoft corporate network all started to browse for resources at the same time and every one sent a broadcast message to every other computer on the network. There would be bedlam! Routers do not let that happen. A router will *usually* not allow a broadcast message to leave the subnet. That is great for the network as a whole because traffic is cut down. It is not so great for browsing the network because it precludes being able to find anything the "normal" way.

Notice I said the router will "usually" not allow a broadcast message to be passed from one subnet to another subnet. Some routers are BOOTP-enabled, which means they can pass broadcast messages. This is great for browsing, but lousy for network traffic. There are ways around the broadcast problem.

The opposite of a packet that is broadcast is a *directed packet*. Take a look at Figure 3.8 below. If a broadcast packet were sent out, and each of the routers were capable of passing the message, each and every workstation on the network would receive the packet, no matter what city the computers were in. On the other hand, if you were sending a directed packet, the packet would be sent directly to the target computer, bypassing everything else.

FIGURE 3.8: Map of a wide area network

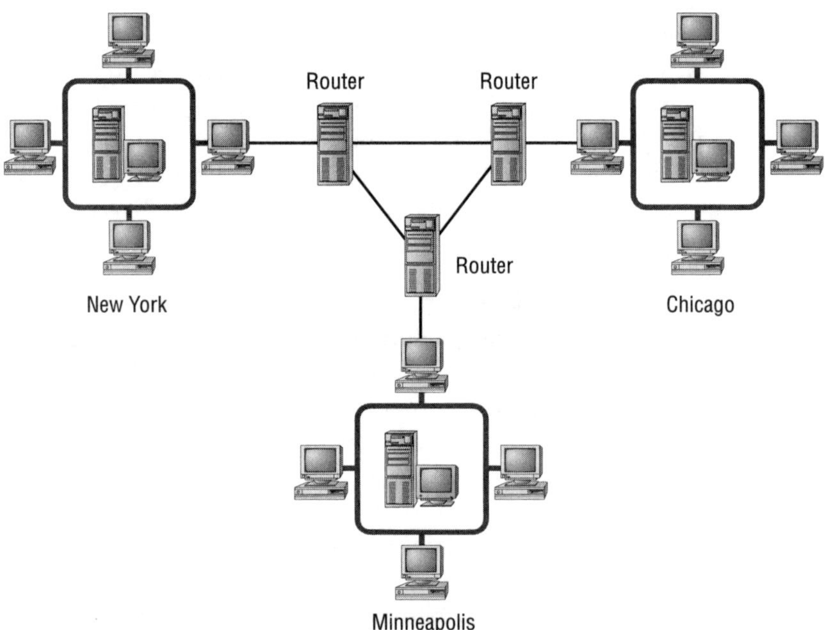

WINS Resolution and the Domain Master Browser

One of the ways that Windows NT resolves network addresses with direct addressing is by using a WINS Server. In this case, a client comes online and dynamically registers with the WINS Server. The WINS Server gets all the information about the NetBIOS name of the client and the services it offers as well as the IP address of the host. The Domain Master Browser uses the WINS Server to update its database of all the domains listed in the WINS database. By querying the WINS Server, the Domain Master Browser gets information on all the hosts on all the domains. The list has only domain names and IP addresses, not the name of the Master Browser on each subnet.

When a client needs a resource, it sends a directed request to the WINS Server and asks for a list of domain controllers for the domain. WINS will respond with up to 25 domain controllers in the domain. The client can then figure out which domain controller it needs to access the resource and send a directed packet. It is simple, neat, and dynamic, which means not a lot of work for the system administrator. System administrators like that!

LMHOSTS and the Domain Master Browser

Just like anything else in computing, there are several ways to approach the same problem. When it comes to browsing, one other way of providing name-to-address resolution is using the LMHOSTS file. The LMHOSTS file is not as neat and clean as the WINS solution, but it does work just as well. The major disadvantage of using the LMHOSTS solution is that it is static, not dynamic. *Dynamic* means the system does the work; *static* means you do the work. If you are a consultant, static means billable hours. If you are not a consultant, static usually translates to overtime!

In order to make the LMHOSTS solution work, there must be an LMHOSTS file on each subnet's Master Browser and in this file there must be an entry to the Domain Master Browser. Any time there is a change to the LMHOSTS list, this change must be manually updated in each LMHOSTS file.

To work across subnets, the LMHOSTS file needs an IP address and the computer name of the Domain Master Browser. Furthermore, this information must be properly formatted using the #PRE and #DOM tags. The appropriate entries would look like this:

```
210.47.26.1      psconsulting    #PRE    #DOM:Corp
210.47.26.33     pscsrv2         #PRE
210.47.26.65     pscsrv3         #PRE
210.47.26.97     pscsrv4         #PRE    #DOM:SalesOff
210.47.26.129    pscsrv5
```

The #PRE tag pre-loads the entry into the NetBIOS name cache. Because this is a static entry, it will be loaded each time and the client will not have to access the domain for information.

By adding the #DOM: tag, every time a computer sends a broadcast message to the domain, a directed message gets sent to every computer listed with a #DOM: tag. These types of messages will be sent across routers.

The Domain Master Browser is a special instance. The LMHOSTS file must have an entry pointing to each of the Master Browsers on each of the subnets. For the Master Browsers, each of these computers should have an LMHOSTS file with #DOM: entries pointing to all the other subnet Master Browsers.

LMHOSTS and Static Mapping

With the LMHOSTS file pointing to WINS Servers, Windows systems are made available by browsing. What about non-Windows systems, such as UNIX hosts? With a UNIX host, you may have to modify both the DHCP scope and the WINS database. In DHCP, if the IP address falls in the middle of a scope, that could cause a problem. Isolating or excluding the static IP address of the UNIX system will solve the problem. How does the system get registered with the WINS Server? All static, non-Windows systems need to be manually entered into the WINS database.

SEE ALSO For more information on the LMHOSTS file, refer to Chapter 2, "Installation and Configuration." Chapter 2 also contains more information on the WINS database.

Necessary Procedures

From the discussion above, you know that there are several browser roles. If there is a Primary Domain Controller (PDC), it is the Domain Master Browser. If your network is made up of domains and workgroups, you only have one Master Browser. If your network is a TCP/IP internetwork (a WAN or enterprise network), there may be more than one Master Browser, with the PDC acting as a Domain Master Browser and Master Browsers designated for each subnet. The other browsers are Backup Browsers, Potential Browsers, and Non-Browsers.

Configuring a Computer to Participate in Browser Elections

To configure a computer to participate in the browser elections, you must modify the \HKEY_LOCAL_MACHINE\SYSTEM\CurrentControlSet\Services\Browser\Parameters\MaintainServerList parameter. Follow these steps to edit this key:

1. Start \%system_root%\system32\regedt32.exe.
2. Select the HKEY_LOCAL_MACHINE hive.
3. Double-click on SYSTEM. This will open HKEY_LOCAL_MACHINE\SYSTEM, which is shown below.

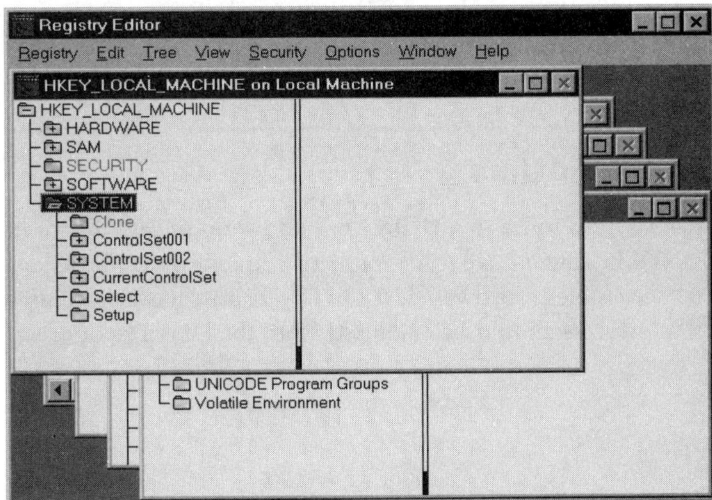

4. Double-click on CurrentControlSet.
5. Double-click on Services.
6. Double-click on Browser.
7. Double-click on Parameters.
8. Click on MaintainServerList. At this point, the String Editor screen appears; it is shown below. Here, you can enter three values: Yes, No, or Auto.

- **No** means the computer will not be a browser.
- **Yes** means the computer will be a Master Browser or a Backup Browser.
- **Auto** means the computer can be a Master Browser, Backup Browser, or a Potential Browser.

If your computer is on a network that does not have a PDC (such as a workgroup), you can force a computer to be the Master Browser by changing the key \HKEY_LOCAL_MACHINE\SYSTEM\Current-ControlSet\Services\Browser\Parameters\IsDomainMaster to TRUE. It is set to FALSE by default, even on a PDC.

Exam Essentials

Know how to have a UNIX host show up in WINS browsing. A UNIX host will have to be manually added to the WINS database to be accessible to browsing. If the UNIX host has a static IP address, that address should be excluded from the DHCP scope.

Know the type of entry that must be made to a WINS database for a UNIX computer. The entry type in the WINS database for a UNIX computer must be unique. A unique entry maps a computer name to one IP address.

Know which types of computers require unique entries in the WINS database. A unique entry is reserved for mapping a computer name to one IP address. This is usually reserved for adding a UNIX computer to the WINS database.

Know the LMHOSTS file entries necessary for systems to be able to browse remote domains. LMHOSTS files on each domain controller must contain one entry for each domain controller on the local domain and the Primary Domain Controller of each remote domain. Remote backup domain controllers can be added as needed.

Know the syntax for adding a domain controller to the LMHOSTS file. This is the proper syntax:

```
IP address  host name  #pre  #dom:domainname
```

Know how browsing is enabled on a totally Windows network. If there is a network that has only Windows 95 and Windows NT clients on it, the system only needs a WINS Server installed and configured for browsing to be enabled across subnets.

Key Terms and Concepts

Backup Browser: A backup to the Master Browser of a subnet. It also responds to browser requests.

Broadcast packet: A packet that is broadcast to each computer on the network

Browser list: A list of all resources on your network. It is maintained by the designated Browsers.

Directed packet: A packet that is addressed to a specific host.

Domain Master Browser: Usually the Primary Domain Controller. It is the server that is responsible for maintaining the master browser list.

LMHOSTS file: A text-based file used to assist in resolving NetBIOS computer names to IP addresses.

Master Browser: The primary browser for a subnet.

Non-Browser: A server on a subnet that does not participate in resolving NetBIOS names to IP addresses.

Potential Browser: A server on a subnet that could become a browser.

WINS (Windows Internet Name Service): Handles dynamic resolution of NetBIOS computer names to IP addresses.

Sample Questions

1. You are creating an entry for a UNIX computer in the WINS database. The system is asking you for the type of entry. You should choose:

   A. Unique entry

   B. Domain Name

   C. Multihomed computer

   D. Multihomed group

   Answer: A. Adding a UNIX computer to a WINS database requires a unique entry.

2. Your network consists of six subnets in a single Windows NT domain. One subnet has the Primary Domain Controller and each of the other subnets have a Backup Domain Controller. You want to ensure that a UNIX host can be accessed by all Windows clients on each subnet. What do you have to do?

   A. You should make sure DNS is enabled on the network.

   B. You should make sure DHCP is enabled on the network.

   C. You should add a static mapping entry to the WINS database.

   D. You should add the address to the HOSTS file on the PDC.

   Answer: C. Add a static entry to the WINS database.

3. By default, the PDC in a domain is also the:

   A. Domain Master Browser

   B. Master Browser

   C. Backup Browser

   D. Potential Browser

   Answer: A. By default a PDC is also the Domain Master Browser.

4. The browser that actually answers browsing requests is a:

   A. Domain Master Browser

   B. Master Browser

   C. Backup Browser

   D. Potential Browser

   Answer: C. Browsing requests are usually answered by a Backup Browser.

CHAPTER 4

Monitoring and Optimization

Microsoft Exam Objectives Covered in This Chapter:

- **Given a scenario, identify which tool to use to monitor TCP/IP traffic.** *(pages 237 – 277)*

Running a computer network is an ongoing task. It is more than just putting out fires and adding new users. It is planning for the future and making sure everything is working at its highest potential in the present. Microsoft TCP/IP is just a microcosm of the network as a whole. As an administrator, you have to take advantage of all the tools at your disposal to make sure your network is making the best use of its available resources.

Performance management is a science. You start out establishing a baseline of network operations. When you know how well your network operates normally, you begin to examine areas that could stand improvement. When you have your opportunity "hit" list, you prioritize the list and start with priority number one. When you begin to make changes, be careful to change just one thing at a time. By changing just one thing, and then reestablishing the baseline, you can determine if your change has had a positive impact on your network. Changing multiple parameters will make the decision difficult because you won't know if everything you did helped or if some of the changes helped and others didn't.

Obviously, Microsoft thinks this is an important topic. Unlike Chapter 2, "Installation and Configuration," which had tons of objectives, this chapter is focused on monitoring traffic. If you have taken other Microsoft exams, you know that monitoring performance is a really big thing. Because Microsoft TCP/IP has some tools that allow for advanced monitoring, it takes on an even bigger role.

Given a scenario, identify which tool to use to monitor TCP/IP traffic.

As you read this section, you may decide to change to a different operating system! It will seem like there is a lot to do and even more to keep track of. Don't let the performance management strategy fool you. NT is very forgiving. NT is also very adaptable. It will sense the operation of the network and if the O/S senses there are some parameters that can be changed, the O/S will change them on the fly. The changes are even for the better.

When you look at the tools available for monitoring Microsoft TCP/IP, you will see that some of the tools are simple command-line utilities. Some are processes that run in the background gathering information, some are programs that take that information and put it into a format that the administrator can understand. Some of the utilities that you will be tested on are included with NT, others are included with the NT resource kit, and some are included with the System Management Server or SMS. In this section, we will look at each type of tool.

As you prepare for the test, keep in mind that while there are multiple questions about performance management on the exam, all the questions seem to revolve around the same utilities. In several cases, there are multiple questions on the same subject, just phrased slightly differently.

Critical Information

The term *network performance* means many things to many people. For most of your end users, it means never having to say, "The network sure is slow today." When we analyze the term from the aspect of Microsoft TCP/IP, it can only mean communication between two hosts somewhere on the network. This can also be defined as the *communication subsystem*.

If you look closely at the network communication "chain" that connects the two hosts, it will look something like this. The signal will leave the first host (the sender) through the network interface card. The NIC will place the packets onto some form of media, usually a cable. The cable can move the packets at varying speeds, from a "slow" Token Ring network of 4 Mbps (megabits per second), to Ethernet speeds of up to 100 Mbps, to FDDI, with speeds greater than 100 Mbps.

Once on the wire, the packet has to know where to go. This may involve some type of name-to-address resolution using NetBIOS or DNS. If a name is involved, it will be resolved to an IP address and the packet will be examined to see if the packet is destined for a host on the local subnet, or if it is destined for a remote network. If the packet is determined to be for a host on the same subnet, the packet will be directed to that host. This procedure is shown in Figure 4.1.

FIGURE 4.1: Communication on a local subnet

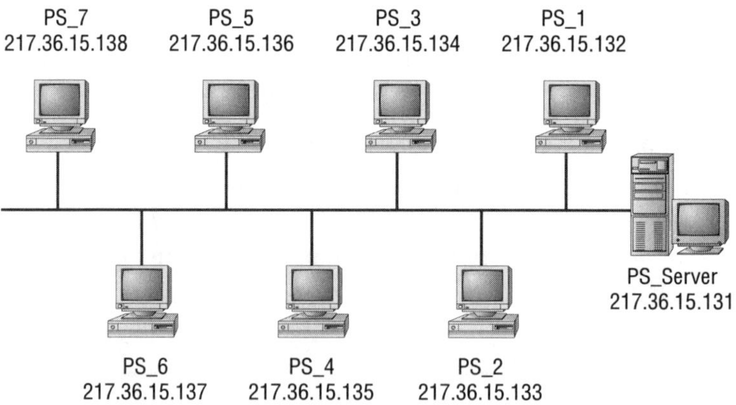

If PS_Server needed to communicate with system PS_6, a packet would be generated and destination address would be checked. Since the address is on the same subnet, the packet would be directed to the appropriate host system without the need of a router or a gateway.

If the packet is bound for a remote network, the packet must pass through some kind of a router or a gateway to get directions. The router will take the packet, strip off some information, add some other information and send the packet on its way to the next stop on the trip to the final destination. When the packet reaches the receiving host, it enters the computer through the network card, and finds its way into the CPU. Look closely at Figure 4.2.

FIGURE 4.2: Map of a small network

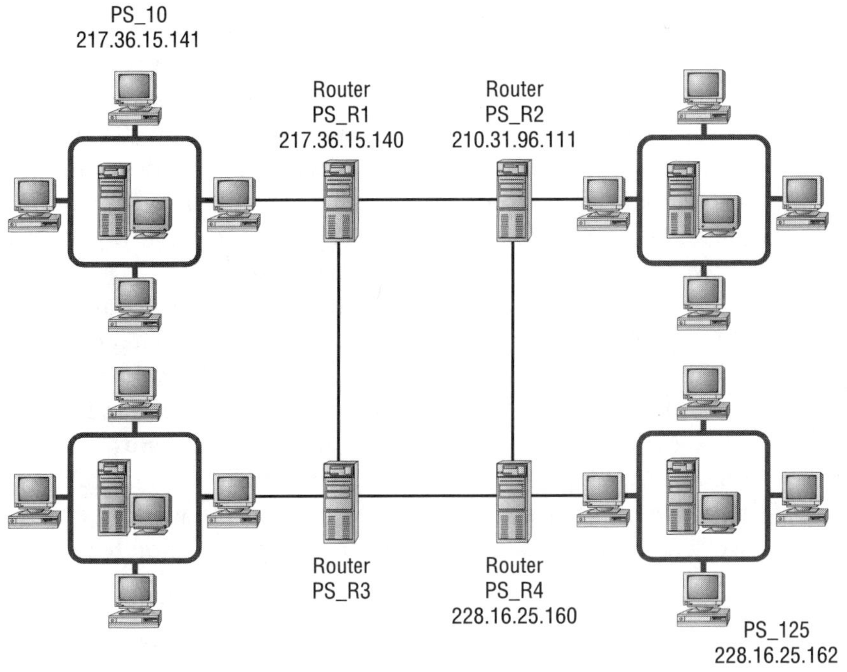

In this case, host PS_10 wants to send a packet to host PS_125. PS_10 checks its HOSTS file, or LMHOSTS file, and finds out that PS_125 has a network address of 228.16.25.162. PS_10 recognizes immediately that this system is not on the same subnet. PS_10 checks its configuration and knows that if a target computer is not on the same subnet the packet is sent to the router/gateway for the router/gateway to worry about it.

PS_10 then addresses the packet for the router PS_R1 at address 217.36.15.140. Once the packet has been addressed, PS_10 sends it off. The packet now has two destination addresses—the address of the router and the final destination address of system PS_125.

When the packet arrives at PS_R1, the router examines the packet and strips off the destination address pointing to PS_R1. When it examines the packet, it finds the IP address of PS_125 and determines the network address that the remote host resides on. Once it has the network address, the router checks its route table to find out how to reach that network. In this case, assume the packet must go through router PS_R2 and onto PS_R4. Once the path to the remote host has been determined, PS_R1 adds the destination address of the next *hop*, or router. In this case it is 210.31.96.111. The packet is then sent on its merry way. When the packet arrives at router PS_R2, the same thing happens. The router strips off its address as a destination, looks at the final destination address, figures out the network number the packet is destined for, checks the route table to see how to get to that network. It then readdresses the packet and sends the packet on to the next hop, in this case router PS_R4. When the packet arrives at PS_R4, it strips off its address as the destination. The router examines the packet and finds that the address is a local address. In this case, the router knows about the hosts on its network, so it readdresses the packet for the destination of 228.16.25.162 and sends it on its way. Finally, the packet arrives at the final destination; the host PS_125 can now act on the message sent by PS_10. And you wonder why the network slows down sometimes. There is a lot going on here!

If you want to check the performance of the network segment, there are a few places along the way that can act as bottlenecks.

First of all, the network cards. If any network card is defective, it can slow down the process. If the card is *chattering*—flooding the network with packets—it can slow down the entire network, not just communication with another host.

The media that the packets travel on is another potential trouble spot. Each type of media can move packets at a maximum speed. That maximum speed is obtainable only in ideal conditions. For example, if your Ethernet segment has too many hosts on it, collisions may occur. When two packets collide, the two "senders" have to step back and wait to resend their packets. Just like a freeway, a collision is going to slow down traffic flow for everyone.

Once the packet gets to the router, it faces another potential bottleneck. If the router is getting more packets than it can handle, packets may be dropped or lost. Once again, the sender will have to resend the packet and the network will become even more congested. Even if the router is not overwhelmed with work, it still has to examine the packet, determine its destination, readdress the packet and send the packet on its way. Routers have ratings and it is not surprising that a router's rating is based on speed. This means that the faster the router, the better. You can also translate that to mean the better the router, the more expensive.

In looking at this subsystem, it appears there are only a few places to check to see how the network is performing: the NICs, name-to-address resolution, the traffic on the media, and the routers. There are more tools at your disposal than you may think. Here is just a partial list:

- GUI (Graphical User Interface) Utilities
  - Network Monitor
  - Performance Monitor
- Command-Line Utilities
  - The ARP command-line utility
  - IPCONFIG
  - NBTStat
  - Netstat
  - PING
  - Route
  - SNMP
  - TraceRT

This is a rather impressive list of tools. It reminds me of the time I went out to my grandfather's machine shop and just stared at the tools. I knew there were a bunch of 'em. I knew they could be used to make wondrous things, because I had seen the things my grandfather had made. I was totally lost when it came to what each tool did and *how* it was used was beyond me.

These network performance tools are easier to use than your average power tool. You just need to know when to use them, and how they will provide the best possible results. Because the objective includes the word "scenario" I will try and give you appropriate times and ways to use each tool.

TIP These tools can be used in conjunction with one another. In some cases, one tool is dependent on the presence of another to perform properly. I will point out these areas as we go along.

GUI Utilities

Network Monitor and Performance Monitor are GUI (graphical user interface) utilities; the rest are command-line utilities run for a command prompt. The descriptions are grouped accordingly, starting with the two GUI utilities.

Network Monitor

Network Monitor is one of the most useful tools for performance monitoring. It allows you to actually capture packets and examine them from the inside out. Network Monitor can be configured to act as an SNMP manager to provide you with network usage statistics. Because Network Monitor is such a useful tool, you would probably love to have it installed on your system. Unfortunately, the full version of Network Monitor is not an integral part of NT; it comes as part of System Management Service or SMS. A limited version of Network Monitor is part of NT. The difference between the full version (which ships with SMS) and the limited version of Network Manager, which ships with NT, is that the NT version can only capture information being sent to or from the computer it is installed on. The full version (the SMS version) can access information from any device on the subnet.

TIP It will pay dividends to understand the inner workings of Network Monitor, even if it is not available on your computer. There will be multiple performance monitoring questions that will revolve around Network Monitor.

The full version of Network Monitor will allow you to view statistics on those processes that are generating the most network traffic. These statistics can be broken down by the device generating the traffic or by the protocol. You can also use Network Monitor to identify routers or even capture, edit, and retransmit a frame.

Network Monitor constantly monitors the *data stream*, or all information going by on the network. You can define filters that tell Network Monitor what types of data you want to capture and save. Once the data has been captured, you can filter it again so that you can further isolate the problem.

Here are some scenarios where Network Monitor may be helpful in monitoring a network:

- **Monitoring amounts of network traffic.** A network administrator is not sure how much TCP/IP traffic is going over the system. Network Monitor can capture and view the protocol statistics on the server for a given time period.
- **Analyzing network traffic.** If you need to analyze traffic by device or by protocol, you can use Network Monitor's capture filters and display filters to get only the information you are looking for.
- **Monitoring specific traffic.** A network administrator wants to monitor specific network traffic going to individual servers. By running Network Monitor on each server, the administrator can see which workstations are generating the most traffic to the servers.

- **Planning for expansion.** A network administrator is planning on expanding the network. The administrator wants to plan for growth and check current usage of the cable bandwidth. By installing Network Monitor on a computer, the administrator can monitor the data stream and make an informed estimate of how the expansion will affect the current network.

Performance Monitor

If you already have had the foresight to install the Simple Network Management Protocol (SNMP) service on computers, you can use Performance Monitor to gather some TCP/IP statistics.

NOTE If you have already passed the Windows NT Server portion of the Enterprise exam (Exam 70-68), some of the following material will be a review. For more information on monitoring performance of a network, check either *MCSE Exam Notes: NT Server 4 in the Enterprise* by Robert King and Gary Govanus (Sybex, 1998), or *MCSE: NT Server 4 in the Enterprise Study Guide* by Lisa Donald with James Chellis (Sybex, 1997).

Performance Monitor, amazing as it may seem, monitors the performance of computers on your network using *counters*. It gathers this data based on *objects*. An object can either be hardware or software. For example, let's assume we are monitoring the performance of a server. One common method of checking the performance of the server is to track what is happening to the paging file on the server. The paging file is to NT what the swap file was to earlier versions of Windows. When the RAM gets filled, and there is more information to go into memory, Windows NT moves that information to a special file on the system's hard disk called the *paging file*. One of the ways to check how hard the system is working is to see how often the paging file is being accessed. Figure 4.3 shows the Add to Chart window of Performance Monitor.

By selecting both %Usage and %Usage Peak, you can track how often the paging file has been accessed and how often the paging file

FIGURE 4.3: Preparing to monitor the paging file

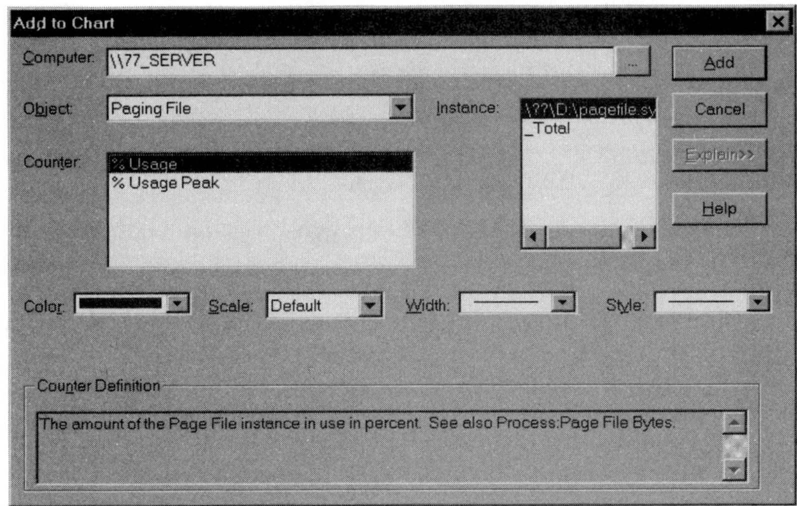

has reached its maximum size. In this case, the paging file is the object and the counters are %Usage and %Usage Peak. The results of monitoring will be sent to a log file or you can configure Performance Monitor to alert one person or one group of people when a threshold has been surpassed.

Performance Monitor can be used to monitor multiple systems at the same time. Suppose you have five servers on your network and you want to ensure that none of the servers are overworked. In this case, you would configure a Performance Monitor alert for each server. An alert tells Performance Monitor that if a counter for a specific object exceeds a certain level, a message should be sent to a designated user. In this case, you would need to configure the Performance Monitor running on your workstation with an alert for each server.

Performance Monitor is a great tool for tracking information about your network, but all this monitoring, logging, and alerting can take up CPU time. If your workstation is suffering from over-monitoring, increase the monitoring interval or set up a separate workstation to do the monitoring. Increasing the monitoring interval means that you will not check statistics as often. SNMP is not installed on Windows NT computers by default; it is a service that must be configured manually. Once it has been installed, Performance Monitor can be used to monitor TCP/IP statistics for the local computer and any other computer with SNMP installed.

Performance Monitor can manage the following tasks:

- Recording the amount of information being handled by the network interface card.
- Tracking Internet Control Message Protocol (ICMP) messages that have been sent or received. The system can be even more granular by keeping tabs on error counts for the ICMP protocol.
- Counting the rates that IP datagrams are sent and received by a specific computer. It will track IP errors as well.
- Counting the rate that TCP segments are sent and received by a specific computer. It will track the number of connections in each TCP connection state.
- Counting the rate that UDP datagrams are sent and received. It will track UDP errors as well.
- Counting WINS objects that include the rates and statistics for WINS name registration and name resolution.
- Counting FTP server requests, logons, and file transfer activities.

Performance Monitor will not only log the data and alert you if there is a problem, it can also chart the data it gathers. If you want to view the information in chart format, Performance Monitor is the tool.

Performance Monitor provides charting and reporting functions necessary to provide a baseline of computer performance. This baseline is necessary to judge the success or failure of any optimization technique.

Suppose you have been monitoring a particular server for a few months and have noticed that you have been receiving more and more page file alerts. To check that you are not imagining things, you take the Performance Monitor information and chart it. You can use the chart function on either current information or by taking information for a Performance Monitor log.

Now that you know you have a problem, you have to solve the problem. You must provide NT Server with more to work with, so you add a lot more memory to the server and adjust the paging file size accordingly. Now, you want to check and find out if your solution actually worked. In this case, you can continue to monitor the paging file and after a week or so, take the statistics that you have gathered and chart them. If you compare the information from the baseline you established before adding the memory, you should see an improvement.

Command-Line Utilities

The rest of the tools discussed in this chapter are command-line utilities. A full description of syntax and options for each utility will be found in the "Necessary Procedures" section.

The ARP Utility

This command-line utility is not to be confused with the ARP protocol. The ARP command-line utility will show what entries are contained in the ARP address resolution table. The address resolution table contains the network card address or MAC address that is routed to each IP address. The ARP command can be used to check that the IP address you *suspect* is mapped to a particular network card actually *is* mapped to the network card. You might consider using ARP if you need to examine the IP address-to-MAC address resolution of outgoing packets from a Windows NT server. Here is an example of the output of the ARP command with the –a parameter, which displays the current address resolution protocol entries:

```
Interface: 209.46.15.148 on Interface 2

Internet Address   Physical Address   Type

209.46.15.130      00-c0-7b-6c-db-c0  dynamic
```

From the information above, you can see the NIC at address 209.46.15.148 found the gateway at address 209.46.15.130. This gateway had a physical address of 00-c0-7b-6c-db-c0. This entry in the ARP table is dynamic and will expire in just a few seconds.

IPCONFIG

This utility displays all the IP configuration parameters for the host on which the command is issued. This includes manually assigned addresses as well as addresses assigned by DHCP. Issuing the command IPCONFIG without any parameters will display the current TCP/IP configuration values, such as the IP address, the subnet mask, and the default gateway. You would use IPCONFIG if you had just changed the configuration on a host computer and you wanted to ensure the host had registered the change. To display the local system's configuration, you would use the IPCONFIG /ALL command.

An example of the output of an IPCONFIG command is shown below:

```
Windows NT IP Configuration
Ethernet adapter CE31:
IP Address. . . . . . . . . : 210.47.26.35
Subnet Mask . . . . . . . . : 255.255.255.224
IP Address. . . . . . . . . : 210.47.26.34
Subnet Mask . . . . . . . . : 255.255.255.224
IP Address. . . . . . . . . : 210.47.26.33
Subnet Mask . . . . . . . . : 255.255.255.224
Default Gateway . . . . . . : 210.47.26.1

Ethernet adapter elpc3r2:
IP Address. . . . . . . . . : 210.47.26.1
Subnet Mask . . . . . . . . : 255.255.255.224
Default Gateway . . . . . . : 210.47.26.62
```

From looking at the information above, you can see that the computer has two network cards—CE31 and elpc3r2. CE31 has several IP addresses bound to it, 210.47.26.33 through 210.47.26.33. It uses a subnet mask of 255.255.255.224 and points to a default gateway of

210.47.26.1. The card, elpc3r2, is address 210.47.26.1 with a subnet mask of 255.255.255.224 and its default gateway is 210.47.26.62.

NBTStat

NBTStat helps to figure out what is causing problems with NetBIOS name resolutions. NBTStat will let you view, remove, and correct the dynamic and static entries in the NetBIOS name cache.

Scenarios where NBTStat might be useful include the following:

- Ooops, someone goofs in the master LMHOSTS file. Somehow, the wrong information has been parsed into the name cache. NBTStat –R purges all the names in the NetBIOS name cache and then reloads the master LMHOSTS file.
- You are trying to view a list of all the NetBIOS computer names stored on your computer. In this case, the nbtstat –c command will list the local cached name, the service name, and the status.

Netstat

The Netstat command-line utility will allow you to check the current connections and protocol-related statistics from your host. It shows information about the amount of data that has been transferred as well as the number of packets that have been sent by several protocols including the following:

- IP (Internet Protocol)
- ICMP (Internet Control Message Protocol)
- TCP (Transmission Control Protocol)
- UDP (User Datagram Protocol)

The Netstat utility can be used to monitor the statistics of packets coming into a host based on the protocol (IP, TCP, and so on) or based on the topology (Ethernet). In addition, the Netstat utility is one of the ways you can view the host's route table. The command to view the route table would be netstat –r.

Some of the reasons to break Netstat out of your tool kit would be if you need to look at the route table of a local computer or if you have a computer with an Ethernet card. You want to monitor the number of TCP/IP related packets being handled by this network card. This is the output of netstat –r:

Active Routes:

Network Address	Netmask	Gateway Address	Interface	Metric
0.0.0.0	0.0.0.0	209.46.15.130	209.46.15.148	1
127.0.0.0	255.0.0.0	127.0.0.1	127.0.0.1	1
209.46.15.128	255.255.255.192	209.46.15.148	209.46.15.148	1
209.46.15.148	255.255.255.255	127.0.0.1	127.0.0.1	1
209.46.15.255	255.255.255.255	209.46.15.148	209.46.15.148	1
224.0.0.0	224.0.0.0	209.46.15.148	209.46.15.148	1
255.255.255.255	255.255.255.255	209.46.15.148	209.46.15.148	1

Route Table

Active Connections

Proto Local Address	Foreign Address	State
TCP psmain:1025	localhost:1026	ESTABLISHED
TCP psmain:1026	localhost:1025	ESTABLISHED

In the case of netstat –r, it shows both the active connections and the routing information that the server knows about. The first two entries to the route table are 0.0.0.0, or the local network, and 127.0.0.0, or the local computer. The gateway address for the local network is the address of the router connecting the network to the Internet, 209.46.15.130, and the interface address is the address of the NIC in the server.

The third listing of 209.46.15.128 points to the subnet of the local network the server resides on. That network uses a subnet mask of 255.255.255.192 and the gateway address is the address of the NIC in the server, 209.46.15.148.

The fourth listing is for the server NIC, 209.46.15.148. In this case, there is no subnet mask because any communication to this network card from this computer would be internal (the card is in the same computer). The gateway address and the interface address is 127.0.0.1, or loopback.

The next listing, 209.46.15.255, points to the local subnet broadcast address, which is why the subnet mask is 255.255.255.255. This means that if there is a broadcast to all systems on the subnet, this is the address the local computer will use.

The sixth listing, 224.0.0.0, is a multicast address. This is when the host would like to find information from multiple locations, for instance when a host is looking for all the routers on a network; it would send out a multicast packet.

The last address, 255.255.255.255, with a subnet of 255.255.255.255, is a general broadcast address. This means the packet will be sent to anyone and everyone on the system.

You will also notice that under active connections, the system has two TCP sessions opened on port address 1025 and 1026 with a foreign host. The connections have been established.

In all cases, the metric of 1 indicates the destination route is 1 hop away.

PING

When it comes to monitoring or optimization, one of the first tricks to pull out of your bag is the PING command. The PING command tests a physical connection between two devices. It can also be used to ensure that TCP/IP is properly configured on your local computer by using the 127.0.0.1 loopback address.

Here's what happens when you ping 127.0.0.1, or a local loopback address:

```
Pinging 127.0.0.1 with 32 bytes of data:
Reply from 127.0.0.1: bytes=32 time<10ms TTL=128
Reply from 127.0.0.1: bytes=32 time<10ms TTL=128
Reply from 127.0.0.1: bytes=32 time<10ms TTL=128
Reply from 127.0.0.1: bytes=32 time<10ms TTL=128
```

The example above shows that the computer pinged the network address 127.0.0.1 with 32 bytes of data. It received a response in less than 10 milliseconds and each packet had a time to live (TTL) of 128 milliseconds. Just to prove the results weren't a fluke, the ping packet was sent four times.

Here are some scenarios where the PING tool may be useful:

- **Communicating with a remote host.** After configuring TCP/IP on a computer, you want to ensure that the computer can communicate with a remote host. To test this communication, you would issue the PING command and the IP address or DNS name of the remote host.
- **Testing your complete network.** By starting with a PING command to the local loopback, progressing to the actual host IP address, and moving out one gateway at a time, you can test to make sure the communication channel is open.
- **Timing packets.** An end user has called to say the network appears slow. The PING command will also return the amount of time it takes to have to the packet sent to the destination host and returned. This can be a useful tool if you have properly set a baseline for your network.

Route

The route command can be used to display, add, or delete entries to the local route table. From a performance and optimization perspective, it can be used in conjunction with other commands to refine the route tables for a network.

Here are some scenarios where the route command would be useful:

- If you are trying to see the complete route table of a local computer, you can use the route print command to display the route table, including the network address, the subnet mask, the address of the gateway, the type of interface, and the metric.
- If you have a solid baseline of the network, you can alter the route table (depending on the communication infrastructure) to find which route will be the fastest.

Here is an example of the output of a route print command:

Active Routes:

Network Address	Netmask	Gateway Address	Interface	Metric
0.0.0.0	0.0.0.0	209.46.15.130	209.46.15.148	1
127.0.0.0	255.0.0.0	127.0.0.1	127.0.0.1	1
209.46.15.128	255.255.255.192	209.46.15.148	209.46.15.148	1
209.46.15.148	255.255.255.255	127.0.0.1	127.0.0.1	1
209.46.15.255	255.255.255.255	209.46.15.148	209.46.15.148	1
224.0.0.0	224.0.0.0	209.46.15.148	209.46.15.148	1
255.255.255.255	255.255.255.255	209.46.15.148	209.46.15.148	1

You will notice this is almost exactly like the netstat –r command without the local connection information. Because it is nearly the same, I will not explain every entry again.

SNMP

Simple Network Management Protocol (SNMP) allows TCP/IP to send information to other tools so the information can be collated and put into some useful format. SNMP is the piece of the puzzle that provides the facts about what is going on with your network. It is up to utilities such as SMS, Performance Monitor, or Network Monitor to make sense out of the information provided.

SEE ALSO An SNMP agent is available with NT Server, but it does have to be installed. For more information on the installation and configuration of SNMP, see Chapter 2, "Installation and Configuration."

Here are some scenarios where SNMP would be important:

- You want to use Performance Monitor on a workstation to gather information from all the NT Server computers on your network. In order to accomplish this task, SNMP would have to be installed on each server computer.
- You want to configure an NT Server computer to use Performance monitor to keep track of all the TCP/IP protocol statistics for that server. In this case, you would have to set up SNMP services for the NT Server computer.

TraceRT

The TraceRT utility is used to trace a route that a packet takes throughout the network. A scenario where using the TRACERT command would be appropriate is if your network includes 10 NT Server computers. Each computer is configured as a static router. You want to verify the path a message takes as it traverses the network. In this case, you would use the TRACERT command.

Here is something Hubert Humphrey could never find—the path from Minnesota to the White House:

NOTE For those of you too young to remember, Hubert Humphrey was a senator from Minnesota, the vice president under Lyndon Johnson, and a perennial presidential candidate. He was the Democrats' choice to run against Richard Nixon. After that defeat, he never made it out of the convention, where he lost to George McGovern and again to Jimmy Carter.

```
Tracing route to whitehouse.gov [198.137.241.30]

over a maximum of 30 hops:

 1  <10 ms  <10 ms  <10 ms 209.46.15.130

 2  30 ms  30 ms  30 ms gofast209-46-15.gofast.net
[209.46.15.1]

 3  30 ms  30 ms  30 ms 209.46.15.49

 4  40 ms  41 ms  60 ms 206.144.128.57

 5  40 ms  40 ms  60 ms grf-ge030.gofast.net
[204.73.51.254]

 6  40 ms  40 ms  40 ms gf-mr-upp-cis.gofast.net
[206.144.128.14]

 7  50 ms  60 ms  40 ms mrnet-GOFAST-2.MR.Net
[204.220.29.37]

 8  50 ms  50 ms  50 ms MUXNet-gw.mr.net
[204.220.31.254]

 9  60 ms  60 ms  60 ms sl-gw12-chi-12-0-
T3.sprintlink.net [144.228.157.41]

 10  50 ms  60 ms  60 ms sl-bb11-chi-1-2.sprintlink.net
[144.232.0.185]

 11  70 ms  60 ms  60 ms sl-bb1-roa-1-0-
0.sprintlink.net [144.232.8.186]

 12  70 ms  51 ms  90 ms 144.232.2.198

 13  80 ms  90 ms  80 ms sl-bb7-dc-6-1-0.sprintlink.net
[144.232.8.46]
```

```
 14  90 ms  101 ms  90 ms sl-bb6-dc-4-0-
0.sprintlink.net [144.232.0.10]

 15  371 ms  190 ms  170 ms 208.28.7.17

 16  80 ms  100 ms  140 ms sl-eop-1-0-T1.sprintlink.net
[144.228.72.66]

 17  90 ms  80 ms  80 ms whitehouse.gov
[198.137.241.30]

Trace complete.
```

You can see the packet leaves the local network, bounces around from an ISP's ISP, gofast.net. From there, it hits another level of ISP, mr.net. Once it leaves mr.net, it makes the big time, hitting the T3 connection (T3=very fast) at sprintlink. Sprintlink kicks the packet from router to router before it finally ends up at 198.137.241.30, the White House.

Necessary Procedures

The information in this chapter revolves around usage. In some cases, services must be installed before other services or utilities can be used. The utilities are presented in the following order, GUI-based utilities first, then the command-line utilities, and everything is in alphabetical order by type. Except SNMP. I know, there always has to be an exception. Because SNMP plays a role in several of the other performance monitors, it is important to get it out of the way first!

Installing SNMP

SNMP is a Windows NT Server service. To install it on a computer, follow these steps:

1. Select Start ➢ Settings ➢ Control Panel.
2. Double-click Network to open the Network window.
3. From the Network window, click the Services tab. Click Add.

4. Scroll down through the Network Service screen until you can highlight SNMP Service. Once it has been highlighted, click OK.
5. Provide the path to set up files and click Continue.
6. At this point, the Microsoft SNMP Properties Agent screen will be brought up.

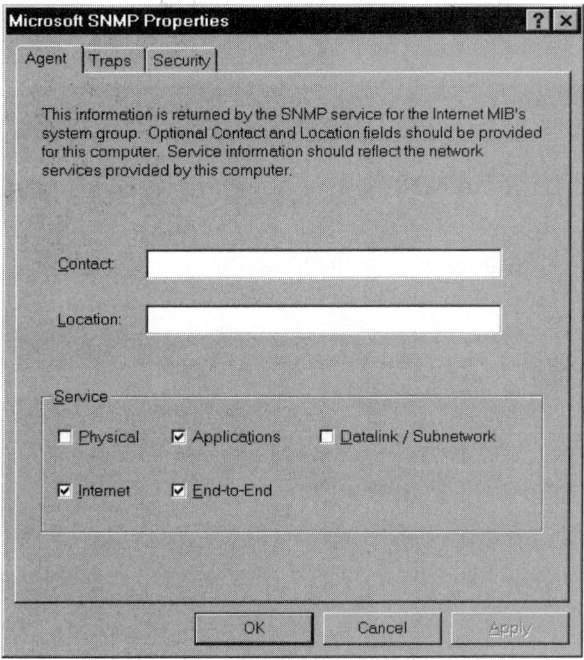

7. The Contact and Location information shown above are optional and for informational use only. The Services include the following:
   - **Physical:** This option is selected if the agent manages a physical device, such as a concentrator or repeater.
   - **Applications:** This option would be selected if the SNMP agent used any TCP/IP applications. This selection should always be checked.
   - **Datalink/Subnetwork:** This option should be selected if the agent manages a bridge.

- **Internet:** Select this option if the agent manages an IP router or gateway.
- **End-to-End:** Select this option if the Agent functions as an IP host.

8. Errors that occur with the SNMP service will be logged automatically and can be viewed in the System Log in the Event Viewer.

WARNING After installing SNMP services, it is very important that you reapply the latest patch. Several older files are copied during the SNMP installation.

---

9. After configuring the SNMP Agent screen, you can click on the Traps tab. The result is shown below.

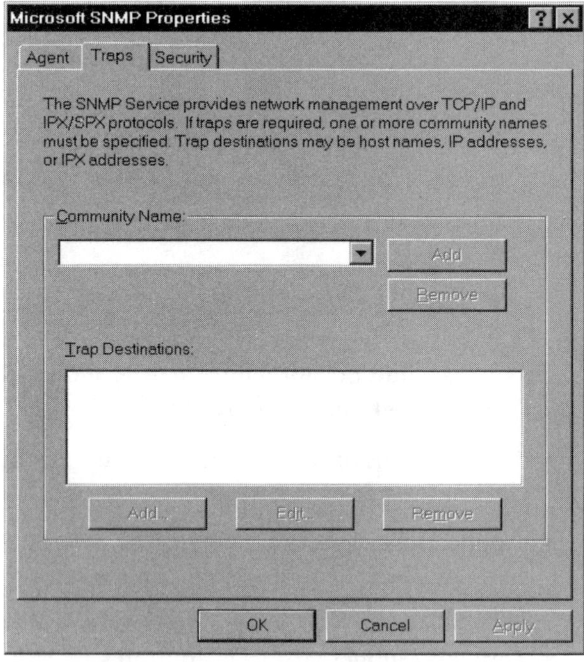

10. Traps may or may not be required. If you enter and add a community name, it will be sent with the trap message. You must then define a management system for the community you defined. The default community name is public. Trap destinations are the IP address of the SNMP manager.

11. Clicking on the Security tab will bring up the screen shown below.

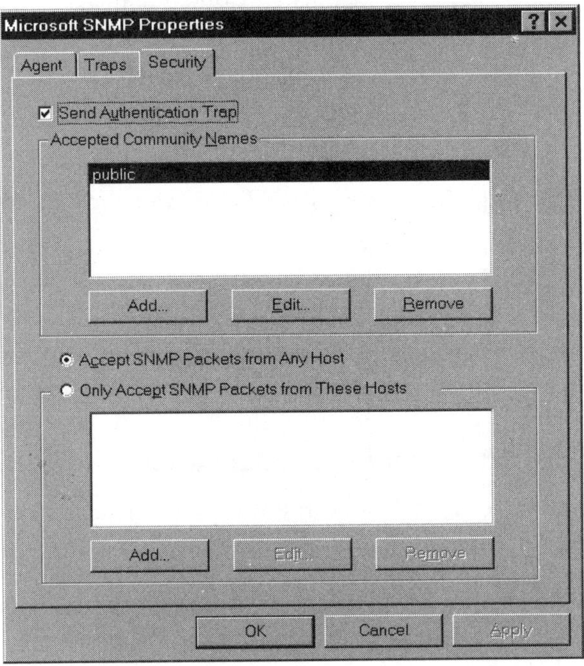

12. When you check Send Authentication Trap, it allows the SNMP agent to send a failed request trap to the SNMP manager when it gets a request for information from an unknown host or manager.

13. Accepted Community Names are the communities the agent belongs to. An agent can belong to multiple communities.

14. Accept SNMP Packets from Any Host allows the agent to accept a request from any SNMP manager in its community.

15. Only Accept SNMP Packets from These Hosts specifies which managers can request information from the agent.

Installing Network Monitor

Unlike Performance Monitor, which is an integral part of Windows NT Server, Network Monitor (even the version that does not come with SMS) needs to be installed. Follow these steps to install Network Monitor:

1. Select Start ➤ Settings ➤ Control Panel.
2. Double-click Network.
3. Click the Services tab.
4. Click Network Monitor Tools and Agent, then click OK.
5. Provide the path to the NT files and click Continue.
6. Click Close to shut the Network window.
7. Shut down and restart the computer.

Network Monitor will let you capture and interpret network traffic that is sent by or received by the local computer.

Capturing Packets with Network Monitor

To use Network Monitor, start by capturing packets processed by the local computer. Follow these steps to capture packets:

1. Click Start ➤ Programs ➤ Administrative Tools (Common), then click on Network Monitor. This will bring up the screen shown below.

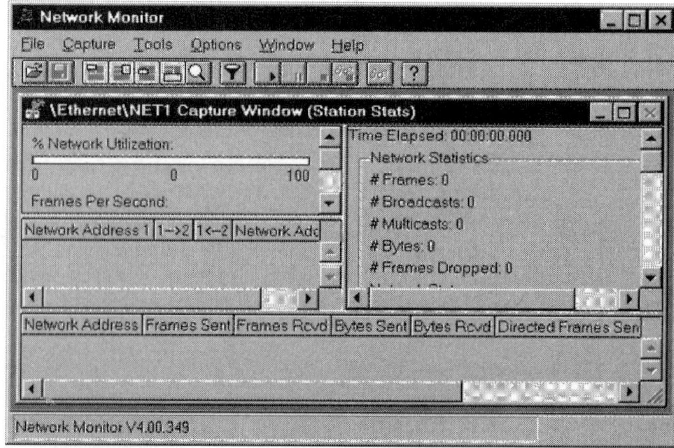

2. To begin capturing packets, select Capture from the Network Monitor menu, then click Start. You can also use the F10 key to start the capture.

3. To stop capturing packets, select Capture from the Network Monitor menu, then click Stop. You can also use the F11 key to stop the capture. When you have completed the capture, your screen will look like this:

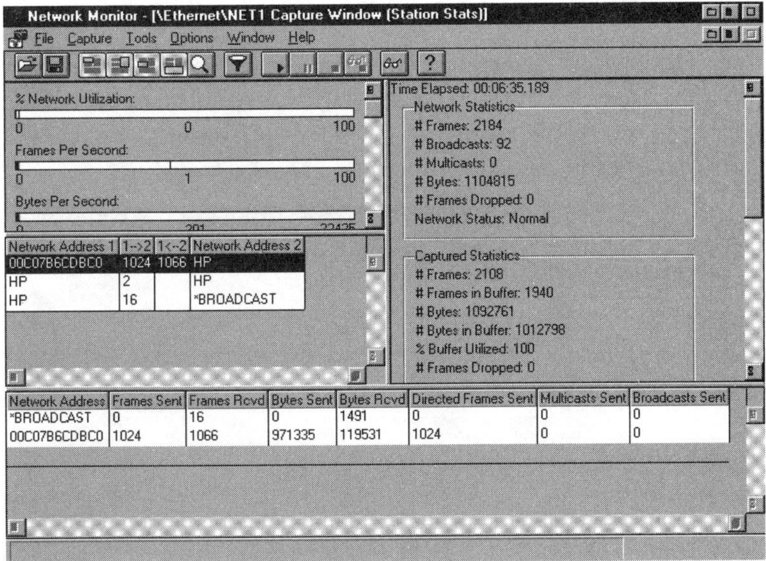

4. To save the captured packets for later review, select File ➤ Save As from the Network Monitor menu and enter a file name and location.

5. Click OK.

Now that you have captured and saved all this data, it is time to use the next piece of Network Monitor, the part that will allow you to manipulate the data. The Monitor tool can allow you to look at the packets captured or just filter out and view those packets that will help in your optimization of the network. Follow these steps to view the captured packets:

1. From the Network Monitor menu, choose Capture ➤ Display Captured Data. You can also use the F12 key.

2. You can display individual packets by highlighting the packet and double-clicking.

Filtering Packets with Network Monitor

If the information shown is a little intimidating, you can simplify your life by filtering out the packets you don't want to look at. For example, if you just want to view all TCP/IP packets, you can create a filter by following these steps:

1. From the Network Monitor menu, choose Display ➤ Filter. The Display Filter screen is shown below. It can be accessed in a variety of ways. In addition to the menu selection, you can use the F8 key, or even the funnel shown on the Taskbar.

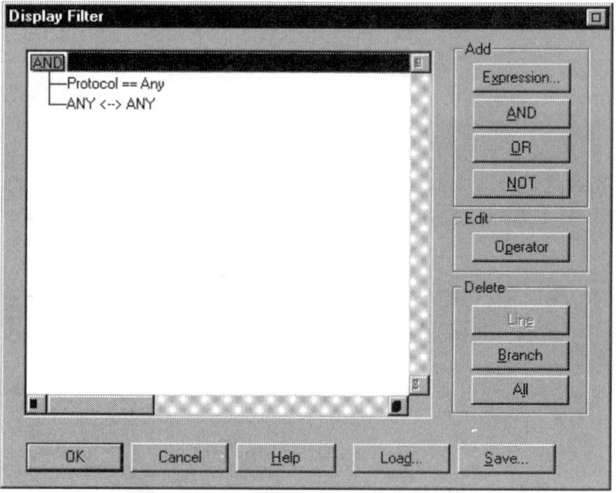

2. To filter DNS packets only, the filter needs to be refined. Start by highlighting the line that says Protocol= Any and then click the Operator button under Edit on the right side of the window.
3. The Expression screen will be displayed. At this time, all protocols are enabled for this filter, so rather than disabling dozens of individual protocols to get to the two we want, click Disable All.
4. From the Disabled Protocols window, scroll down and find DNS. When you find the selection, highlight it, click Enable, and it will

move back to the Enabled Protocols side of the screen. After this has been completed, click OK to return to the Display Filter screen.

5. You can save the Protocol filter for later use by clicking the Save button on the Display Filter screen and giving the filter a name.
6. From the Display Filter screen click OK.
7. While this screen seems to give a lot of information, there is even more off to the right margin. Slide the bar at the bottom of the screen and you will see several other columns including source address, destination address, and type of address.
8. To display the contents of a particular packet, double-click on the packet. You can also use the Window option for the Network Monitor menu to look at information in the packet in detail, summary, or even in hex. Throughout this entire book, we have been talking about packets. Below is an example of some information contained in the average packet. Entire books have been written on the information contained here; suffice it to say, this packet contains all the data it needs to bring information from one spot to another.

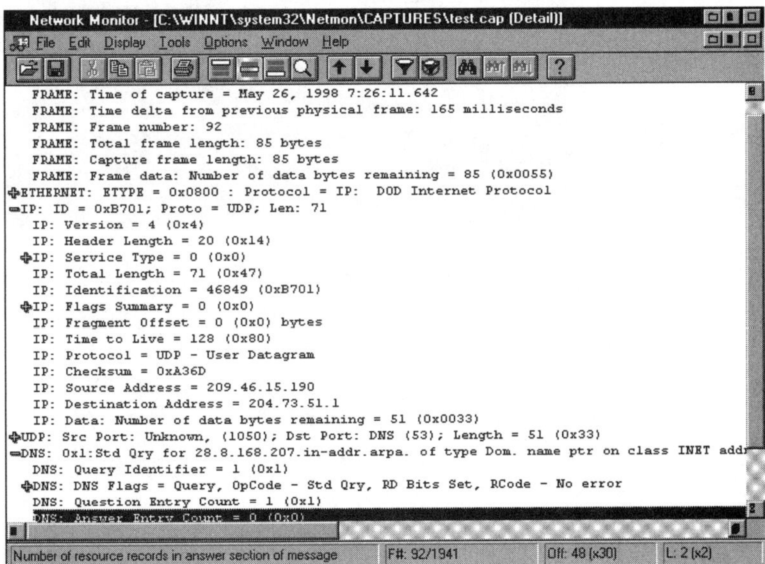

TIP For the sake of the exam, it is important to remember that Network Monitor comes in two flavors, one from Windows NT and one from SMS. The SMS version can gather information from remote computers. Also, SNMP needs to be installed before Network Monitor can perform adequately.

Creating Charts with Performance Monitor

Follow these steps to create a chart with Performance Monitor:

1. Start Performance Monitor by clicking Start ➤ Programs ➤ Administrative Tools (Common), then click on Performance Monitor.
2. To add items to check, click on the plus sign (+) on the Performance Monitor Taskbar. This will bring up the Add to Chart screen shown below.

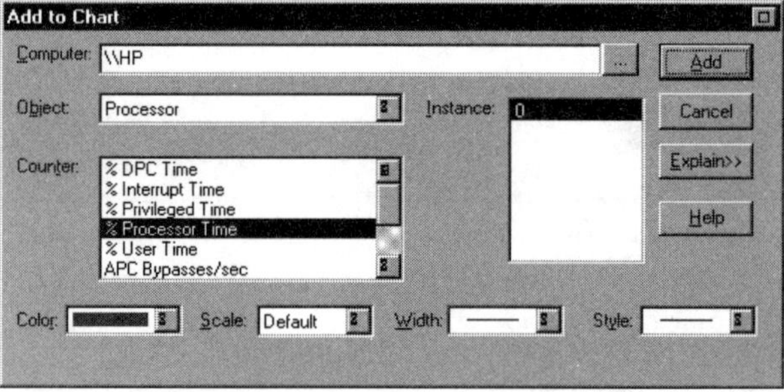

3. Using the drop-down menu from the Object section, you can choose what you want to monitor. For example, you could choose to monitor the network segment total frames received per second, total bytes received per second, and the percentage of network utilization. The choices you make are totally configurable for whatever baseline you want to construct. Clicking Done will start the monitoring process.

Once you have gathered the information, you can use it in raw form, or if it needs to be manipulated, you can export the information from Performance Manager and import it into either an Access database or an Excel spreadsheet.

TIP For the sake of testing, understand that Performance Monitor is used for setting baselines. Baselines should be gathered over those parts of the day when the network is in use, after all we want to find out how much the network is currently being used before we make any changes. Don't fudge the statistics by only running your baseline during peak periods either, that is cheating.

Using ARP

Depending on the given scenario, the ARP command can be useful in several ways. This is the syntax for the ARP command:

```
ARP -s [ipaddress][ethernet_address][target_address]
ARP -d [ipaddress][target_address]
ARP -a [ipaddress][-N target_address]
```

Table 4.1 explains all of the command-line options.

TABLE 4.1: ARP command-line options

Options	Descriptions
Ipaddress	Specifies the IP address to resolve.
Ethernet _address	Specifies the MAC address to resolve.
Target_address	Specifies the IP address of the network interface card whose ARP table should be changed.
-a	Displays the current ARP table data.
-d	Deletes the host specified by the ipaddress.
-s	Adds the host specified by the ipaddress using the ethernet_address as the MAC address. The MAC address should be 6 hexadecimal bytes separated by hyphens.
-N	Displays the ARP address for the NIC specified by the target_address.

Using IPCONFIG

This is the syntax for IPCONFIG:

```
ipconfig [/all][/release adapter][/renew adapter]
```

Table 4.2 explains the IPCONFIG command-line options.

TABLE 4.2: IPCONFIG command-line options

Options	Description
/all	Displays full configuration information.
/release	Releases the IP address for the specified adapter.
/renew	Renews the IP address for the specified adapter.

Using NBTStat

The NBTSTAT command has the following syntax:

```
Nbtstat [-a remotename][-A IPAddress][-c][-n][-R][-r][-
S][-s][interval]
```

Table 4.3 explains all the NBTStat command-line options.

TABLE 4.3: NBTStat command-line options

Options	Description
Nbtstat –a *remotename*	Lists the remote computer's NetBIOS name table.
Nbtstat –A *ipaddress*	Using the remote computer's ipaddress, lists the remote computer's NetBIOS name table.
Nbtstat –c	Lists the contents of the NetBIOS name cache by IP address.

TABLE 4.3: NBTStat command-line options *(continued)*

Options	Description
Nbtstat –n	Lists the local NetBIOS names.
Nbtstat –R	Purges the NetBIOS name cache and reloads the LMHOSTS file.
Nbtstat –r	Lists name resolution statistics for WINS resolution.
Nbtstat –S	Displays workstation and server sessions. All remote computers are listed by IP address only.
Nbtstat –s	Displays workstation and server sessions. All remote computers are listed by name as well as IP address. All name resolution services are used, including HOSTS and LMHOSTS.
Interval	Reshows selected statistics, pausing a specific number of seconds between each display.

The output from an NBTSTAT command is displayed in a table format. Table 4.4 shows what each of the column headings mean.

TABLE 4.4: Table column headings for NBTStat

Column Heading	Description
IN	Number of bytes received by the local computer.
OUT	Number of bytes sent by the local computer.
IN/OUT	Tells if the connection is inbound or outbound.
LIFE	Remaining Time To Live (TTL) before a computer name is purged.

TABLE 4.4: Table column headings for NBTStat *(continued)*

Column Heading	Description
Local Name	Local NetBIOS name associated with the connection.
Remote Host	Computer name or IP address of the remote computer.
Type	The type of name; it can be either unique or a group name.
<03>	Each NetBIOS name is 16 characters long. The 16th byte is used to indicate the NetBIOS applications that identify themselves using the NetBIOS computer name.
State	State of the NetBIOS connection.

The possible states of a NetBIOS connection are contained in Table 4.5.

TABLE 4.5: NBTStat connection states

State	Description
Connected	A session has been established.
Associated	A connection endpoint has been established and it has been resolved to an IP address.
Listening	The connection end point is available to inbound connections.
Idle	The end point has been opened, but it is not able to accept any connections.
Connecting	The name-to-IP address resolution of the destination is being completed.
Accepting	An inbound session is in the process of being connected.

TABLE 4.5: NBTStat connection states *(continued)*

State	Description
Reconnecting	A session is attempting to reconnect after a failure.
Outbound	A session is still in the Connecting phase; the TCP connection is now being created.
Inbound	An inbound session is being created.
Disconnecting	The session is in the process of terminating.
Disconnected	The local computer has issued a disconnect and is awaiting the confirmation from the remote computer.

Using Netstat

The Netstat utility has parameters that can be helpful. This is the syntax for the NETSTAT command:

```
NETSTAT [-a][-e][-n][-s][-p protocol][-r][interval]
```

Table 4.6 gives a summary of these parameters.

TABLE 4.6: Netstat options

Options	Description
-a	Shows all connections to the host. Server connections are not shown.
-e	Shows statistics based on the Ethernet adapter. May be used with the -s parameter.
-s	Shows statistics based on the protocol. Default protocols are UDP, ICMP, IP, and TCP.
-n	Shows addresses and port numbers in numerical format rather than computer or DNS name.

TABLE 4.6: Netstat options *(continued)*

Options	Description
-p protocol	Shows connections and statistics by a specific protocol. Can be used with the –s parameter
-r	Shows the contents of the routing table
Interval	Refreshes the statistics at this interval, in seconds.

Using PING

This is the syntax for the PING command:

```
PING [-t][-a][-n count][-l size][-f][-I TTL][-v TOS][-r
count][-s count][[-j host -list][-k host -list]][-w
timeout]destination -list
```

Table 4.7 explains how each option can be used.

TABLE 4.7: PING options

Options	Description
-t	Pings the specified host until stopped. To stop, press Ctrl+C.
-a	Resolves IP address to host names.
-n count	Number of echo requests to send.
-l size	Specifies the buffer size.
-f	Sets the Don't Fragment flag in a packet.
-I TTL	Displays Time To Live (TTL).
-v TOS	Display Type of Service.
-r count	Records the route to count the hops.
-s count	Timestamp for hop counts.

TABLE 4.7: PING options *(continued)*

Options	Description
-j host-list	Loose route along a host list.
-k host-list	Strict route along a host list.
-w timeout	Time in milliseconds to wait for reply.

Using Route

This is the syntax for the route command:

```
route [-f] [-p] [command [destination] [MASK netmask]
[gateway] [METRIC metric]]
```

Table 4.8 explains the options for the route command.

TABLE 4.8: Route options

Options	Description
-f	Purges the route table of all entries. If this parameter is used prior to using a command, the tables are cleared before the command is run.
-p	Enables persistent routes. This parameter will enter the route into the route table and the route will remain after the system has been reset. This parameter will keep the route in the table until route –f is run.
MASK netmask	Specifies that the next entry will be the subnet mask associated with this entry. The default is 255.255.255.255.
Gateway	IP address of the gateway to the destination.
METRIC *metric*	Associates a cost/hop count with this entry.

In addition to the parameters listed above, there are several commands that can be used in conjunction with the route command. These commands are summarized in Table 4.9.

TABLE 4.9: Route commands

Command	Description
Print	Prints a route.
Add	Adds a route.
Change	Changes a route.
Delete	Deletes a route.
Destination	The host or network to which you are going to route.

Using TraceRT

This is the syntax for the TRACERT command:

```
Tracert [-d][-h maximum hops][-j host-list][-w timeout]
target_name
```

Table 4.10 explains the options that can be used with TraceRT.

TABLE 4.10: TraceRT options

Options	Description
-d	Putting in the –d switch tells the command not to resolve addresses to hostnames.
-h maximum hops	Maximum number of hops to search for target.
-j host_list	Loose source route along host_list.
-w timeout	Wait the timeout number of milliseconds for each reply.
Target_name	The name of the target host for the trace route.

Exam Essentials

Know when to use Network Monitor. Network Monitor can capture and view the protocol statistics for TCP/IP traffic for a given time period. An administrator can then use that information to analyze traffic by device or by protocol. You can use Network Monitor's capture filters and display filter options to choose just what you want to monitor.

Know when to use Performance Monitor. Performance Monitor charts the data it gathers. If you want to view the information in chart format, Performance Monitor is the tool. You can also export the information you have gathered into other formats, such as a spreadsheet.

Know when to use ARP. You would use the ARP command if you needed to examine the IP address-to-MAC address resolution of outgoing packets from a Windows NT Server.

Know when to use IPCONFIG. Use this command-line utility if you have just changed the configuration on a computer and you want to ensure it has registered the change. To display the local system configuration, you would use the IPCONFIG /ALL command.

Know when to use NBTStat. If misinformation has been parsed into cache from a corrupted LMHOSTS file, this information can be purged using the NBTStat –R command. This purges all the names in the NetBIOS name cache and then reloads the LMHOSTS file. To see the local cached computer names, use the NBTSTAT –c command.

Know when to use Netstat. The NETSTAT command is best known for being able to view statistics based on a particular network card. Besides that use, you can also use netstat –r to view the local route table.

Know when to use PING. The PING command is used to check the physical connection between two cards. It can be used to check a network by progressively working your way out from a workstation to a remote host through a maze of routers and gateways. It can also be used as a low-level verification of the speed of the network.

Know when to use Route. The primary purpose for the route command is to add routes to a route table. You can also use the route print command to display the route table, including the network address, the subnet mask, the address of the gateway, the type of interface, and the metric.

Know when to use SNMP. You want to use Performance Monitor on a workstation to gather information from all the NT Server computers on your network. In order to accomplish this task, SNMP would have to be installed on each server computer.

Know when to use TraceRT. Consider this scenario. Your network includes 10 NT Server computers. Each computer is configured as a static router. You want to verify the path a message takes as it traverses the network. In this case, you would use the TRACERT command.

Key Terms and Concepts

ARP: A command-line utility that shows IP address-to-hardware address resolution.

DHCP (Dynamic Host Configuration Protocol): Provides dynamic configuration of TCP/IP hosts by providing an IP address and other information, including the subnet mask, default gateway, and WINS Server.

ICMP (Internet Control Message Protocol): Handles error messages when datagrams or packets have been corrupted or discarded. The ICMP will also provide messaging in the case of systems that are overworked.

IP (Internet Protocol): The routable protocol that computers use to communicate over the Internet.

IPCONFIG: A command-line utility that shows the current IP configuration for a network card or for a host.

LMHOSTS: A text file that aids in the resolution of NetBIOS computer names to IP addresses.

Loopback: A reserved IP address of 127.0.0.1 that is used to check the IP configuration on a local host.

MAC address: The Media Access Control layer or hardware address.

NBTStat: A command-line utility that shows the effectiveness of the NetBIOS-to-IP address resolution.

NetBIOS: A protocol used on Windows networks to provide host identification by computer name.

Netstat: A command-line utility that shows the current state of the network.

PING: A command-line utility used to test the physical connection between two hosts.

Route: A command-line utility used to add, delete, or print information from a static routing table.

SNMP (Simple Network Management Protocol): A protocol used to control or monitor devices on a computer network.

TCP (Transmission Control Protocol): A connection-oriented communications protocol that is used by hosts on the Internet.

TraceRT: A command-line utility that is used to show the route a packet takes from one host to another host.

UDP (User Datagram Protocol): A connectionless-oriented protocol used by hosts. As a connectionless protocol, delivery of packets is not guaranteed.

Sample Questions

1. Before starting to optimize a network, you must establish:

   A. Which utilities you will use.

   B. Which protocols to monitor.

   C. Which hosts to monitor.

   D. A baseline.

   Answer: D. Before you can optimize a network, you must know how the network is currently performing. This is done with a baseline.

2. There are two ways of displaying a static route table for a local host. These are:

   A. By using the route print command

   B. By using the route display command

   C. By using the netstat –r command

   D. By using the netstat –d command

   Answer: A and C. The two ways of displaying a local static route table are by using the route print command or the netstat –r command.

3. You want to check the physical connection between host 125.4.5.6 and host 201.7.8.9. The command you would use to do that is:

   A. TPING

   B. WINPING

   C. TCPING

   D. PING

   Answer: D. The PING command will check the physical connection between the two hosts.

4. You want to check the route a packet takes between host 125.4.5.6 and host 201.7.8.9. The command you would use to do that is:

   A. TRACEPING

   B. TRACERT

   C. TRACEIP

   D. TRACEUDP

   Answer: B. The TRACERT command will show the route a packet takes between two hosts.

CHAPTER 5

Troubleshooting

Microsoft Exam Objectives Covered in This Chapter:

- **Diagnose and resolve IP addressing problems.** *(pages 281 – 287)*

- **Use Microsoft TCP/IP utilities to diagnose IP configuration problems.** *(pages 288 – 300)*
  - Identify which Microsoft TCP/IP utility to use to diagnose IP configuration problems.

- **Diagnose and resolve name resolution problems.** *(pages 301 – 306)*

Now let's see if I can sneak this past the editors. Sometimes, they think I don't like end users, but in reality I love end users. They help me pay my bills. The first law of network computing states: End users lie! Always! There are no exceptions. Now, before you get too big a smile on your face, remember, system administrators are the world's best end users. Therefore, logic says system administrators are the best liars.

Now, don't take this personally. Just think about the last time you did any troubleshooting. The first question we are trained to ask is, "What has changed?" Whenever I have asked that question, I have only received one answer. That answer has never varied, ever, and the answer is, "Nothing." After asking some deep probing questions such as, "Was the motherboard always laying on the floor?" I usually found that someone had in fact changed something immediately before the problem started.

Now, don't get me wrong, I lie as much as the next person. What makes it even worse is that I lie to myself. How many times have you been troubleshooting a problem and spent hours on it absolutely convinced it had nothing to do with the new vertical "ferbliztser" you just installed. Been there, done that, got the tee shirt. That is how we learn troubleshooting.

Effective troubleshooting of TCP/IP is a strange mixture of science and art. On a good day, it's 75 percent art and 25 percent science. On a bad day the figures may be more 90 percent science and 10 percent art. *Art* in this context means looking at a problem, immediately recognizing the symptoms, making one small change, and everything works. You walk away congratulating yourself on a job well done and how wonderful it is to know the answer to a question right away. Of course, you have long since forgotten the 10 times you worked on the same problem before, usually for an hour at a time, to solve it.

The *science* comes in when you look at a problem and while maintaining your cool exterior in front of the client you are screaming inside, "I have no clue what is going on here!" At that point, you start at the beginning and test each piece of the subsystem, one step at a time, before you find the piece that fails. This takes a lot longer, is not as exciting, but usually when finished is just as ego gratifying.

TCP/IP problems can be solved the same way; try and find what has changed and take things from the beginning, one step at a time until you see what fails. The trick here is to recognize the infrastructure so you can see what pieces need to be tested. That is some of the material we will cover in this section.

When you get to the troubleshooting part of the exam, the questions are usually straightforward. There are a few of those, "Given the following situation…" kinds of questions, but when you weed through all the excess information and get to the meat of the issue, things usually become clear.

Diagnose and resolve IP addressing problems.

IP addressing problems are usually pretty easy to diagnose. Something isn't able to talk with something else. That is usually the first clue that something is wrong on your network.

Critical Information

Addressing problems usually come in two flavors. Something or someone has hosed a network address, or something or someone has hosed a host address. Because every host address is made up of just those two pieces, that pretty much covers it. This is also a fairly insidious problem because Windows NT won't recognize an improper IP address. It will just boot and go on like it's supposed to. It may even be sending the packets out the back of the machine, just like it's supposed too. The only problem is that the packets might as well be falling out on the floor for all the good it's doing.

Network Addressing Problem

In the case of an incorrect network address, you would have two computers on the same subnet with a different network address. If you remember the section on subnets back in Chapter 2, "Installation and Configuration," you recall that some different network numbers can be just a couple of addresses apart. When a host sends a packet, it looks at the destination address of the packet. It ANDs the destination address and if the destination address does not appear to be on the same subnet, the packet is sent to the gateway and out to the rest of the world to bounce around until the TTL expires and the packet is thrown out. Having a workstation with the wrong network address will cause just that sort of thing to happen.

For example, say I am installing a new workstation on someone's desk. I install the workstation and check the next nearest down stream neighbor (for example, the cube next door) to see what IP address that computer is using. I note that the IP address is 210.47.15.30 with a subnet mask of 255.255.255.224. Logically, because the two computers are right next to each other and plug into the same subnet, the two numbers should be close. You use the PING utility to check 210.47.15.29 and find that it has been assigned. You try 210.47.15.31 and don't get a response. You figure the number has got to be unassigned, so you assign it to the new computer. Unfortunately, 210.47.15.30 is on the edge of the subnet. This means 210.47.15.31 is an invalid address and therefore will be accepted by Windows NT, but not used by IP in any worthwhile way.

Symptoms of network addressing problems: The systems will not be able to communicate with other computers on the network.

Solution to the network addressing problems: Use the appropriate network address for the subnet. When in doubt, figure it out.

Host Addressing Problems

While using the wrong network address is common, using the same host address is even more common. Consider this scenario. You have a valid network address and a valid host address; the problem is the host address has already been assigned. This problem rears its ugly head in several ways.

The first exposure is the easiest to troubleshoot. In this case, you assign the same host address to two different Windows NT–based computers on the same network.

Symptoms of a host addressing problem: Windows will recognize the problem at start-up, generate an error message to the screen, and make an entry to the log. The second system to come online will not initialize TCP/IP and will not be able to communicate.

Solution to the host addressing problem: Assign unique host addresses. Documentation is always a good thing here.

NOTE I am truly sorry, but there will be times when I will have to use vulgar, base, disgusting language to describe how to solve a problem. For those of you with strict sensibilities, I apologize for the use of the word "documentation."

The next exposure to the host addressing problem is when you assign the same host ID to two computers on the same network running different operating systems.

Symptoms of the host addressing problems: Both computers will have trouble communicating across the network. The trick to solving this problem is to be aware of what is happening on your network. This may show up as an intermittent problem (after all, both computers may not be on at the same time). It is difficult sometimes to realize that the dual address is the problem.

Solution to the host addressing problem: Change the IP address of one of the hosts to a valid, unassigned address and see if the problem goes away. Be sure to document the new assignment.

What would happen if a sender tried to send information to a system with a duplicate address?

Symptom of the host addressing problem: The transmission would flat-out fail. The sending hosts seems to work just fine when communicating with other systems on the network; the problem arises when it tries to send a message to the hosts with the duplicate address.

Solution to the host addressing problem: Change the IP address of one of the hosts to a valid, unassigned address and see if the problem goes away. Be sure to document the new assignment.

Finally, what would happen if a system had already been booted up and was happily communicating with other systems on the network and another system with the same IP address was brought online?

Symptom of the host addressing problem: The established session might end unexpectedly and the host systems might freeze up.

Solution to the host addressing problem: Change the IP address of one of the hosts to a valid, unassigned address and see if the problem goes away. Be sure to document the new assignment.

Necessary Procedures

NOTE This section does not involve any installations or reconfigurations. If you are unsure of the syntax for the PING command, see the "Necessary Procedures" section of the objective, "Use Microsoft TCP/IP utilities to diagnose IP configuration problems," later in this chapter.

Exam Essentials

There are some questions asked on this section. The questions usually revolve around "What happens if...?"

Know what happens when a host has the wrong network address. A host with the wrong network address will not be able to communicate with another host.

Know what happens when two Windows NT systems share the same IP address. In this case, each system will display an error message and the message will be written to the log.

Know what happens when two hosts, using two different operating systems, share the same IP address. Both systems will be unable to communicate. The systems may freeze up or stop working.

Key Terms and Concepts

Duplicate address: Two computers sharing the exact network and host address.

Host address: An IP address is made up of a network address and a host address. The host address uniquely identifies a single host computer.

Network address: An IP address is made up of a network address and host address. The network address uniquely identifies a network segment.

Sample Questions

1. You have just finished configuring a Microsoft NT Workstation to use TCP/IP. You have manually assigned an IP address. Unfortunately, it is the same IP address that one of your coworkers has previously assigned to another Windows NT Workstation computer. The other computer is currently online. You restart your workstation. What is the expected result?

   A. The first computer to come online will continue to work. The second computer will not finish its start-up procedures.

   B. An error message will be displayed on the screen of the newest computer to come online.

   C. The computer that is already logged onto the network will be immediately restarted.

   D. If the computer that is already logged in is using DHCP, it will ask for and receive a new IP address.

   Answer: B. An error message will be displayed, saying that a duplicate address has been detected.

2. Two computers, one running Windows NT and another running UNIX, share the same IP address. What is one of the expected outcomes of this situation?

   A. Both systems will have trouble communicating on the network.

   B. Only the last system to be authenticated will not be able to communicate on the network.

   C. Only the first system to be authenticated will not be able to communicate on the network.

   D. Both systems will automatically restart, no matter what the systems are currently doing.

Answer: A. When the second computer comes on the network, both systems will have problems communicating.

3. You have just finished configuring a Microsoft NT Workstation to use TCP/IP. You have manually assigned an IP address. Unfortunately, the host address is correct, but the network address is wrong. What is the expected result?

   A. The computer to come online will continue to work.

   B. An error message will be displayed on the screen when the computer comes online.

   C. The computer will not be able to communicate.

   D. If the computer that is using DHCP, it will ask for and receive a new IP address.

   Answer: C. The computer will start, but it will not be able to communicate.

4. A host on a different subnet is communicating with a host on the subnet you manage. Your assistant starts a Windows computer with an IP address of the computer that is already working and communicating with a different subnet. What are the expected results?

   A. The established session may terminate.

   B. The hosts may lock up.

   C. The second computer may automatically restart.

   D. The second computer will not complete start-up.

   Answer: A and B. The established session will terminate and the hosts may lock up.

Use Microsoft TCP/IP utilities to diagnose IP configuration problems.

- Identify which Microsoft TCP/IP utility to use to diagnose IP configuration problems.

So far, we haven't talked about the utilities that Microsoft provides to work with IP. There are several and they are all helpful. In this section, each will be discussed, as well as when is the best time to break out the utilities and put them through the paces.

Critical Information

In the previous objective section it was shown that there are several reasons why two hosts would not be able to communicate because of addressing problems. There must be other ways to check the communications links.

Using Microsoft TCP/IP Utilities to Diagnose IP Configuration Problems

When Microsoft TCP/IP is installed, it adds several command-line utilities to your troubleshooting arsenal. These utilities are listed below:

- **PING** is used to check a physical connection between two hosts.
- **ARP** is not to be confused with the acronym for the Address Resolution Protocol. The ARP utility will allow you to look at the ARP cache on a machine to determine if there are any invalid entries.
- **Netstat** is designed to check the protocol status and the number of TCP/IP connections.
- **NBTStat** helps display the status of NetBIOS over TCP/IP. NBTStat has several switches that enhance its performance.

NOTE NBTStat will be discussed in more detail as part of the next objective.

- **IPCONFIG** is an all-purpose workstation utility. It shows the status of how the workstation is configured. It allows the user to release a DHCP address or renew the lease.
- **TraceRT** will let you verify the route between the sender and the receiver.
- **Route** will add routes to the local route table, delete routes, or view the table.
- **NSLOOKUP** is one of the more powerful TCP/IP command-line utilities used specifically for troubleshooting. It will allow you to access information from DNS servers and display the information it receives. If you wanted to find the computer, education.microsoft.com, you could use the NSLOOKUP command to do so. NSLOOKUP will also return information on the DNS server itself or information on individual domain names. For example, I needed to know how my e-mail was being sent to my ISP. Using NSLOOKUP, I was able to find the records pointing all e-mail to my ISP's server.

SEE ALSO See Chapter 4, "Monitoring and Optimization," for details on the command-line utilities listed above.

Identifying Which Microsoft TCP/IP Utility to Use to Diagnose IP Configuration Problems

When troubleshooting problems with TCP/IP or any other protocol, the first thing to determine is who or what is affected. If it is one or two hosts, the troubleshooting is much different than if a group of hosts or an entire network segment is down.

As strange as this may sound, it is usually much easier to arrive at the source of a problem if an entire network segment is down than it is to work with just one or two isolated workstations. After all, if 100 workstations cannot communicate, there are very few common points of failure to test. With one or two workstations, the possibilities may seem endless!

For the sake of this discussion, refer to Figure 5.1, which is a very simplified map of a network.

FIGURE 5.1: A simple network map for troubleshooting

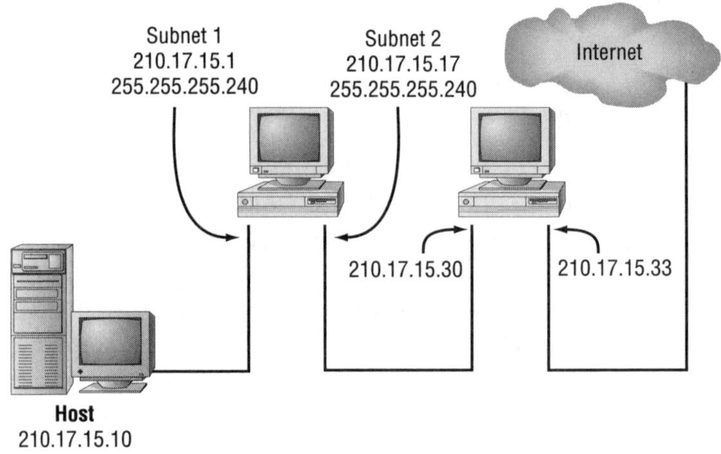

Let us assume that you are at host 210.17.15.10 and you are trying to find the Web site, http:\\www.microsoft.com. Now, because you are a geek (admit it), instead of using the URL, you are going to use the IP address of 207.46.130.17. For some reason, it just doesn't go through and you want to know why.

Now, there is always more than one way to troubleshoot a problem, that is a fact of life. When taking an MCSE test, however, there are exactly two ways of doing everything: the Microsoft way and the wrong way. Here is the Microsoft way of solving this TCP/IP problem.

First, you determine if TCP/IP is configured right on the host. This can be done by going to the command prompt and using the IPCONFIG /ALL command. This will tell you if your network cards have an IP address, if they have a path to the default gateway, and if the subnet mask is correct. Assuming that all this is correct, while you are the command line, you can use the PING utility to ping 127.0.0.1. That is the local loopback address. A *local loopback* means, is this sucker working? (The term "this sucker" is a highly technical name for the host you are sitting at.)

If the ping to 127.0.0.1 is working, then you begin to branch out. You start by pinging the local gateway on your side of the router or 210.17.15.1. If you can ping that address, you then begin to work farther and farther out the system, one IP address at a time, until you come to Microsoft or to the IP address that will not let you ping it. That *could* be where the problem lies. So, after pinging 210.17.15.1, the next step would be to ping 210.17.15.17. If that system responds, move on to 210.17.15.30.

WARNING Pease keep in mind, this is for Microsoft testing purposes only. PING uses UDP and some routers will not let UDP or PING requests through the system. You may not be able to receive a response to your ping, but the infrastructure may be up and working fine. For testing purposes, this *never* happens.

What if you are doing this in the real world and you suspect the system is in fact working, you just cannot ping it? Try using a TRACERT command with the IP address of the target system. This may be a more realistic test. If you find a problem with a router, you can use the route print command to check the route table.

Necessary Procedures

Each one of the utilities mentioned in the previous section provides another look at the IP configuration.

Using PING

When troubleshooting TCP/IP configuration issues, one of the most useful utilities is the PING command-line utility. The syntax for PING is simply

```
Ping ipaddress or ping hostname
```

If the ipaddress is 127.0.0.1 or local host, it can be used to check the configuration of IP on the local computer. Otherwise, it can be used to check the communication link between the host and other machines.

Using ARP

The ARP command will let you view the ARP cached on a machine to detect invalid entries. This command displays and modifies the Media Access Control (MAC) or hardware address translation tables used by the Address Resolution Protocol (ARP).

This is the syntax for ARP:

```
arp -a [ipaddress] [-N [interfaceaddress]]
arp -d ipaddress [if_addr]
arp -s ipaddress physicaladdress [interfaceaddress]
```

Parameters

-a: Displays current ARP entries by querying TCP/IP. If the ipaddress is specified, only the IP and physical addresses for the specified computer are displayed.

-d: Deletes the entry from the ARP cache table that is specified by the ipaddress.

-s: Adds an entry in the ARP cache to associate the ipaddress with the physical or MAC layer address. The physical address is given as 6 hexadecimal bytes separated by hyphens. The IP address is specified using dotted decimal notation. The entry is permanent, that is, it will not be automatically removed from the cache after the timeout expires.

-N [interfaceaddress]: Displays the ARP entries for the network interface specified by interfaceaddress.

Physicaladdress: Specifies a physical address.

Using Netstat

The Netstat utility displays the current protocol status and connections. This is the syntax:

```
Netstat
```

It is also possible to determine the status of the connection by running the Netstat utility and looking at the State column.

The State explanations as shown in Netstat are shown in Table 5.1.

TABLE 5.1: Netstat's state of the protocol

State	Explanation
SYN_SEND	Indicates active open. SYN indicates a request to open or establish a communication session.
SYN_RECEIVED	Server just received SYN from the client.
ESTABLISHED	Client received server's SYN and the session is established.
LISTEN	Server is ready to accept connection.
FIN_WAIT_1	Indicates active close. FIN indicates a close connection request.
TIMED_WAIT	Client enters this state after active close.
CLOSE_WAIT	Indicates passive close. Server just received first FIN from a client.
FIN_WAIT_2	Client just received acknowledgment of its first FIN from the server.
LAST_ACK	Server is in this state when it sends its own FIN.
CLOSED	Server received ACK from client and connection is closed.

This is the syntax for Netstat:

netstat -a displays all connections.

netstat -r displays the route table plus active connections.

netstat -n tells Netstat not to convert addresses and port numbers to names.

netstat –e displays Ethernet statistics.

netstat –s displays per protocol statistics for UDP, TCP, and IP.

The following is sample output:

```
C:\>netstat -e
Interface Statistics

   Received Sent
Bytes   3995837940 47224622
Unicast packets 120099 131015
Non-unicast packets 7579544 3823
Discards  0  0
Errors   0  0
Unknown protocols 363054211

C:\>netstat -a

Active Connections

Proto Local Address Foreign Address State
 TCP davemac1:1572 172.16.48.10:nbsession ESTABLISHED
 TCP davemac1:1589 172.16.48.10:nbsession ESTABLISHED
 TCP davemac1:1606 172.16.105.245:nbsession ESTABLISHED
 TCP davemac1:1632 172.16.48.213:nbsession ESTABLISHED
 TCP davemac1:1659 172.16.48.169:nbsession ESTABLISHED
 TCP davemac1:1714 172.16.48.203:nbsession ESTABLISHED
 TCP davemac1:1719 172.16.48.36:nbsession ESTABLISHED
 TCP davemac1:1241 172.16.48.101:nbsession ESTABLISHED
 UDP davemac1:1025 *:*
```

```
 UDP davemac1:snmp *:*
 UDP davemac1:nbname *:*
 UDP davemac1:nbdatagram *:*
 UDP davemac1:nbname *:*
 UDP davemac1:nbdatagram *:*

C:\>netstat -s
IP Statistics

 Packets Received  = 5378528
 Received Header Errors = 738854
 Received Address Errors = 23150
 Datagrams Forwarded  = 0
 Unknown Protocols Received = 0
 Received Packets Discarded = 0
 Received Packets Delivered = 4616524
 Output Requests  = 132702
 Routing Discards  = 157
 Discarded Output Packets = 0
 Output Packet No Route = 0
 Reassembly Required  = 0
 Reassembly Successful  = 0
 Reassembly Failures  = 0
 Datagrams Successfully Fragmented = 0
 Datagrams Failing Fragmentation = 0
 Fragments Created   = 0

ICMP Statistics
    Received Sent
 Messages   693 4
 Errors   0  0
 Destination Unreachable 685 0
 Time Exceeded  0  0
 Parameter Problems 0  0
 Source Quenchs  0  0
 Redirects  0  0
```

```
 Echos   4  0
 Echo Replies  0  4
 Timestamps  0  0
 Timestamp Replies 0  0
 Address Masks  0  0
 Address Mask Replies 0  0

TCP Statistics

 Active Opens   = 597
 Passive Opens  = 135
 Failed Connection Attempts = 107
 Reset Connections  = 91
 Current Connections  = 8
 Segments Received  = 106770
 Segments Sent  = 118431
 Segments Retransmitted = 461
UDP Statistics

 Datagrams Received = 4157136
 No Ports  = 351928
 Receive Errors = 2
 Datagrams Sent = 13809
```

Using IPCONFIG

The IPCONFIG utility allows the user to see how TCP/IP is configured for a particular computer. In addition, you can use IPCONFIG to release all DHCP address leases, renew all DHCP address leases, or release and renew individual DHCP addresses.

This is the syntax for IPCONFIG:

IPCONFIG: Displays current configuration for the installed network card.

IPCONFIG /ALL: Displays detailed information.

IPCONFIG /BATCH *[filename]*: Provides output of the information from the IPCONFIG request to a file.

IPCONFING /RENEW ALL: Renews the leases for all adapters.

IPCONFIG /RELEASE ALL: Releases the leases for all adapters.

IPCONFIG /RENEW *N*: Renews the lease for the IP address for adapter N.

IPCONFIG /RELEASE *N*: Releases the IP lease for adapter N.

Using TraceRT

The TraceRT utility will verify that a route exists between a sender and a receiver.

This is the syntax for TRACERT:

```
tracert [-d] [-h maximum_hops] [-j host-list] [-w
timeout] target_name
```

tracert –d: Specifies to not resolve addresses to host names.

Tracert –h *maximum_hops*: Specifies the maximum number of hops to search for the target computer; in other words, trace the route to the remote computer over five hops.

Tracert -j *host-list*: Specifies the loose source route along the host list.

tracert -w *timeout*: Waits the number of milliseconds specified by the timeout for each reply.

Tracert *target_name*: Displays the name or IP address of the target host.

Using Route

The route command can be used to view the local route table, as well as add or delete routes from the local route table.

This is the syntax for the route command:

```
route [-fs] [command [destination][gateway]]
```

route –f: Clears the route table.

route –s: If there is a packet with no destination address, it is forwarded to the smart gateway.

route add: Adds a route.

route delete: Deletes a route.

route print: Prints a route.

route change: Changes an existing route.

Exam Essentials

There are several commands that the exam writers appeared to be enamored of, certainly the PING command topped this list.

Know how to use the PING command for troubleshooting. Ping the loopback address first, then work your way through the network to the destination. That is the Microsoft way.

Know what the ARP command does. The ARP command views the Address Resolution Protocol cache on a machine to detect invalid entries.

Know what the NETSTAT command does. The NETSTAT command displays the current status of the protocol and its connections.

Know what the IPCONFIG command does. The IPCONFIG command is used to view the TCP/IP configuration on a computer.

Know how to use IPCONFIG to release a DHCP address. The command for this is ipconfig /release.

Know how to use IPCONFIG to renew a DHCP address. The command for this is ipconfig /renew.

Know how to view a local route table. The command for this is route print.

Know how to verify a route between a sender and a receiver. The command for this is tracert *ipaddress*.

Key Terms and Concepts

ARP: A command-line utility designed to show the Address Resolution Protocol cache for a local machine.

IPCONFIG: A command-line utility designed to show the current IP configuration of the local machine.

Netstat: A command-line utility designed to show the status of the protocol and the network.

PING: A command-line utility designed to establish a physical connection between hosts.

Route: A command-line utility designed to print, add, and delete entries from a route table.

TraceRT: A command-line utility designed to show the route a packet must take to reach a destination host.

Sample Questions

1. You are troubleshooting a host computer that is unable to connect to one particular host on the network. The rest of the computers appear to be communicating without a problem. You have checked the IP configuration running IPCONFIG. You now want to test and see if the local computer can respond to IP commands. The command you would issue is:

   A. WINIPCFG

   B. PING *local_ipaddress*

   C. PING *remote_IP address*

   D. PING 127.0.0.1

   Answer: D. PING 127.0.0.1 or the local loopback will check the IP configuration to see if it will respond to IP commands.

2. IPCONFIG /release *ipaddress* produces what results?

A. Releases all IP addresses bound to any network card in a computer.

B. Releases all IP addresses, whether assigned manually or through DCHP.

C. Will only release all IP addresses assigned through DHCP.

D. Will just release the designated IP address.

Answer: D. The command specified will release just the designated IP address.

3. You want to check the local address resolution cache on a Windows NT Server. Which of the following commands would use?

A. ARP

B. Route Print

C. TraceRT

D. IPCONFIG

Answer: A. The ARP command-line utility will show the local Address Resolution Protocol cache.

4. The TRACERT command does what?

A. Displays the current ARP cache.

B. Displays the route table stored on the local machine.

C. Displays the IP configuration for the local machine.

D. Displays the route a packet must take to get to its destination.

Answer: D. The TRACERT command displays the route a packet must take to reach its destination.

Diagnose and resolve name resolution problems.

Diagnosing and resolving name resolution problems is not nearly as scary as it sounds. Before you start with the troubleshooting process, there are two very important things to keep in mind. The first is: Where is the name resolution supposed to come from? The second is the ability to realize that sometimes you just have to accept the fact the name cannot be resolved.

Where the name resolution is supposed to come from is the first thing you look for in name resolution. If the name is supposed to be resolved by a DNS root domain server and it still keeps coming back as an unknown address, there is little if anything you can do about it. In this case, the end user will have to accept the fact that the name cannot be resolved. Actually, the majority of these kinds of problems are usually related to the carbon unit interface anyway. It seems some end users have trouble spelling www and other key things. We are getting ahead of ourselves.

When it comes to testing, this section gets attention in an offhanded kind of way. It is another way to point out that WINS works best on all Windows networks and WINS and DNS can work together to resolve name problems.

Critical Information

When a user is having problems resolving a name to an IP address, the first question that should come to mind is: Where is the resolution supposed to come from? If the user is trying to resolve a local printer name using the Windows Network Neighborhood, the troubleshooting steps are much different than if the user is trying to find http:\\www.favoriteweb.com.

Where is the resolution supposed to come from? What are the choices? A DNS server, a WINS Server, an LMHOSTS file, or a HOSTS file. That pretty much covers all the options.

Troubleshooting a DNS Server

If the user is attempting to resolve a host name that should be stored on a DNS server, check first to make sure the DNS server is actually online. After you know the DNS server is online, ask the age-old question, "What have you done to your system recently?" The answer you will get is, "Nothing," but probe deeper. (Remember the laws of computing that state, "end users lie.") Perhaps they were poking around in the Network Neighborhood properties and changed an IP address. Perhaps someone was poking around on your DNS server and changed an IP address. Perhaps someone was messing with the DNS database and changed the spelling or IP address of a favorite site. If DNS resolution is supposed to go up the directory for resolution, make sure all the pieces are online and working. This can be done by using PING, or if the servers are on the local network, through the network neighborhood.

Finally, if you still can't resolve the DNS question, look very, very closely at what the end-user has typed. It is amazing how often www comes out vvv or something equally as strange.

Troubleshooting a WINS Server

Troubleshooting a WINS issue can be more complicated, simply because there are more places for the WINS Server to get information. DNS is a static database; that means it doesn't change much. WINS is a dynamic database, which means it changes all the time. The WINS database can get information from other WINS databases, from an LMHOSTS file, or from a client on boot up.

When you start troubleshooting name resolution issues, remember the steps the system goes through to resolve the name. With WINS, the host comes up and registers with the WINS Server, if the name is unique. If the name is not unique, the WINS Server does not recognize the computer. Check to make sure the NetBIOS name on the target computer is a unique name.

One of the problems that can come up using WINS is the existence of computers still showing up in the browser, long after they have been shut off. This is especially prevalent in networks with several WINS Servers. Suppose a resource on the network suffers a catastrophic failure. Because the resource did not shut down properly, its name still shows up in the NetBIOS cache. By default, WINS keeps information in cache for at least 15 minutes before checking to see if it is still valid. If it sends out a request and does not get a response, the system still does not remove the resource from the browser. It waits and checks again. When the primary system finally removes the resource from the browser, that change needs to be replicated across the network.

If the backup WINS Server is configured as a pull partner, that replication is usually initiated by a time interval. After the time interval expires, the change is finally replicated out to the backup WINS Server, and the resource is removed from the browser. The interval between the time the resource fails and the time it is removed from the Network Neighborhood can be lengthy. In most cases, this is not a serious problem, unless you are one of the people trying to access the resource. Then it can be an issue. If you suspect, or know, that a resource is not available and it still shows up in the browser, the best way of solving the problem is to force a replication using WINS Manager.

Other issues with WINS can occur if the server is configured to import an LMHOSTS file into the WINS database. If the entry in the LMHOSTS file is not correct, obviously, the entry in the WINS database will not be correct. The LMHOSTS file cannot be directly imported into the WINS database; it must be a copy of the file. If you attempt to import the LMHOSTS file, the system will return a message saying the file was imported successfully, except nothing shows up in the database. This falls under the category of: The operation was a success, except the patient died.

WINS works with DNS to provide resolution of both NetBIOS names and host names. By default, the NetBIOS computer name is used as the host name. If this default is not followed, there may be some confusion. Just one more thing to add to your checklist.

Troubleshooting the LMHOSTS File

The LMHOSTS file is a text-based file. Each entry in this text-based file is manual and any time you have a manual entry, you have the opportunity for a typo. This is the usual reason for problems with the LMHOSTS file. When checking name resolution, be sure to check spelling and syntax.

Resolution using the LMHOSTS file occurs when the file is parsed from the top down. If there is a problem with the resolution for the file, make sure it is the only file that is being parsed. For example, LMHOSTS can reference other files. There is even the opportunity for alternate selections. Make sure you check the syntax of each and every entry in each and every LMHOSTS file.

Troubleshooting the HOSTS File

The HOSTS file is also a text-based file. Each entry in this text-based file is manual and any time you have a manual entry, you have the opportunity for a typo. This is the usual reason for problems with the HOSTS file. When checking name resolution, be sure to check spelling and syntax.

Resolution using the HOSTS file occurs when the file is parsed from the top down. If there is a problem with the resolution for the file, make sure there is only one entry for the host in question. If your HOSTS file is large, there can be duplicate entries.

Key Terms and Concepts

DNS (Domain Name System): Resolves non-Windows–based host names to IP addresses.

HOSTS: A text-based file used to resolve DNS names to IP addresses.

LMHOSTS: A text-based file used to resolve WINS computer names to IP addresses.

WINS (Windows Internet Name Service): Resolves NetBIOS-based computer names to IP addresses.

Sample Questions

1. A host is having a difficult time finding another UNIX computer named GEORGE. Your network is not configured to communicate with the Internet. You check the local DNS server and GEORGE does not show up. Which file would you check on the local machine?

   A. HOSTS

   B. LMHOSTS

   C. GATEWAY

   D. SERVICES

   Answer: A. Because this is a non-WINS–based resolution, you would be checking the HOSTS file.

2. In the example above, the listing should appear as:

   A. Alias, computer name, IP address.

   B. Computer name, IP address, alias.

   C. IP address, computer name, alias.

   D. None of the above.

   Answer: C. The syntax of a HOSTS file is IP address, computer name, alias.

3. How do you designate a comment in both a HOSTS file and an LMHOSTS file?

   A. # (pound sign)

   B. ; (semicolon)

   C. REM

   D. REMARK

   Answer: A. The # (pound sign) is used to designate a remark or a comment in both the LMHOSTS file and the HOSTS file.

4. The most common cause of name resolution using a HOSTS file or an LMHOSTS file is:

A. The file has been imported into the WINS database and therefore no longer exists.

B. The #DOM tag in the HOSTS file references a domain that does not exist.

C. The #PRE tag in the LMHOSTS file cannot be loaded into memory.

D. Syntax.

Answer: D. The most common cause of a name resolution issue in a HOSTS file or LMHOSTS file is syntax, or human error.

Index

Note to the Reader: First level entries are in **bold**. Page numbers in **bold** indicate the principal discussion of a topic or the definition of a term. Page numbers in *italic* indicate illustrations.

A

B

C

D

E

F

G

H

I

J

K

L

S

U

V

W

Z

NT® IN THE REAL WORLD

HE INFORMATION YOU NEED TO BUILD, SECURE, AND OPTIMIZE NT NETWORKS

ISBN: 0-7821-2163-2
1,664 pp; 7 1/2" x 9"; Hardcover
$59.99

ISBN: 0-7821-2123-3
544 pp; 7 1/2" x 9"; Softcover $44.99

ISBN: 0-7821-2006-7
929 pp; 7 1/2" x 9"; Hardcover
$59.99

ISBN: 0-7821-2156-X
624 pp; 7 1/2" x 9"; Hardcover
$54.99